THE SEARCH FOR
JOHNNY NICHOLAS

THE SECRET OF NAZI PRISONER
NO. 44451

THE SEARCH FOR JOHNNY NICHOLAS

THE SECRET OF NAZI PRISONER NO. 44451

HUGH WRAY McCANN
DAVID C. SMITH

ARBOR COVE PRESS· MICHIGAN

2011

First published in Great Britain by:
Sphere Books Limited
30-32 Gray's Inn Road
London WC1X 8JL
Copyright © Hugh Wray McCann,
David L. Matthews and David C. Smith 1982

Book design by heatherleeshaw.blogspot.com

Cover Photo: Jean Marcel Nicolas, age 10 in 1928, at the
St. Nazaire boarding school in Brittany, France.
Courtesy of the Nicolas family.

ISBN: 9781456464417

Printed in the United States of America

To our fathers;
and in memory of the
men who lost their lives
in the Massacre at Gardelegen

*A human life is like a
single letter in the alphabet.
It can be meaningless; or it
can be part of a great meaning.*

—from 'Who Takes Delight in Life,'
New York Herald Tribune, Sept. 5, 1956

CONTENTS

AUTHORS' NOTE

The Search for Johnny Nicholas may not be considered complete until the lost memoir that he personally penned in his hospital bed before his death has been found. Only then will we be in a position to fill the many blanks in his story that are currently completed on a speculative basis.

We have it on the assurance of his late brother, Vildebart, that Johnny underwent a lengthy debriefing by anonymous Allied Intelligence officers in 1945, in the course of which he compiled a detailed account — in English, French and German — of his war-time activities. Despite our best efforts we have never unearthed this account.

When the book was first published in Europe it was our hope that someone reading it might know where to find this potentially invaluable account so that we could make use of it. To date, however, this has not happened, and the passage of the years makes it increasingly unlikely that it ever will.

Interlochen, Michigan
Auburn Hills, Michigan
December, 2010

HOW THE SEARCH BEGAN

In 1965 my husband, Hugh, and I first heard about Johnny Nicholas during a dinner with David Matthews in Detroit, a visiting attorney from South Bend, Indiana. Matthews had heard the name 18 years earlier when he was a young U.S. Army public information officer covering proceedings of the 1947 Nordhausen War Crimes Trials at the former Dachau Concentration Camp near Munich. Matthews' interest was piqued when he heard numerous witnesses refer to a fellow slave laborer, Johnny Nicholas, as a black American airman and perhaps a spy who also treated them as a prisoner doctor.

Matthews sensed a mystery worth telling. Outside the courtroom he interviewed witnesses whose testimony had prompted the U.S. Military Tribunal conducting the trials to order a search for Nicholas, assuming he'd be a star witness against the Nazis. However, the post-war years fully absorbed Matthews with acquiring a law degree, wife and family, and tending to a growing legal practice. Johnny Nicholas's story remained lost in the six pages of notes he kept in his attic.

Earlier in 1965 Hugh had his book, *Utmost Fish*, published by Simon & Schuster, and was ready for a new challenge. He offered to co-author the Nicholas book and Matthews agreed. Hugh soon realized that he had little except the book subject's name to go on and that a dedicated effort would be necessary to flesh out the story. He invited his former University of Michigan classmate, close friend and fellow journalist David C. Smith to join the effort.

It was slow going initially as both journalists were working full-time at the *Detroit Free Press*. The story assumed broader dimensions during July 1967 when they worked around the clock covering the Detroit race riot. The *Free Press* staff won the Pulitzer Prize for its Local Reporting effort.

Previous to that tragic episode, Hugh was assigned to interview the husband of a Michigan civil rights activist, Viola Liuzzo, who was shot and killed while volunteering as a transport driver following the Selma to Montgomery march. It was difficult for him to visit the Detroit home they had shared with five children. We had four of our own at that time, and were sobered by those events and stunned by the revelations of continued injustices and brutality we saw almost daily on TV as the Civil Rights movement gained momentum. Belief that this emerging awareness of racial and social inequality should continue, fueled our decades of involvement in this and other efforts.

Both Hugh and Dave witnessed prejudice up close as teenagers. After the war and his father's death, Hugh migrated from his home in Northern Ireland to work for a gold mining company in Johannesburg, South Africa, where he learned the meaning of apartheid up close. In high school, Dave left his home in integrated Michigan one summer to work in the tobacco fields of a then totally segregated southern state, where blacks were denied the most basic rights.

Hugh was an engineer as well as a journalist. Actually, we befriended two gentlemanly Haitian fellow students at Indiana Tech in Fort Wayne, often inviting them to breakfast after Sunday mass. Memories of them later became a reference for trying to fix a cultural image of the name Johnny Nicholas.

Hugh, in mid teens, had burrowed beneath his blankets in boarding school as German bombers, flew over to destroy the docks and ship building areas of nearby Belfast, Northern Ireland. His close, attention to the air war was intensified when the Nazis added V-2 rockets to the assault on England.

He could not have known then that the V-2 would become intrinsic to telling the Johnny Nicholas story. During the 1980s and '90s he covered space launches at Cape Canaveral for the *Detroit News*. This experience added yet another significant dimension to the story for him as he became increasingly aware of the connection between the slave laborers who died by the thousands making V-2 production possible and the German scientists led by Wernher von Braun who, after the war, helped establish the U.S. space program that resulted in landing on the moon in 1969.

In 2006 we were approached by a young American attorney of Haitian descent practicing in New York City, Caroline Memnon. She was eager to produce a movie about Johnny's life, having been inspired by the story while working on a French documentary entitled "Noirs dans les Camps

Nazi," about prisoners of African descent in German concentration camps. She has used her knowledge of both language and cultural history to help us navigate in France and Haiti for this new edition.

Caroline also traveled to Germany seeking resolution of the many remaining mysteries of Johnny's existence as he transitioned from a life of privilege to one of murderous, suffering slavery. She attended the 60th commemoration of Buchenwald and Camp Dora, where she spoke with former deportees whose lives had been touched by Johnny. Among them was a Dora prisoner who had suffered gangrene in his leg. "Dr. Johnny," he told her, operated successfully on the leg and then hid him from hard labor while he recovered.

We told her that Johnny, based on his family's accounts, was no stranger to the French film world during the early 1940s, and had socialized with the pre-Cannes crowd, in particular popular movie star and Miss Paris of 1930, Viviane Romance. Caroline introduced his story to today's Cannes movie contingent, hoping that perhaps one day Johnny's gifted, optimistic, chameleon-like life of daring would find audiences in need of hope and inspiration, especially now in beleaguered Haiti.

While attempting recently to interview the frail, reclusive Dr. Hans Pape, Johnny's friend and medical school classmate in Paris, Caroline sought help from his nephew, Dr. Jean William Pape, in Port-au-Prince. Thus we learned of his recognized role in Haitian medical care, now and before the recent disasters. When he was interviewed for the original edition of this book in 1972, but then lacking details of the still-unfolding chronicle, Dr. Hans expressed disappointment that Johnny hadn't finished his medical studies and returned home to serve Haiti's suffering poor, as he had done and as his nephew does so prominently today.

A portion of the income from this account of the short, dynamic life of Jean Marcel Nicolas (Johnny Nicholas) will be contributed to two Haitian medical relief organizations,* putting to rest Hans's regrets and allowing Johnny to return to Haiti in spirit after 65 years, helping to bring his message of hope that he persistently instilled in his fellow prisoners.

I contribute these thoughts in my husband's name. A stroke in 2002 claimed his ability to speak, read and write adequately. It may be that Johnny's message of perseverance also has reached Hugh during these past nine years, helping him to endure his own sense of isolation and loss of freedom. He continues to be involved in the progress Dave has made in planning, writing and editing this revision. We wish to dedicate the book to the Smith children and ours, who have lived with Johnny Nicholas most of their lives and have made valuable continuing professional contributions; and to Dave Matthews, deceased since 1990, who first brought the story to our attention, sending Hugh and Dave on their long quest (see Afterword, p.286). We also give our thanks to Heather Shaw for her guidance through the new technologies of publishing, and to the scores of friends and colleagues who have shared and contributed to this long mission.

We have witnessed that the ultimate act of rebellion in a violent world is love.

Beverly and Hugh Wray McCann
Interlochen, Michigan
December 2010

* Donations may be sent to Dr. Jean William Pape's organization:
GHESKIO
The Center for Global Health
Cornell Medical College
440 East 69th Street
New York, NY 10021
 Phone (212) 746-6680 or email globalhealthweb@med.cornell.edu.

Also contact Dr. Paul Farmer's organization, active in Haiti for 20 years:
PARTNERS IN HEALTH
888 Commonwealth Avenue, 3rd Floor
Boston, MA 02215.
Phone (617) 998-8922 or email info@pih.org.

Donations also may be made to the Haitian relief organizations of your choice.

THE SEARCH FOR JOHNNY NICHOLAS

CHAPTER ONE

FIND JOHNNY NICHOLAS!

Q. Tell me all you know about Johnny Nicholas?

*A. He was working as a doctor in the hospital, and I worked for him.
He told me that he had parachuted from a damaged American plane into
France, where he had a secret-service assignment to perform in the nature of set-
ting up a medical practice in Paris, communicating information to the Allies....
He also told me that after landing he was arrested by the Germans and that he
did establish in Paris a medical office which he operated for a period of time that
he did not disclose to me.* — Testimony from the Nordhausen War Crimes
Trial, 1947

Find Johnny Nicholas!

That brusque order came from U. S. Army Lieutenant Colonel William Berman, chief prosecutor in the Nordhausen War Crimes Trials.

It was the summer of 1947, more than two years after World War II
had ended. In preparation for the upcoming trials, Berman and his
staff had interrogated hundreds of witnesses who had been prisoners in
Dora, a concentration camp in north-central Germany near Nordhausen, a beautiful medieval town.

Dora was unique in the annals of the some 2,000 holding pens where
Germany warehoused human beings who had run afoul of the Nazi state.
It was a slave-labor camp where thousands died tunneling out a secret
underground factory inside a hill in the Harz Mountains. In that factory thousands more were worked to death on sprawling assembly lines
along which sped V-2 rockets, the world's first ballistic missiles.

German scientists had been researching and refining the V-weapons
since the early 1930s. Now, in mid-1943, Adolf Hitler, staring in the face
of certain defeat by the Allied armies, bet everything on these gigantic,

46-foot long rockets to save his 12-year-old Third Reich that he had arrogantly boasted would last a thousand years.

When Berman, a New York lawyer in civilian life, got assigned to the Nordhausen case, Hitler was already dead and Germany lay in ruins. His mission was to prosecute Camp Dora SS officers and men responsible for heinous crimes against prisoners from 32 nations who had excavated the subterranean factory and then been forced to assemble the V-2 weapons. From August 1943, when the slaves began quarrying rock from inside the Kohnstein Hill, as it was known to the citizens of Nordhausen, until its liberation by the U. S. Army in April, 1945, more than 60,000 prisoners had passed through Dora and its 31 outlying subcamps. An estimated 15,000 to 20,000 died from malnutrition, diseases, beatings, hangings and SS men's Lugers and Mauser machine pistols.

Among the luckless denizens of Dora was Johnny Nicholas, a black man claiming to be an American.

Nicholas' name and his exploits while in the camp were cited frequently by prisoners who had arrived to testify at the Nordhausen proceedings. Their stirring accounts of his courage, his bearing, his high morale and his knowledge of what had gone on inside Dora convinced Berman that the black prisoner, the only American known to have been a prisoner at Dora, could be the prosecution's star witness — if he could be found.

But where was he?

Colonel Berman ordered William Aalmans, a Dutch civilian investigator employed by the U.S. 7708th War Crimes Group, to find Nicholas and bring him in.

It was a daunting assignment. Germany's social and economic infrastructure still lay in a state of almost total ruin caused by ceaseless Allied air attacks and the devastation wrought by the collision of vast armies. The country thronged with millions of refugees and displaced persons.

The four Allied victors — the United States, Britain, France and the Soviet Union — had carved the defeated Reich into four military occupation zones, each administered differently by a different Ally. But beyond the neatly typed articles of occupation and paper plans for rehabilitating the stricken nation, chaos and confusion abounded.

Aalmans[1] began his search for Nicholas by interrogating ex-Dora prisoners who had volunteered to testify at the Nordhausen trial. He quickly discovered that the black man had been a legend at Dora, an innovator capable of the most audacious acts in outwitting his captors, a wellspring of confidence in Allied victory. He endlessly evangelized this gospel for the benefit of his miserable and dejected fellow slaves. He continually promised them that they would all go back home one day and eventually be reunited with their families.

While many prisoners completely lost their spirit under the backbreaking labor of boring the massive tunnel complex where the V-2 was built, Nicholas — they told Aalmans — refused to be cowed. And later, as a prisoner doctor, they said, he kept his patients alive not so much with the sparse medicinals available as with his wide smile and repeated transfusions of his indomitable personality.

Under the most wretched conditions of hunger, starvation and brutality, where despair was more infectious then typhus and tuberculosis, the large black man became an oasis of hope. Fellow prisoners drank from the font of his verbal swagger and his repeated assurances that the Americans eventually would free them. And when U.S. planes eventually flew over Dora on their bombing runs to Berlin, his credibility soared to unprecedented heights.

The long and circuitous search by Aalmans, the Dutch investigator, for Nicholas led him to a large barn several hundred miles from Dora; a barn that, two years previously, had been littered with charred corpses as the result of a fiery massacre.

Aalmans's next clue was a photograph shot by an American soldier who had taken pictures at the soot-blackened barn the morning after the massacre. Signal Corps Sergeant P. R. Marks of Swayzee, Indiana, had gotten to the scene as more than 1,000 bodies were being removed. His camera had scanned the cavernous, still-smoking interior, the remnants of mess gear, the caps and clogs, the precious soup cans and other personal items hoarded by desperate men through years of deprivation and hell on earth.

His shutter had also clicked on a lone, contorted figure on the straw-littered ground. It looked as if, in his final agony, the victim had

1 Aalmans, whose home was in Kerkrade, the Netherlands, had worked in the Dutch Resistance movement. He prepared a booklet entitled, "The Dora-Nordhausen War Crimes Trial." He was last reported as serving in the Dutch embassy in Lima, Peru.

grabbed a handful of shirttail in the front and had been trying to rip off his clothes when the flames overtook him. There were bullet holes in his head, chest and stomach.

The corpse immediately arrested Marks' attention: It appeared to him to have the facial features of a Negro. However, most of the corpses were badly charred and several others could also have been mistaken for the bodies of Negroes.

Aalmans returned to Berman and reported what he had found. Correct identification was crucial, so Berman had Aalmans develop blow-ups of Sgt. Marks' 35-millimeter prints and showed them to ex-Dora prisoners who had known Nicholas.

A few shook their heads: Definitely not; lips too thick, features not fine enough. Johnny was tall. This poor bastard looks too short.

But most of them nodded. Yes, they said, it's "Dr. Johnny."

For Aalmans, the search for the "star witness" was over; and, as far as Berman and the Dutch investigator were concerned, from then on the fortunes and fate of Johnny Nicholas were of academic interest only.

The Nordhausen War Crimes Trials — Case No. 000-50-37: Kurt Andrae et al vs. United States of America — opened on the hot, sunny morning of August 7, 1947. What continues to befuddle many historians of the period is that the Nordhausen trials were not convened in Nordhausen, as one would assume, but in Dachau, which itself was the venue for another infamous Nazi-era concentration camp. In fact the Dachau War Crimes Trials had recently concluded, and because the SS sessions hall that had served as an ideal courtroom was no longer in use, the U.S. Army elected to conduct the Nordhausen trials at the Camp Dachau venue.

The hall was a beamed-ceiling room with high windows, heavy dark drapes, globed lamps and Kleig lights strategically spotted to aid in filming the proceedings for history. A large American flag tacked to the rear wall looked down on a raised platform of chairs seating the seven-member tribunal — all senior U.S. Army officers.

Hear ye! Hear ye! By authority of Allied Council Law No. 10, promulgated 20 December 1945 and signed by the Commanders of Occupation of the Republic of France, the Union of Soviet Socialist Republics, the United Kingdom of Great

Britain and Northern Ireland, and the United States of America, this honorable tribunal is in session, Colonel Frank Silliman III presiding. Please be seated! [2]

An Army clerk read the opening statement: "A special military court appointed by Special Order No. 144 Par. 17 dated 5 August 1947, Headquarters European Command, APO 207-1, met at Camp Dachau, Germany, on 7 August 1947 at 0915 hours as directed by the president thereof ..."

SS Master Sergeant Arthur Kurt Andrae, 13 other SS men, four prisoners and one German civilian — the general manager of the underground factory — were "each individually accused of murder" of inmates at Camp Dora and its subcamps where, the indictment read, 15,000 prisoners perished.[3]

"May it please the court," began Prosecutor Berman, a tough-talking rotund New Englander, "the evidence will show that the accused, as part of a common plan with others, subjected Russians and Poles, Frenchmen, Dutchmen, Belgians, Italians and Jews to indignities, tortures and to enforced slave labor in Dora and its subcamps. Among these prisoners of war were Italians and Russians, Frenchmen — and even one American."

The accused each heard the charges lodged against him and impassively entered a "not guilty" plea. A decidedly nonmilitary-looking formation

---

2 Col. Silliman was from Philadelphia, Pa. The other six members of the tribunal were Col. Joseph W. Benson of Los Angeles, Calif.; Col. Claude O. Burch of Petersburg, Ind.; Lt. Col. David H. Thomas of East Palestine, Ohio; Lt. Col. Roy J. Herte of Floral Park, N.Y.; Lt. Col. Louis S. Tracy of Hartford, Conn.; and Major Warren M. Vanderburgh of Boston, Mass. The trial was one of 489 cases involving 1,672 defendants conducted by U.S. Army military courts and commissions in the U.S. Zone of Occupation in Germany. These cases were sometimes called the Petty War Crimes Trials to distinguish them from the Inter-Allied Nuremberg Military Tribunal that tried major German civilian and military leaders in 1945-46. The venue of the trial, however, was not Nordhausen itself; it was the former concentration camp at Dachau, 220 miles to the south.

3 The exact death toll at what became known as the Dora-Mittelbau complex was never determined and remains controversial. It was claimed that the figure according to official German records fell far short of actual deaths. Actual fatalities went as high as 20,000. In settling on the 15,000 figure the tribunal took a conservative position on the controversy.

in baggy cast-off GI clothing, they were fresh from a POW stockade and the hair clippers of unsympathetic U.S. Army barbers.

None appeared even slightly remorseful. Andrae, 47, and former SS Capt. Heinrich Schmidt, 35, sported Hitler mustaches. Strings around the defendants' necks suspended six-inch-square cards bearing their numbers starting with "1" for Andrae and progressing alphabetically to number "19," the civilian Willi Zwiener, a stern-faced man of 59, who parted his hair to one side as had *Der Fuehrer*.

Appointed to defend the accused were Maj. Leon B. Poullada of Los Angeles and Capt. Paul D. Strader Jr. of Salem, Ohio, assisted by three German civilian lawyers. Berman's chief assistant was Capt. William F. McGarry of New York City.[4]

Witnesses and observers occupied rows of seats directly facing the tribunal. Among them sat Corporal David Matthews. He would become a key figure in the search for Nicholas. A 19-year-old from South Bend, Indiana, assigned to the Public Information Office (PIO) of the 7708th War Crimes Group, he was reporting on the trial at the behest of his commanding officer, Colonel Clio E. Straight. Matthews' assignment was to write glowing press releases about the trial in order to induce American and British newspaper and radio correspondents to come to Dachau and report on the trial.

"The problem," Matthews explained nearly 25 years later, when he had become a highly successful attorney in his home state, "was that after months and months of the big showdown in Nuremberg of Goering and all those top Nazis, you couldn't give away another war-crimes story — particularly when dozens of hotter stories were breaking all over postwar Europe at the time."

From a journalistic standpoint, the trial was shaping up as "pretty boring stuff," he said. "A bunch of third-rate Nazis nobody ever heard of robbing prisoners' Red Cross packages." The only reason that he

---

4 Poullada contended that centuries of ingrained animosity among European nationalities made it impossible for ex-prisoners to give unprejudiced testimony against their former German guards. In his summation he urged the tribunal to throw out the testimony of many Dora ex-prisoners as being automatically suspect and therefore unreliable.

stayed in the courtroom, he explained, was that Straight, his C.O., had ordered him to do so.

When the name Johnny Nicholas began surfacing, the chore gradually became a consuming personal priority for Matthews.

The trial recessed at noon and reconvened at 1:30 p.m., and the prosecution called its first witness, Cecil Jay, an Englishman who had been a prisoner in Dora.

The assistant prosecutor, Capt. McGarry, asked him: "Did you know a person named Johnny Nicholas?"

Jay: "Yes."

McGarry: "What was his nationality?"

Jay: "He was a nigger. He told me he was an American, sir. I spoke with this man almost every evening."

This is how the Nordhausen tribunal was introduced to Johnny Nicholas. Over the next four months, witnesses from England, France, Germany, Poland and Hungary — Nazis and former prisoners alike — would testify as to their recollections of the mysterious black man.

Matthews's boredom with the trial vanished as soon as Jay began to testify, and from there on his interest never flagged. When court recessed again, Matthews followed Jay out of the courtroom and, notebook in hand, took him aside to quiz him for more details about Nicholas. As the trial progressed and successive witnesses testified that they had known Nicholas, Matthews made a practice of sequestering them beyond the ambit of the courtroom, where they were free of legal constraints, and interviewed them in depth about "the black American doctor."

"The stories they told about him were spine-tingling," recalled Matthews. And they were what set in motion in 1968, the second search for Johnny Nicholas.

Matthews's exclusive interviews, the substance of which he relayed orally to co-author McCann in 1968 and which survive only in McCann's recollections, are dubbed for convenience the Nordhausen Notebook[5] and are so cited throughout this narrative.

---

5 Those interviewed are believed to include Romuald Bak, Poland; Geza Bondi, Hungary; Vincent Hein, Poland; Cecil Jay, England; Boruch Siedel, Germany; Jean Septfonds, France; and Aurel Zobel, Hungary.

Among Nicholas' associates at Dora was Wincenty Hein, a lawyer from Krakow, Poland. He had been a clerk responsible for keeping statistics in the hospital for prisoners. Hein, then 38, proved to be a walking encyclopedia on the subject of Dora. He was recovering from a heart attack when War Crimes Investigation Team No. 6822's Captain Robert G. McCarty arrived at Dora shortly after the camp's liberation.

Hein conducted McCarty on a tour of Dora and its subcamps. Entering the barracks used by the SS as a prisoner post office,[6] McCarty opened a large, wooden filing cabinet containing five-by-seven-inch index cards.

Thumbing through them, he flipped up a card made out in the name of Nicholas, Johnny; nationality American. The card would surface later in the Nordhausen trials as Prosecution Exhibit No. 81.

In a legal deposition McCarty questioned Hein about the card, and the Pole's answers, excerpted at the beginning of this chapter, would become part of the Nordhausen trial record.

Q. "Tell me all you know about Johnny Nicholas, who had Prisoner No. 44451 and whose card you have found.

A. "Johnny Nicholas, a Negro, appears from the card to have been born on 5 October 1918.[7] He was an acquaintance of mine at the camp. He told me he had parachuted from a damaged American plane into France, where he had a secret service assignment to perform in the nature of setting up a medical practice in Paris, communicating information to the Allies.

"He was very conspicuous because he was the only Negro there. He was a tall man about six feet in height.

"I met him the first part of November 1944, although he had been present at the camp for a period of what he told me (was) one year prior thereto.

"At the time I became acquainted with him he was working as a doctor in the hospital (at Dora), and I worked for him.

"I did not ask Nicholas what sort of plane he was in at the time of parachuting into France, or in what part of France he landed. I never questioned his story, although he indicated to me that his original ar-

---

6 Mail from home and food packages from the International Red Cross arrived at Dora for the prisoners but was systematically plundered by the SS. There was rarely any out-going mail from the prisoners.

7 The date was in error. Nicholas was born on October 20, 1918.

rival in France was prior to the entry of the United States into the European war....

"From Dora he was transferred to [Subcamp] Rottleberode ... and that is the last I saw of him."

Before the Nordhausen trials ended in December 1947, Corporal Matthews wrote a six-page account of the exploits of Dora's black American doctor. Based on testimony and his interviews with witnesses, it was, he thought, a surefire way of luring British and American journalists to the trial. Failing that, he would submit the story to *Stars and Stripes*, the U.S. Army newspaper, and it could be his ticket to a career on some Indiana newspaper.

Neither ever happened. The army rotated him back home to South Bend. In the meantime the bloom faded from the rose of journalism. He chose the legal profession instead and graduated from The University of Notre Dame law school.

His intriguing sketch of "Dr. Johnny" would yellow in an old army duffel bag in his attic before it would see the light of day again, when the second search for Johnny Nicholas would begin.

JUDGE ADVOCATE SECTION
WAR CRIMES BRANCH

HEADQUARTERS
EUROPEAN THEATER OF OPERATIONS
UNITED STATES ARMY

File No. 000.5 (JA-1023)   APO 887

SUBJECT: Interrogation of Alleged American Inmate of DORA Concentration Camp

TO   : The Judge Advocate General
        Washington 25, D. C.
        (Attention: War Crimes Office)

    1. Attention is invited to the inclosed copy of letter from Twelfth Army Group to this branch, dated 21 June 1945, File No. 000.5 (JA-1023). Machine Records Units in this theater have no record of "Johnny NICHOLAS."

    2. Notwithstanding the somewhat incredible nature of NICHOLAS' story to the witness Wincenty HEIN, it is requested that an effort be made to identify and interrogate NICHOLAS about conditions at DORA and that his sworn testimony, preferably in question and answer form, be forwarded to this branch in triplicate.

    3. In the event NICHOLAS in his testimony names as either witness or perpetrator any American military personnel or German prisoners of war now in the United States, it is requested that such person or persons also be interrogated and their sworn testimony be forwarded to this branch in triplicate.

    FOR THE THEATER JUDGE ADVOCATE:

JOHN A. HALL
Colonel, JAGD
Chief, War Crimes Branch

1 Incl:
    Copy of ltr from 12th Army
    Group dtd 21 June 1945.

11 11 JUL 1945

DECLASSIFIED–DOD Directive
No. 5200.9, 27 September 1958

Having learned that Johnny Nicholas had been a slave laborer and prisoner physician, the U.S. Army was anxious to locate him and sent out this letter on June 21, 1945, two years before the Nordhausen Trials. It got no response. (National Archives)

The Chief prisoner physician was a Czech Dr. Jan CESPIVA, the Dutch
prisoner doctor GROENEVELD was head of the Internal Ward, the French
prisoner doctor POUPOULT from Dieppe was head of the Surgical Ward,
the French prisoner doctor GIRARD was the specialist for otho-laryng-
ological cases, French prisoner doctor LEMIERRE together with French
prisoner doctor MOREL took care of the sick call. The Camp for the
entire prisoner hospital was a German political prisoner by the name
of Fritz PROELL. The first Clerk who took care of all the statistics
was a Czech prisoner by the name of PIESALA. Clerk stenographer was
Josef ACKERMANN, the head nurse in the Surgical Ward was Hans SCHNEIDER.

Q   Did you know a negro doctor by the name of Johnny NICHOLS?
A   Yes.

Q   Was he a doctor for a certain time at DORA?
A   For a certain time when I came there he was working in the sick call
     department.

Q   Tell me what you know or heard about this man?
A   He told me that he was an American officer and had been shot down over
     France during a bombing mission. He had been hiding in French for quite
     a while and knew French very well. He told me that he had been picked up
     during a raid by the Gestapo in France and had been sent to a concentration
     camp. I think it was BUCHENWALD. As far as I know he was transferred out
     of DORA late in 1944.

Q   Where was he sent to?
A   To an out-camp.

Q   Did you hear what happened to him eventually?
A   I saw him the last time in OSTERODE on the 7th or 8th of April 1945 when
     we were loaded on trains in the station of OSTERODE together with the
     whole details, there were about 300 or 400 men, he was marching away from
     the station with the SS. I do not know where.

Q   Do you know whether this detail was the prisoners which came from
     ROTTLEBERODE?
A   No, I don't know what detail it was and where they came from.

Q   Do you happen to know who was in charge of the detail?
A   No.

Q   Did you know a man by the name of BRAUNY who was at one time in DORA?
A   No.

DR. KURZKE: Johnny Nickols was transferred out of DORA in December 1944 because
     he had had some trouble with the Capo Hans SCHNEIDER. He was assigned to
     ROTTLEBERODE and I personally talked to him there end of February or
     beginning March 1945. At that time he was together with a French prisoner
     doctor whose name I do not remember.

MR. KARPIK: I personally was assigned to the Surgical Ward in Block #38 and
     there had to set up the "Aseptic" Surgical Room since I had been doing
     similar work for two years in DACHAU. The building was a so-called
     Air Force Barrack made out of wood about 40 meters long and 12 meters
     wide, one floor with a path in the middle and rooms on both sides. The
     Operation Room was at the end of the barrack and had a preparation room
     attached to it.

Q   Describe these private rooms that you say were on both sides of the aisle?
A   The patients' rooms in this Surgical Ward were not bad but in very good
     shape because there were not so many patients. Altogether there were six
     rooms with about 120 beds altogether. Three rooms had beds, regular iron
     beds with mattresses, the other rooms had double decked wooden beds with
     straw sacks. This Surgical Ward was the only part of the prisoner hospital
     where the beds and patients' rooms were in almost normal condition. During
     the first time I had to try to collect all the necessary instruments

Excerpt from the official transcript of the Nordhausen Trials in 1947 with
testimony regarding Johnny Nicholas, his role as a prisoner doctor, and the same
story he'd told repeatedly to his colleagues at Buchenwald, Camp Dora and Camp
Rottleberode. (National Archives)

CHAPTER TWO
NIGHT AND FOG

As an aspiring actress, Florence didn't mind stories. But a girl did like to know fact from fiction in a love affair.

Johnny Nicholas' stories always amused or entertained her. Sometimes they amazed her.

How could someone so young have done so many things, been so many places, had so many adventures?

He told them with polish and finesse, as if he had rehearsed them. He told them with a great grin on his face and a twinkle in his eye, as if exploring the limits of her credulity.

Or was it her stupidity he was testing? She never knew when to believe him. That was her problem. And it was the problem of almost everyone who knew him.

Florence had seen her acting career come to a halt when the Germans had goose-stepped into Paris. The German High Command had completely taken over movie-making in France and had a stranglehold on the nation's cinemas. The only way she could get in front of a camera now was by warming up to some middle-aged propaganda officer on the staff of Paris Military Headquarters whose job was to produce films on how much Parisians loved their conquerors.

Florence's yearning to act, however, was still being fulfilled. But not in front of camera.

To any Gestapo or *Sicherheitsdienst* (SD) security man who might have been prying, she was a bespectacled and proper French schoolmarm type. But to her associates she was a link in a chain of thousands of French women whose cunning and courage were daily saving American and British pilots shot down over France.

There were lethal risks in the work. If they caught you, it was your final curtain call. And there was another kind of risk. A girl couldn't allow herself to become emotionally involved with the men whose lives she saved. But it was hard not to.

Big American kids who had been the romantic terrors of the little English towns where their airfields were. Or the less-assertive Royal Air Force boys who looked so lost.

Florence's acting ability helped her to maintain a pose of professional detachment. Until she meet Johnny.

Who knows how these things start? Certainly she was shocked to come across an American who spoke French like a native. Most of them had atrocious accents. She was terribly curious. But the group leader kept telling the girls: Don't get involved! Don't say too much! Don't ask too much!

The less you knew about the others and the less they knew about you, the safer it was for both women and pilots. If the Gestapo nabbed a girl, they could do their exquisite worst. And if they did, she might reveal a name. One name. All it took was the leak of *one* for the security of the entire escape network to be blown wide open.

Women formed the backbone of these networks, which stretched across France, Belgium and Holland.

Males of the Underground, civilians continuing the fight against the German occupiers, harvested the downed airmen from trees, bushes, lakes or wherever the caprice of parachute had deposited them, and handed them over to the women. It was the women who found homes, barns, farmers' outbuildings or other refuges where they could hide from the German soldiers scouring the countryside for them.

It was left to the women to find and cook food for the hapless airmen in a country where food was severely rationed.

Many of the airmen were wounded, often suffering from severe burns. It was left to women to treat their injuries as best they could, or find local doctors brave enough to risk torture and imprisonment if the Germans caught them aiding the enemy.

The women ventured into the black market to buy civilian clothes, which the airmen would exchange for their uniforms before they set out on their long, dangerous and circuitous trek south toward the Spanish frontier.

Typically one woman would lead a group of about 20 airmen, none of whom spoke a word of recognizable French. She would be armed with false papers usually identifying the airmen as foreign workers. And it worked perfectly—as long as the airmen kept their mouth shut, and as long as the Gestapo, the dreaded German secret police, and the *Milice*, their French counterparts, did not inspect the documents too rigorously or scrutinize the English and American faces too closely.

En route the escape line stashed Allied pilots in all sorts of places, moving them at night from barn to barn, house to house, town to town, until weeks later they'd be close to the French border with Spain, which was a neutral country.

In peacetime, one could drive straight through from Paris to the frontier in about eleven hours. But in wartime Europe, with the Germans on the trail, waiting to trap them at every major highway intersection or train station, a girl and her little party of escapees had to take the byways and the back roads. Consequently, it could take her as long as six weeks to smuggle them over the Pyrenees Mountains and into Spain.

The favorite hideouts along the way were usually the haylofts of remote farmhouses or the dank cellars of working-class homes. Certainly not the elegant apartment that Johnny maintained in a high-priced address near the Eiffel Tower.

Florence wondered about that.

And there was something else that didn't add up: For all his insistence that he couldn't wait to get back to his squadron in England and start fighting the war again, he didn't seem too anxious to leave.

Johnny had been with white women before. Where he came from, their complexions ranged from ebony and coffee to amber and cream. The lighter-skinned ladies had always been his downfall.

But whiteness had ceased to be the fixating novelty it had been for him in his teens. Nowadays a girl had to have something more. A lot more. And Florence had it all.

Women were essential vitamins for his ravenous ego. But no matter how hard he tried to prevent it, the longer he stayed with one, the sooner she got the idea that she owned him. A possessive woman was dangerous; there was no telling what she might do.

Their voices drifted across the pillow to each other.

He couldn't put his finger on it. Maybe he had told her too much. His street instincts stirred.

Outside, Paris lay unchanged from the morning before. Spires and chimney pots and bluish haze rose from the cook stoves of early risers. It was November 1943 and the City of Light, under Nazi occupation for three and a half years, was cold, hungry, miserable, afraid. Every day the Gestapo knocked down front doors and dragged off men and women to God knows where.

Florence had her own questions about the strapping young black man, six feet tall or more, possessing a cat's grace and agility in his two hundred-pound frame. How was it that he had such an elegant apartment? Who owned it? With several million Parisians cramped in the most abrasive austerity, who in Paris had a luxurious, green carpet on his bedroom floor? Who had a living room big enough to hold a ball in? And a grand piano?

Black marketeers. Gamblers. Pimps. Abortionists. That's who.

In the escape network, it was well understood that pilots were instructed to reveal to their French rescuers only name, rank, serial number and date of birth and unit. This information would allow the escape organization to radio London to check out whether a man was genuine, or a German infiltrator in disguise, and there were many of those. Time and again infiltrators had succeeded, and women, young and old, had been dragged off to horrible fates along with the airmen they had hoped to rescue.

Still, curiosity couldn't prevent Florence from wondering. Whoever was hiding him was obviously rich and probably very influential. In the shadow of the Eiffel Tower, the Avenue de Lamballe was a much-envied location — or had been until the war. And the elegant clothes in the wardrobe: black market, certainly. Were they Johnny's? They were his size. He used them as if they were his own.

A woman captivated by a man yearned to know all the little things: Tell me about your father? Your mother? Where did you grow up? Tell me the things you did as a little boy. Tell me about America.

With her, as with all who knew him, his answers would have been perfunctory, general. He would, as always when backed verbally into a corner, have detoured the conversation along a different route.

The questions of name, rank, serial number and military unit were as vital to the operatives of the escape network as they were to the German Gestapo. Nicholas could be a plant, a cunning contrivance of the Germans to infiltrate the escape network and destroy it. If he answered these questions, the escape network could radio his answers to the Allies in London and verify that he was indeed who he claimed to be.

As long as he withheld the answers to those questions, he was in danger from both sides: The escape network could eliminate him as quickly and indifferently as could the Gestapo—and would if necessary. Anyone as shrewd, as worldly-wise and as calculating as he eventually would prove himself to be should have recognized the danger he was in.

But these were not his most imminent peril. As it turned out, he was his own worst enemy. He had led Florence to believe that she was his one-and-only. Which she wasn't. And when she found that out, according to his brother Vildebart, she turned him in to the Gestapo.

It was November 23, 1943.

Just before dawn in the courtyard of 9 Rue des Saussaises, Gestapo headquarters in Paris, a black car with men wearing civilian suits in the back seat raced out through the gates. It cut across the Rue St. Honore, the Rue de Rivoli and then the Champs Elysees, heading south for the Pont de la Concorde across the Seine.

It was still very dark and there was little traffic. The car's blacked-out headlamps threw slits of light along the vacant streets. As it reached the south end of the bridge, the driver wheeled right along the Quai d'Orsay, and then drove down the Boulevard de la Tour Mauborg. As the bulk of the Ecole Militaire showed up in the headlamps' skimpy illumination, the driver slowed and came to a halt by the curb.

The Ecole, no longer an academy for French officer-cadets, was the most magnificent barracks that German Army troops ever enjoyed. The car, its motor idling, parked behind an empty canvas-topped army truck. On the snow-covered lawns of the Ecole, a dozen German soldiers stamped their feet and briskly rubbed their hands against the pre-dawn cold. In the back of the car the civilians waited....

An officer shouted an order to the troops. Tailgates clanked tonelessly. The soldiers, bulky in their greatcoats, their rifles and equipment jangling and clicking, clambered into the trucks. The car, followed by the truck, rumbled away from the curb and headed down the Avenue de Lamballe. The vehicles barely changed into high gear when the car swung over to the curb, dutifully followed by the truck.

They parked on the avenue near some ancient but magnificent townhouse buildings. Rising from the clutter of their roofs was the steel skeleton of the Eiffel Tower like an apparition in the foggy dawn.

In a few minutes the soldiers were deployed in and around the building. Then the two civilians left the car and entered the building....

Five minutes later they came out with Nicholas, handcuffed between two soldiers.

He had no way of knowing that he has been arrested in a category re-served for very special offenders of the Third Reich. Thereafter, in every official German document in which his name would appear, the initials "N-N" would be appended.

N-N stood for *Nacht und Nebel*, which means Night and Fog, the in-formal title of a decree from the German leader, Adolf Hitler, specifi-cally targeting Resistance fighters in all countries occupied by Germany. The words were adopted by *Der Fuehrer* for his executive order — *Nacht-und-Nebel Erlass* (Decree) — issued in 1941, authorizing that all those charged with committing offenses against the German state be secretly deported to Germany for execution.

N-N appended to any prisoner's name was the code for: "Dangerous Terrorist: To Be Eliminated."

CHAPTER THREE

DOCTOR? ACTOR? SPY?

There was no need to ask where they were taking him. He knew: the Rue des Saussaises or Avenue Foch.

Both meant the absolute worst.

From the rear of the car, seated between the two Gestapo agents, the city he knew so well didn't look the same. Familiar yet strange — like something viewed through the wrong end of binoculars.

What the hell! They were just two pig-headed Germans. He'd handled their kind before. He had a distinct advantage over them because they took one look at his black skin and leaped to all their smug, Aryan conclusions. He always delighted in watching their stunned expressions when he opened up on them in his fastidious German *Hochdeutsch* and announced that he was on a first-name basis with a senior officer on the personal staff of the Paris military commandant.

When you sparred with the Germans, it was a matter of exceeding them in arrogance. You name-dropped profusely, scattering ranks and titles around with abandon. They might have their doubts — but they were scared to risk offending some higher-up.

He hadn't liked Germans particularly — not since the headmaster at the private school he had attended, a huge man of German ancestry, had whipped him in front of the entire class, humiliating him woefully. And now that he was in France, he had more reason than ever for his feelings: The occupiers were taking every possible opportunity of humiliating the occupied.

The Mercedes droned on through the brisk morning, and he found himself thinking about the incident on the Metro several months earlier. He'd been standing at the station with his little friend, Hans Pape, the medical student, waiting for a train. It was always the same for French civilians: if there were any Germans waiting, they got preference. A civilian would stand for more than an hour while train after train pulled in, filled up with Germans, and pulled out.

He'd waited for a long time that day. "I don't give damn," he told Pape. "I'm getting on the next train that pulls in."

The next one was full — except for a single car in the middle. It was painted red, and everyone in wartime Paris knew this meant that the car was reserved for senior German officers, explained Pape, recalling the incident many years after the war.

"You're crazy!" Nicholas heard Pape call out as he headed toward the car, pulling his little friend into the car with him.

There were a half-dozen Nazi officers inside.

One wore a monocle, a chestful of ribbons and a haughty expression. Sitting apart from the others, he obviously outranked them. As Nicholas entered, all six looked up inquisitively. The senior officer, seeing a pair of Negro civilians, screwed his monocle into his eye socket and impaled the intruders with an outraged stare.

Nicholas froze. Slowly he brazenly slipped his hand into his jacket and withdrew an old-style pocket watch, startling the Germans who feared he may have had a weapon. Pretending it was a monocle, he raised it to his eye and stared right back at the German. Except for the clacking of the wheels of the train and muffled gasping, there was silence in the car.

Nicholas advanced toward the monocled Nazi and halted snappily in front of him. From his commanding height, he looked down at the man's medal-bedecked tunic. He tapped the first medal with a probing finger.

"What's this?" he demanded in German. "In what campaign did you win it?" He tapped a second medal, then a third, asking the same questions.

The German was flabbergasted by the effrontery of a civilian in a reserved *Wehrmacht* car. A black-skinned one at that. In the lexicon of the Nazis, blacks ranked at the bottom of the *untermenschen* heap, about the same level as Jews. Totally at a loss for any other response, the German invited Nicholas to sit down.

For the next fifteen minutes, as the subway train glided through Paris, the officer recited the circumstances of his battlefield citations while Nicholas gave him his undivided attention.

The other German officers sat in shocked silence.

When the train arrived at the next station, Nicholas rose, clicked his heels smartly, bade the German *auf wiedersehen* and, towing the quaking Pape behind him, disembarked....

In the back of the Mercedes the two Gestapo men ignored him. Maybe they were handling him with kid gloves because he had claimed to be a close friend of Colonel Schmidt. Or it could be part of their psychology: Let the black bastard sweat it out, not knowing what was ahead for him.

To anyone staring through the car windows it was obvious how the German Occupiers had desecrated Paris with their ubiquitous trappings. Swastikas fluttering everywhere. Hardly a public building without one. If you didn't trip over the flag, you tumbled into one of their thousands of black-and-yellow sentry boxes. It was impossible to stroll the arcades of the Rue de Rivoli as in the old days without bumping into them.

Funny, though. As much as the morning ceremonial march down the Champs Elysees by the First *Sicherungeregiment,* with its blaring brass band, raised his hackles, something else provoked him even more: asinine names a meter long that any civilized nation would long ago have broken into manageable syllables: *Der Militarbefehlshaber in Frankreich ... Hauptverkehrsdirecktion Paris.*

The flared muzzles of the 40-millimeter anti-aircraft cannons poked over the edge of the parapet atop the sacred Arc de Triomphe. The guns' presence there wasn't a military necessity; the Germans did it just to rub French faces in the dirt.

They'd done it in many other ways, too, like shutting down the magnificent Metro from eleven to three o'clock each day and completely on weekends. They'd cut off most of the gasoline supplies and driven nearly all civilian cars off the streets. If you wanted to go somewhere, you could take a velo-taxi, an enclosed cab pulled by bicyclist.

Mostly you walked. If you did and were out after the eleven o'clock curfew, German patrols could hear you a mile away, clop-clopping home on your wooden-sole shoes. If they caught you, the least that could happen was a night spent in the local station of the field police. But if the Resistance happened to have knocked off a few Nazis that night, you might wind up as one of the hostages shot the next morning in retaliation.

It was beautiful to watch how hard Parisians worked at ignoring the Germans. Even at rock bottom, when there was almost no food, little electricity and people were cooking on their Rechaud '44s — 10-gallon cans welded together and filled with balls of crushed newspaper sprinkled with water — they continued to put on their act. They'd sit in pavement bistros such as the Cafe de la Paix and sip an *erzatz* coffee brew called Cafe National, pretending the war had never happened. On weekends, they'd head for the paddocks at Auteuil and Longchamps and watch their ribby ponies race. They pretended that they didn't know there was a war on.

Probably his two Gestapo escorts wanted him to humiliate himself by bowing and scraping to them and initiating conversation. Or maybe they expected him to volunteer some information. Even ask for a cigarette. He wouldn't lower himself. The droning silence of the car demanded to be broken, but he'd be damned if he'd be the one to do it.

It was much too soon to think about escape. Indeed, escape might not be necessary. He would wait and see if Colonel Schmidt was at Gestapo headquarters when they got downtown. If Schmidt *was* there, he'd be home free. If not? Well, he wasn't sure. Still, he'd been arrested before and been able to talk his way out of it. He could do it again. He'd been talking his way out of all kinds scrapes ever since his teen years; so long and so successfully, in fact, that he didn't for an instant doubt his ability to talk his way around the "stupid Germans," as his Underground friends always called them.

He and Colonel Schmidt had an understanding that went way back.

He hadn't always gone by "Schmidt." When they'd first met, which had been on the other side of the Atlantic some years earlier; "Gardemann" was the name he'd been using. *Major* Gardemann.

Nicholas chuckled inwardly, remembering how unpleasantly shocked the major had been to see him strolling into his office in Paris Military Headquarters, requesting an audience with him.

Gardemann, or Schmidt, as he was now calling himself, was on the personal staff of the most powerful German in Paris: General Hans von Boeineberg-Lengsfeld, the commandant of Greater Paris. From the general's colonnaded headquarters — the Hotel Majestic — on Avenue Kleber, fluttered the largest Nazi flag in the city. That day, as Nicholas walked confidently up the steps, the two young German soldiers on guard raised their eyebrows suspiciously. They'd never seen such a well-dressed French civilian: elegant grey fedora, shoes that shone like a mirror. Surely an official of the Vichy French government, which was collaborating with the German conquerors? Maybe an agent of the

Milice, the Gestapo-like auxiliary composed of Nazi-loving Frenchmen who were delighted that France had lost the war?

The black man, addressing the sentries in faultless German, gave them his name and requested to see Colonel Schmidt. They looked at his papers, found them in order, frisked him — standard procedure to prevent some crazy Underground fighter from blowing up German Army Headquarters — and showed him inside.

Nicholas wasn't gone long. In ten minutes he emerged with Colonel Schmidt, and they'd driven off together in a staff car.

In the months that followed, the Hotel Majestic sentries became accustomed to seeing the tall black civilian come and go at headquarters, sometimes with the colonel, sometimes without him. But Nicholas' French friends couldn't get used to it at all. They began to wonder about their black friend: If he's so cozy with the *Bosche*, whose side is he *really* on?

If they had known the origin of the two men's acquaintance, they might have been less anxious. But maybe not.

In 1933, the year that the National Socialist Party assumed full power in Hitler's Germany, Gardemann suddenly appeared on the staff of the German embassy in Haiti; his occupation was listed as "engineer." In Port-au-Prince, as in other national capitals, embassy personnel from around the world tend to socialize within their own community. Nicholas' father, Hilderic, worked for the British embassy, and he and Gardemann met at one of these international get-togethers.

Hilderic, who spoke not only perfect French, his native tongue, but also excellent English, considered himself something of a linguist. It may have been that he hoped to escalate his command of German by associating with Gardemann. In due course Gardemann was invited to the Nicolas home and met the rest of the family, including the young Jean Marcel.

Whatever the reason, it is certain that had as consecrated a Francophile as Hilderic Nicolas suspected that the German diplomat was operating under false colors, he would never have permitted himself and his family to become socially involved with him.

In 1941, following Haiti's declaration of war against Germany, Gardemann mysteriously disappeared from the island. Haitian newspapers speculated that, under the guise of a diplomat, he had been operating as an agent of the *Abwehr*, the secret intelligence-gathering service of the German armed forces, possibly reporting to Berlin spymasters the movements of British and American military convoys sailing the Caribbean.

Lending weight to this speculation was the revelation that Gardemann, prior to his arrival in Port-au-Prince, had spent time on the other side of the border separating Haiti from her perennial enemy, the Dominican Republic.

For years the two tiny nations had furiously disputed the location of their common border. Countless times Haitian peasant farmers, innocently wandering across the poorly marked demarcation line, had been shot and killed by Dominican border guards.

The two countries had almost gone to war in 1937 following the massacre of thousands of Haitian peasants who had come across the frontier.

Intelligence reports reaching the British embassy in Port-au-Prince at the time detailed plans for the immigration of 40,000 Germans to the Dominican Republic for settlement along the disputed frontier.

In 1934, after the U.S. Marines had departed Haiti, Hilderic Nicolas, along with hundreds of thousands of Haitians, had seen with his own eyes the German cruiser anchored for several weeks in Port-au-Prince bay. He had learned, too, that after the warship's departure, the city's small German-Haitian community had split into two camps — pro-Nazis and anti-Nazis.

Adding fuel to the fire, the local press ran stories claiming that Gardemann had been an advisor from the German government on the staff of Dominican dictator Rafael Trujillo in the early 1930s. During this period, the papers reported, Hitler, the new Nazi leader, had been wooing Trujillo for permission to build a German naval base on the Dominican coast of the island.

Anything threatening to enhance Dominican superiority over Haiti was anathema to Hilderic Nicolas. The report of Gardemann's dealing with Trujillo would have been reason for Hilderic Nicolas to sever his relationship with Gardemann. As it happened, Hilderic had been dead four years when Haiti, in 1941, declared war against Germany. The declaration emboldened Port-au-Prince newspapers to publish extravagant speculation that Gardemann, under his cover as a diplomat, had been a German secret agent throughout his years in Haiti.

What happened a few days after these stories broke seemed to support press speculation: Gardemann disappeared. A search was launched, and the German diplomat's car was found on a desolate stretch of beach not far from Port-au-Prince. Newspapers reported it abandoned, keys still in the ignition, all four doors wide open, gas tank drained dry.

Gardemann had apparently left in such a hurry that he hadn't even taken time to turn off the engine. He had simply vanished.

But why? How? Where to? Rumor had it he was picked up by a German submarine.

Police broke the locks on the German embassy, which, by this time, had been impounded by the Haitian government, and searched the premises. What they found fed the conjecture that Gardemann had been an intelligence agent; that he had gone back to Germany, either voluntarily or involuntarily spirited aboard a U-boat that had surfaced off a remote beach.

The mystery surrounding Gardemann took on startling new dimension after news leaked that he been secretly living in common law with a beautiful black Haitian and had sired several children by her; startling because the German had been a diplomatic representative of Nazi Germany, a dictatorship that trumpeted the superiority of Aryans over all other races.[1]

This grossly prejudicial common-law connection, which Gardemann probably thought he had successfully left far behind him, suddenly surfaced in a threatening way right in front of him when Nicholas strode into the Hotel Majestic headquarters that day in 1941. Only now, the German wasn't in the mufti of a civilian; he was wearing the field-gray of a *Wehrmacht* officer on the staff of the German Military Kommandant. If he were ever to get anywhere in his military career, all information regarding his liaison with the beautiful Haitian would have to be expunged.

The car slowed down and curved into the courtyard of 9 Rue des Saussaises, then stopped. The two Gestapo men checked his handcuffs, hauled him out of the car and led him into the main lobby. Throngs of French civilians were being signed in. Convicted of petty offenses against the German occupation authorities, they were parolees under suspended sentences and forced to register each morning with the Gestapo.

---

1 In 2006, the authors located Gardemann's Haitian daughter, Gisela Magones-Vallat, in Orlando, Florida. She was only a year old when he left Haiti for Germany in 1939 and says she never heard about him again.

They shunted Nicholas through the crowd and down a hallway where he was photographed and fingerprinted. About twenty minutes later, a cell door on the fourth floor clanged behind him. He was manacled hands and feet and chained to a ring low in the wall.

The cell was dark. The floor was damp and hard. His mind whirred.

Where the hell was Gardemann?

He heard screams from the floor above.

It was an old trick. They often kept a suspect penned up for days, letting the sound of others' agony soften him up for interrogation. The fifth floor was famous for a sadist they called the Prince de Merode.

The prisoner hadn't been born that Rudi Merode couldn't break, they said.

They say a lot of things. There's always a way out. Somebody closes a door, somebody else opens a window....

They said the Germans' chief weakness was their predictability; that they went by the book; that you could play them like an organ if you knew the stops to pull.

If Schmidt couldn't or wouldn't intervene on his behalf, there had to be a way. He'd bide his time and wait, as he had so often, for Lady Luck. When she came calling, he'd be ready.

Whenever he got himself in a jam and Jaques Coicou or Hans Pape, his medical-student friends, couldn't help, he would turn to his big brother, Vildebart. But how would Vilde know he had landed himself in trouble again — much less know where to find him?

Vilde lived at 135 Rue de Charonne, a working-class residential section of the city. It wasn't too far from the Eiffel Tower area, yet he and Vilde didn't see much of each other. Two or three times a year at most. But with Johnny's odd temperament and mysterious involvements, that was to be expected.

The two brothers had never gotten along. Vilde had always been the student, Johnny the goof-off. Vilde the meticulous preparer, planner and list-maker. Johnny the gambler, the eternal flipper of a coin to decide which move to make in life.

Vilde was four years older and had a wife. As far back as high school he'd never approved of his younger brother's antics and friends. He knew they were too different in personality to be really close. They kept in touch mostly from a sense of family duty. So when Johnny would

---

2 Not a German but a Frenchman named Frederic Martin, he was tried by a French tribunal at the end of the war and executed.

knock on his door at six in the morning with three days' growth of beard on his face, and he was hungry, dirty and bedraggled, Vilde didn't do cartwheels when he saw him. But blood was thicker than Vilde's fear of the Germans, and he and his wife were always good for a bite, a bunk and a few hundred francs to tide Johnny over.

They'd tried to pump him on his first few visits, but he hadn't told them anything, and they finally gave up. Other than saying that he was taking some medical courses at the University of Paris, he always kept them in the dark. That annoyed Vilde, but in wartime Paris the less you knew about a friend's or relative's activities, the better it was for you and them.

Whenever Johnny left after one of his highly infrequent visits, Vilde wouldn't have the faintest idea when he'd see him again — if ever. So if Johnny waited for his brother to come looking for him, he knew he'd rot in jail.

Vilde never knew what to expect, and Johnny delighted in surprising his straight-laced brother. He'd show up dressed as a fashion plate, swaggering with the confidence born of a pocket full of cash, spreading around rolls of five hundred-franc notes as thick as cigars.

Maybe Pape and Coicou would miss him when he failed to show up in their favorite Latin Quarter bistro. If he was missing for any length of time, would the two of them come hunting for him as they had once before?

Pape was loyal and had courage. He hadn't fled when Nicholas had brazenly encountered the *Wehrmacht* officer on the Metro; the poor devil had just sat there and sweated.

Jacques Coicou was just as dependable. He'd let Nicholas hide in his apartment at 116 bis, Champs Elysees, for several months. Nicholas had shared an attic room with a rescued B-17 pilot[3], and had picked up knowledge about his squadron in England and his life in the States.

---

3 When Coicou was interviewed by the authors in 1971 he identified the U.S. airman as Lt. Warren P. (Pete) Edris. However, when contacted in 2010 Edris said he never met Nicholas, suggesting that Coicou may have had him confused with another downed American he had helped. Now 89, Edris maintains a vivid memory of his World War II experiences, which are chronicled in a new book entitled "Dying for Another Day." Although Coicou and his wife were released by the Gestapo, Edris was arrested in May 1943 and eventually sent to a stalag in Germany. He was liberated by the U.S. Army's 14th Division in April 1945, survived the ordeal and later became an American Airlines pilot. In 2010

Coicou worked for the Resistance as a doctor. After the American had bailed out of his plane and been injured parachuting, Coicou had taken care of his injuries.

The phone had rung in the apartment late the night before. Coicou had answered. The voice had said that his "aunt" had taken a turn for the worse. Could he come and see her? It was the Resistance code: an Allied pilot had been shot down and needed medical attention.

As a senior medical student at the University of Paris, Coicou was permitted by the German military administration to practice medicine — up to a point — because of a shortage of civilian doctors. This meant Coicou qualified for a ration of gas for his car and an *ausweis*, the all-important little piece of paper from German headquarters permitting him to be travel after curfew.

Coicou had made the trip across Paris in his Citroen with his heart in his mouth. While the *ausweis* kept him from being arrested, it didn't stop the patrols from flagging him down and questioning him. He always tried to keep off the big, empty boulevards. He preferred the narrow, twisting back and side streets; they offered more chance of escape if pursued. Unfortunately his muffler was blown, and this left a trail of high-pitched decibels in his wake.

Amazingly, Coicou arrived at the "safe" house where the U.S. airman was hidden without being intercepted. But he learned on arrival that the Germans had the house under surveillance: They were in great danger. Everyone would have to scramble — and fast. But nobody had a place to take the injured lieutenant, so the burden fell on Coicou.

He couldn't refuse. First, though, he had to find out from his wife Suzanne if she would agree to take the young pilot. But he couldn't use the phone: the Germans routinely tapped the lines, and it would be too risky. So he had to drive all the way across the city again to tell her personally what was happening.

Aware that the Gestapo was closing in, Coicou found himself emotionally exhausted as he headed back to his wife. Again, no patrols. That in itself, however, doubled his fears that the Gestapo was on to him. He felt that they were going to zero in on him in their own good time; that they had arranged for army street patrols *not* to blunder into him and foil their exquisitely contrived capture plan.

---

he resided in Kennersville, NC. He visited Coicou in Port-au-Prince during the 1950s.

Coicou's wife agreed without hesitation to take in the young American pilot and suggested he could share the attic room with Nicholas. But could Coicou once again make the trip across town to the "safe" house where the injured pilot lay and bring him back without the Germans catching him?

Nicholas didn't have to look twice at Coicou to diagnose exhaustion, so he volunteered to go along. This time, however, he insisted that they take *his* car, and that *he* would do the driving.

Good old Gardemann. Through him Nicholas had obtained a car, gasoline coupons and his own personal *ausweis*.

When Coicou got into the car, he was shocked. Not just that in car-famished Paris it was a large Citroen; Nicholas had large French tri-color flags fluttering from both front fenders!

Coicou spluttered his protest, but Nicholas waved it away. Relax, he said, explaining that, if stopped by a German patrol, they would pretend to be three high-ranking Vichy government officials on a top-priority mission.

Who was the third?

They were about to find out.

In the Passy area of the city Nicholas guided the car into a darkened street lined with elegant apartment houses. He leaned back and opened the door to the rear seat.

A young man slipped out of the shadows and entered. Nicholas identified him as the son of Paris Police Chief Amedee Bussiere, Coicou would recall years later.

When they arrived at the "safe" house, they bundled the injured American into the back of the car and threw a traveling rug over him. Nicholas gunned the Citroen back to the Champs.

Coicou sweated in the back seat with the American. It seemed to him as if Nicholas was deliberately looking for German curfew patrols. And he got them. Each time they were flagged down, all three produced their *ausweis*. If it looked as if some *Wehrmacht* N.C.O., with nothing to do but kill time, was going to give them the third-degree, Nicholas addressed him haughtily in German, lacing his explanations with military protocol, alluding to his personal association with Colonel Schmidt (Gardemann) and identifying his back-seat passenger as the police prefect's son.

About a month later, when the lieutenant had fully recovered, someone knocked on the front door of Coicou's apartment. He opened it, and a squad in SS uniforms barged in. They arrested everyone in the house — except Nicholas, who was elsewhere at the time. But when Nicholas returned to the house a few days later, the SS were waiting for him. They slapped handcuffs on him and took him to Gestapo headquarters.

Germans in general — and the Gestapo in particular — nurtured a special hatred for anyone caught helping Allied airmen. The more fliers returning to their bases in England, the more the merciless aerial bombing of German cities would continue. So Coicou and his wife could expect very harsh treatment.

But they were released!

Why?

Coicou explained his release years afterwards. As a medical student in his final years, he was almost fully trained as a doctor and therefore too valuable to be shot or sent to a concentration camp. So he was given a suspended sentence by the Gestapo and assigned to work in a German military hospital in the Paris region. Like all parolees, he had to sign the register at Gestapo headquarters each day.

The German army takeover of Paris in June 1940 had thrown the vast city's administration into chaos. Its health-care infrastructure was stretched far beyond its needs, particularly in terms of doctors. In recognition of the emergency, the German military administration relaxed the rules to allow medical students to open limited practices.

"All the French doctors and many medical students were at the front," said Coicou, a Haitian and a medical student at the time. "So all that was left were the foreign students who came to Paris to study.

"In one year all French doctors were prisoners-of-war, and you had no doctors in Paris or anywhere else in France, so you were obliged to treat people if you were in your third, fourth or fifth year of medical school.

"I know that Johnny had a medical practice, but I didn't see a diploma on the wall. I didn't have a diploma either, but it was possible for us to practice because we were in the hospitals, and we had patients. Patients would come to our apartments. We would examine them, diagnose them and prescribe treatment."

During this period of extreme shortage, when medical students were legally permitted to stand in for qualified physicians, Coicou said that

Nicholas had worked before his arrest by the Gestapo as a substitute doctor at The American Hospital in the wealthy western Paris suburb of Neuilly-sur-Seine.

"We were trying to make a living," Coicou said. "No one questioned this at the time. It was perfectly normal.

"Johnny had clientele. His specialty was gynecology."

How could he have gotten away with it? Yes, he had had some experience — mostly of a menial nature — working in a small local hospital in his late teens and as a non-registered medical student, but how could he have convinced the German administration that he was a *bona fide* medical student?

One had to know Nicholas to understand how he could have pulled the wool over German bureaucratic eyes, Coicou explained. "He knew so much that he could outsmart you at any time. Very quickly he could learn ten times more than you, and he could put you in a chair and tell you all about it. If he read something on a medical theme, it was possible for him to speak authoritatively on it within an hour — as if he knew everything about it. And he could speak for an hour on almost any medical subject."

The toilets in the cells at Gestapo headquarters frequently overflowed. The place stank. Chains threaded through the low wall-rings prevented prisoners from standing upright and exercising. Most of them couldn't stomach the pannikins of mangel-wurzel soup and grew weaker every day.

Any prisoner mulling over the prospect of escape realized that he had to force down the slop if he hoped to be strong enough to make a break — if and when the opportunity presented itself.

That was Nicholas's situation if Colonel Schmidt didn't show up.

Like every prisoner, he would have wondered how long it would be before they started interrogating him. It was part of Gestapo operating philosophy to make them wait and wonder. It broke them down psychologically.

When would Pape and Coicou miss him? Were they already looking for him? Would Vilde even notice that he had disappeared?

Pape and Coicou had become accustomed to meeting Nicholas in the cafes and student haunts of the Latin Quarter and in Montparnasse. They recalled him inevitably surrounded by a party of theater or motion-picture people, and never without some charming female on his arm.

He had a personal style, a grinning, brimming self-confidence, a *savoir-fair* that their classmates of both genders found irresistible. He often seemed as if he were performing; as if he were on stage before an audience, testing them to see how far along he could coax and cajole them into his fantasies.

He flattered his medical-student guests with his hungry interest in their course of study. He knew so much already about his chosen profession that some figured that he might be a former army medic making a pile in whatever business he was in, but whose first love was really medicine. On several occasions he had hinted that he was taking some medical courses at the university, but neither Pape nor Coicou had ever seen him in class.

He would seek Pape out in his modest apartment in the Quarter, and they'd talk medicine for hours.

But they never talked about the war. They studiously avoided any discussion of Resistance activities, preferring to ramble on about movies, actors, actresses, directors; subjects in which Nicholas excelled. He even bragged about socializing with some of filmdom's leading lights.[4]

From these conversations Pape concluded that his big friend hung around Paris' movie colony.

The French movie industry was lethally stricken when the country surrendered to the Germans. Even before the conquerors had captured Paris, many of its top talents had fled to Hollywood. French filmmakers, to survive as an industry and to avoid the leaden hand of German military censorship, developed a strain of poetic romanticism in films having nothing to do with the war. One of the most widely acclaimed and controversial films of the period was *less Visitors du soiree* (The Devil's Envoy), directed by the fabled Marcel Carne.

For many French men and women, the film embodies their country's most eloquent passive resistance against the Occupiers. It was a *cause célèbre* in France in 1942, when it premiered, and during the years of the Occupation; so much so that anyone with any interest at all in movies couldn't avoid getting into arguments over it.

---

4. Nicholas had always been a film enthusiast. He reportedly mingled at the first Cannes Film Festival in 1939 — before the start of World War II — and was photographed with starlets and others.

In this medieval fable, two minstrels, who are actually servants of the Devil, arrive at a castle during the betrothal feast of a baron's daughter and a knight. One minstrel falls in love with the bride-to-be. The Devil turns him and the bride-to-be of into stone — but permits their hearts to continue beating.

Throughout the war, many French people claimed that Carne had pulled one over on the Occupiers by turning the seemingly innocuous tale into an allegory of the Occupation, with the Devil representing the Germans, and the lovers the indomitable French spirit. However, just as many others insisted that Carne had done nothing of the sort. Hence the controversy.

It typified the arguments that engaged Pape, Nicholas and their circle of artsy and sophisticated friends for hours. And if it wasn't movies, it was likely to be medicine.

Pape recalled a night when Nicholas turned up at a party some medical students were throwing for their professors. Early in the evening he drew Pape aside and asked him the best procedure for doing an abortion. Pape told him. A few hours later Pape found Nicholas in a group, authoritatively describing modern abortion techniques.

Pape and Coicou, like most of those who were drawn to Nicholas, had heard the troubling rumors: Their friend was a frequent visitor at German Army headquarters. He associated with German officers. He had been seen riding around with them in their staff cars. French Resistance people took a very poor view of such proximity to the hated enemy. So Pape and Coicou were afraid to be seen too often with Nicholas; it tended to cast doubt on *their* patriotism.

Yet Nicholas was not only fascinating, sophisticated and at home in glamorous circles; he was also very generous with money when he had it, always good for a loan. To perennially destitute university students on austerity budgets it was a quality usually sufficient to mollify all but their gravest reservations about him.

Pape and Coicou hadn't seen him for a long time prior to his arrest by the Gestapo. When the days of his absence lengthened into weeks, they decided they'd better check and see if anything was wrong. They'd never been to his apartment before; he had always come to theirs. But they had his address.

When they went there, they found he'd left — without leaving a forwarding address.

As senior medical students, they were busy with their studies and had patients to attend to in their capacity as doctors in limited practice. So it took a while until they could arrange for time off to hunt for him.

Their search took them a long way from the Latin Quarter. They worked their way through a succession of landladies and concierges, bartenders, waiters and hatcheck girls. They crossed the Seine to the Right Bank and into the clubs and cabarets of Piglet and Montmartre. Their questions led them through the working-class districts of La Chapelle and La Villette west to the middle-class area north of the Arc de Triomphe known as Les Batnigolles.

They found him there in a small office in a fairly modern building. It was adequately but not extravagantly furnished, and on the wall above his desk hung an impressive, framed document bearing a red-wax seal.

Behind his enthusiastic greeting they sensed that he was not entirely happy to see them. He adroitly sidestepped any explanation for his mysterious movements or his long absence by bombarding them with questions about their medical studies.

Under the circumstances Pape and Coicou felt a little ill at ease, but they didn't let that inhibit their curiosity about the document. They got close enough to read it. Setting aside all the ornate language, it said that "John Guy Nicholas" was licensed to practice medicine and that his specialty was gynecology. There was no diploma on the wall but on their way out they picked up one of his calling cards. It stated that he'd obtained his M.D. at the University of Heidelberg, Germany.

Gestapo Headquarters was always a busy place beginning at sunrise, when those unfortunate French men and women caught overnight in the finely meshed German net widely cast over the city each night were brought up from their cells for processing. They ran the gamut from prostitutes and pimps to innocent housewives caught outdoors a few minutes after the 8 p.m. curfew and Resistance fighters caught in the act.

Usually they formed several lines in front of a long table, where three or four bored German army NCOs quizzed them on their names, addresses, dates of birth, etc. and recorded these particulars on a preliminary questionnaire.

An armed German soldier usually stood near the table, guarding a group of petty offenders. But those charged with serious offenses, such as Resistance fighters, appeared in chains and were escorted by two armed guards.

Nicholas was prodded into place in the line by the two armed soldier escorts. He wore handcuffs and a short chain connected cuffs on his feet. As he waited his turn, he likely mulled over in his mind all the stories he had heard about how the Gestapo could make the strongest man talk.

A Gestapo officer had many interrogating techniques, most of them brutal. Every French man and women in Occupied France had heard of them. The question facing every prisoner with something to hide always was: Do I tell them now, and save myself the torture? Or do I refuse, only to have them torture it out of me?

Sometimes they jammed cotton batten between the toes and lit it. Or they pulled out fingernails or toe nails one at a time. Or they held a stubborn prisoner's head underwater until he was almost drowning. ... Stories abounded about the German ingenuity for extracting the truth from those unwilling to tell it. Usually they liked to apply their techniques to parts of the body where the damage wouldn't show when the prisoner was fully clothed. But impatient interrogators often became indiscriminate, and the brutality would show on a prisoner's face.

Nicholas was too fond of his creature comforts and his good looks to want to have anyone become *that* impatient with him. ...

Now it was his turn. He decided to tell the truth, a tactic to steer the Germans away from connecting him with the Resistance and his "American" cover story.

Name?

Jean Marcel Nicolas (not Nicholas, which he later adopted as his surname).

Date of birth and birthplace?

20 October 1918. Port-au-Prince, Republic of Haiti.

Nationality?

French.

Why French?

French parentage.

Parents' names?

Hilderic and Lucie Nicolas.

Mother's maiden name?

Dalicy.

Date of arrival in France?

First arrival 1928. Second arrival 1938.

Explain.

In 1928 to begin education; in 1938 to join French navy.

Late in the fall of 1938, the French naval vessel finally docked at Martinique. He grabbed his bag and excitedly hopped aboard the inter-island ferry for the 100-mile trip.

Bon voyage at long last: Climbing the ship's gangplank, turning his back on the boredom. He surely exuberated in his final freedom from all who would have tied his hands and blinded his extravagant imagination.

A few weeks later found him aboard the training ship *Courbet*. Later he transferred to the *Ocean*. Life as a naval cadet. Out on the briny. The Atlantic. The Mediterranean. Salt spray stinging his face. The thrill of a ship in full sail, the solidity of oak underfoot in a heavy swell.

Aloft in the *Ocean's* rigging, he lost his footing, crashed to the deck, almost killing himself.

In March 1939, after he recovered, the navy boosted his ego with a Certificate of Good Conduct, then slapped it down with a notation on the back: "UNFIT FOR FURTHER SERVICE."

After discharge he moved to Paris and holed up at 97 Boulevard Diderot in the 12th Arrondisement, plotting his next move.

The German *blitzkrieg* into Poland that launched World War II was five months away, but war clouds loomed across Europe. Talk of hostilities against the *Boche* buzzed in every Paris sidewalk cafe. Thousands of young French army reservists daily dusted off their uniforms — including his brother Vildebart. But *macho* Jean, good with his dukes, always ready for a fight, afraid of no one? He was busy mothballing *his* uniform.

A youth of his temperament must have felt humiliated, but he would have psyched himself out of it before too long. He would have been able to turn his mind around: What a fabulous stroke of luck — setting him loose in the most beautiful and most civilized city in the world, with so many marvelous young women to be danced, dined and loved — and all the competition going off to war!

Who was keeping him financially afloat all this time?

Surely not the modest nest egg that this parents had pressed on him when he sailed from Port-au-Prince. More likely the well-heeled Uncle Fortune, who had engineered his nephew's emigration in the first place. And Uncle's advance could have been parlayed multifold through Jean's legendary luck at the gaming tables.

Easily bored, quickly impatient, chronically in search of new experiences, he quit Paris, got himself a car and headed for the south of France. Friends and relatives in Port-au-Prince and Paris had him sampling *en route* the casinos and fleshpots of Nice, Marseilles, Cannes, Toulon and Bordeaux. In the sunny, monied revelry and abandon of the Riviera, it seems, Jean Marcel Nicolas of Port-au-Prince began his transformation into "Johnny Nicholas" of Boston, USA.

Uncle Fortune was comfortable with anecdotes of his nephew flashing his engaging grin around the cocktail bars, buying drinks "on the house" from his winnings and consecrating himself to lasting friendships on the strength of a single night-on-the-town.

Local legend has him gate-crashing society parties in his velvet-glove style and wedging his big frame in the door of the colony of screenwriters, producers and movie actors populating the exotic Mediterranean coastline. They discovered their new-found "medical student from Paris" an urbane host, a witty conversationalist and — for an "American" — unbelievably facile among the international set with his command of French, German, English and Spanish.

Until his money began to run low.

Then, according to Coicou, his medical-student friend in Paris, a newspaper ad caught his eye: A Paris motion-picture company shooting on location in the Riviera needed the consulting services of a freelance producer.

The little that Nicholas knew about movie making had been picked up strictly from watching the finished product at the Rex back home, but that didn't stop him. He answered the ad, invented his experience as a producer and embarked for Nice, whose library books apparently taught him everything he knew about producing movies. For three days and nights he lived with the books, said Coicou, hardly bothering to eat or sleep, preparing to smart-talk his way into the job.

On the appointed day he dressed himself in his impeccable "American" ensemble, which he fashioned after the wardrobes of his gangster-movie heroes. He conned the interviewer with his false credentials, got the job and scooped up 500,000 francs for his services, said Coicou.

Sometimes, however, as he discovered in an auction at Nice, it was a liability to be American.

In a conventional auction, the highest bidder is the only one to pay out any money. However, in some private auctions held in upper crust circles in France to raise money for charity, Coicou explained, it was the custom for *every* bidder to pay into the kitty, even though the highest bidder was the one to get the item.

On this occasion Nicholas was low on funds and high on champagne, but that did not deter him from bidding. Continually upping the bid, he found himself in competition with a French philanthropist unwilling to be outdone by an American. Each time the philanthropist upped the bid, Nicholas raised him. His last raise was 9.5 million francs, which the philanthropist topped with a bid of 10 million, and the auctioneer banged his gavel.

The next day, according to Coicou, two husky men from the charitable organization came around to collect their 9.5 million francs from the "wealthy American Negro." Nicholas confessed that he wasn't really an American but a poor Haitian medical student unfamiliar with that type of auction.

The charity men turned mean and threatened to strong-arm him. He reminded them that this type of auction was illegal and pointed out that the philanthropist's bid would not have reached the 10 million mark had not he, Nicholas, kept upping the ante.

In the end — or so goes Coicou's recollection — they commended him and withdrew, apologizing for the inconvenience.

His wandering lifestyle took him back to Paris, which is where he was in June 1940, when the war was nine months old and German armored columns trundled ominously close to the city. He, like hundreds of thousands of Parisians, fled on his bicycle.

Pedaling south toward Chartes, he found the road choked by hundreds of thousands of refugees. All he could do was to get off his bicycle and begin walking. Eventually all forward movement stopped.

Looking out over the heads of the refugee horde packed in around him, he would have wondered: Now what?

The German NCO handed the completed questionnaire to one of Nicholas' guards, who took him to a private office where a man in civilian clothes sat behind a desk. The escort handed the man Nicholas' questionnaire. He studied it as the escorts prodded Nicholas into a chair facing the civilian. When the armed guards stepped back, the civilian looked up.

What was the nature of the medical discharge from the French navy?

A head injury.

Repeat the name of the training ship?

Le Courbet.

Where had he received his education?

The Aristide Briand School at St. Nazaire and the College de Garcon at Grasse.

When had his father arrived in Haiti?

He couldn't remember.

How was his father employed?

He was deceased.

When had he died?

1937.

What had his employment been?

Secretary at the British Embassy in Port-au-Prince.

The Gestapo officer pressed for details on his father's work for the British. Nicholas told him that he was very young at the time and that he didn't really know much about his father's activities, except that he had held a very important job.

What had Nicholas done after his discharge from the French Navy?

Attended medical school at the University of Paris.

Where had he been when the war broke out?

In Paris.

Where had he been when the German army entered Paris?

He had left with hundreds of thousands of other refugees for Chartres.

And then?

To Marseilles in the Unoccupied Zone.

What did you do in the Unoccupied Zone?

Loafed around. A little gambling. Baccarat. Blackjack, that type of thing. Had fun.

Why did he return to the Occupied Zone?

Germany and France had signed an armistice. He wanted to come back to Paris and continue his medical education.

How was he supporting himself?

His family in Haiti had been sending him money to a bank in Marseilles, but when the German Army took over the Unoccupied Zone, they could no longer do so.

What diploma did he hold?

Baccalaureat Part I and Part II.

What lycee had he attended?

The Tippenhauer Academy.

Who was the headmaster there?

Harry Tippenhauer.

What was Haiti's national anthem?

La Dessalinienne.

What were its opening lines?

Pour le Pays, pour le Ancetres/Marchons unis, marchons unis

Dans nos rangs point de traitres/Du sol soyons seuls maitres ...

Had he ever been outside France since his discharge from the navy in March, 1939?

No.

Did he ever visit his old teachers at the Aristide Briand School?

No.

Or at the College de Garcon in Grasse?

No....

From the standpoint of the Gestapo officer, the aspects of the interrogation that merited special vigilance included the prisoner's membership in a military organization — the French navy; his father's employment at the embassy of Germany's sworn enemy — England; his familiarity with St. Nazaire — a major German U-boat base; and his perfect command of French, German and English. Confronted with any one of these aspects, an experienced intelligence officer would have immediately placed him in a high-risk category for being an Allied agent and duly handed him off to others for more highly specialized interrogation.

There is no record that was ever done.

Nor is there any evidence that he was ever tortured to make him confess to charges based on Florence's betrayal. More than a few Gestapo interrogators, aching for the excuse to brutalize their prisoners, welcomed the stubborn ones. For the time being the one female Nicholas would never have dared two-time — Lady Luck — smiled on him. He got through the interrogation with his good looks and his "family jewels" intact. But gambler that he was, he knew that somewhere, sometime, his winning streak had to break.

And it did. The Gestapo determined that while his Haitian story may have been compelling, it was perhaps rehearsed to well and that he was indeed as Florence had alleged: an American agent sent to France to commit sabotage and espionage against the German armed forces. And this made him a perfect candidate for punishment by extermination under *Nacht und Nebel.*

Nicholas climbed into the back of a big French police "Black Maria" van with a crush of other prisoners. The vehicle groaned under its load and whined out of the courtyard of the Rue des Saussaises.

Through the long, narrow window slits the prisoners could see the sides of buildings, people on the sidewalks, traffic flowing by. The Avenue Marigny, then the Champs, now the Boulevard St. Germain, now the Boulevard Raspail. Any old denizen of Paris would have recognized from the order in which the streets were appearing that they were heading south. Gradually the heavy traffic sounds waned. Fields and trees showed through the slits....

A long time later the vehicle bucked and lurched over cobblestones, then came to a halt. When the rear doors jerked open, Nicholas and his fellow prisoners faced a platoon of German soldiers staring up at them. *Heraus! Schnell!*

The prisoners, stiff from the long ride, climbed clumsily down from the truck and were ordered to line up for roll call.

When roll call was over, they were marched down an underground passage at the end of which they entered a mammoth hall. They looked around apprehensively. Over their heads they saw gallery upon gallery of cells rising to a far distant ceiling, and all they could hear was the clanging of iron cell doors and the metallic zing of guards' boots along the steel catwalks.

Looking debonair, six-foot-tall Johnny Nicholas cut a dashing figure in Paris around 1940. He attended medical school at the University of Paris and later set up a medical practice. (Nicolas Family Photo)

Johnny Nicholas was a movie buff, reportedly also a producer and hung out with the movie crowd, including famed French actress Viviane Romance, who is believed to be on the far left with the dog. He's seen here strolling with members of the Parisian film set during the early 1940s in Nice.

Vildebart Nicolas and his wife, Andree, at their home in a Paris suburb during the mid-1970s. When Johnny went missing, they boldly went to Gestapo Headquarters seeking information concerning his whereabouts but hit a blank wall. (Authors' Photo)

Viviane Romance (nee Pauline Ronacher Ortsmanns) was named Miss Paris in 1930 and made her first picture in 1931. For more than 25 years she reigned as one of France's most popular actresses, often playing a flirt, vamp or femme fatale. She reportedly palled around with Johnny Nicholas. Ms. Romance made dozens of movies, her last in 1974. She turned down Hollywood and died at age 79 in 1991. (Image from Internet; L'ECRAN, translates to THE SCREEN).

Johnny Nicholas and unidentified friend in Paris during the early 1940s. Nicholas had a wide range of friends in movie and medical circles. (Vildebart Nicolas)

CHAPTER FOUR
COMPIEGNE

In the prison at Fresnes Nicholas lived in a tiny, dark cell that had an iron bed with a filthy mattress. There was a flush toilet without a lid, above it a single faucet and a small table nearby. The walls were filmed in grime and scored with initials, names, dates and slogans.

The prison staff included a huge German Army sergeant who specialized in victimizing N-Ns. He would burst into a cell first thing in the morning and announce to the occupant: You are dirty spy and we will kill you slowly! With that, he would punch the N-N in the face, kick him in the groin, then depart.

Being an N-N, a prisoner had one big strike against him. Bearing in mind the German attitude toward people of color, Nicholas had two, so he surely received his share of visitations from the brutal *feldwebel*.

All his instincts would have screamed for him to take the hulking German on, but common sense would have told him that it would be a no-win contest for him.

By this time his hopes of being rescued by his patron, Colonel Schmidt, would have waned considerably, and he would have been getting used to the idea that he was all on his own. If he was going to get out, it would be up to him — and him alone. So, despite his cramped quarters, he would continue with his daily calisthenics, determined to be in top physical condition when he got his chance to make his break.

However, it would be almost a year and a half before that happened.

In the meantime he was pushed into the back of truck one day and driven to a place that, to hundreds of thousands of French men and women, marked their entry into the German concentration-camp pipeline: the Royal Lieu transit camp near Compiegne, about forty-five miles north of Paris.

This former French Army barracks was enclosed by barbed wire and gangly guard towers — but the library was still in operation! The Germans held roll call every morning and evening in the big parade ground. During the day, prisoner work details marched out of camp after breakfast and returned well before the seven o'clock curfew.

Nicholas, probably because he was an N-N, was never among them, and his main problems were boredom and uncertainty. There was the daily sweeping of the dormitory, with its double rows of twin-tiered bunks on both sides and the long table down the middle. And there also was an occasional potato-peeling detail in the camp kitchen. Beyond that, more boredom. More waiting and wondering.

Compiegne was the last stop on the way to the Third Reich. Every prisoner knew it, so every prisoner's overriding pre-occupation was escape: Everything Nicholas did, everything he saw, everything he heard he sifted and evaluated and categorized in terms of how it could get him through the barbed wire and out.

The Germans, past masters in understanding the prisoner psyche, had meticulously taken care of all the unauthorized ways out of the camp.

Whoever escaped, Nicholas knew, would have to come up with something completely different. There had to be a way! It was only his first day. He'd give himself a few days to look around, and then something would come to him. He knew it. Something would work out for him. It always did in these kinds of situations. His luck never left him alone for too long.

The other men in his quarters hailed from every province in France, every page in the social register: Resistance leaders, government officials, doctors, priests, writers, policemen, pimps, fairies, whorehouse operators, black-market racketeer....

He'd watch them at the open-air washing trough in the morning. Snow on the ground. Cold as an ice cube. It made the bruises look blacker; the weals look purpler on their pallid, goose-pimply flesh. The men who shuffled along slowly with an odd way of walking, almost as if they'd been riding a horse for a week straight; they were the ones who had been kicked in the balls so often and so long they'd never walk or make love properly again in their lives.

The old hands insisted that there was no way of telling how long they'd keep you at Royal Lieu. Some were there barely a week when they were shipped out. Others had been there for months. But it didn't take long for a prisoner to figure out that what they were in was a pipeline operation between French prisons and German concentration camps. When the camps were full, everything else along the line jammed up. When they emptied out, they were restocked with shipments from places like Royal Lieu.

Of course, whispered the old timers, there were always ways of slowing things down — if you knew the right people. Like arranging with someone in the camp office to "lose" your records. Or when it came to the physical that the fastidious German medical officers insisted a prisoner had to pass before going on a shipment: You could flunk it — if you knew the right strings to pull.

But you had to have money. Once you found the string-puller, it cost you plenty to buy his services.

Royal Lieu's long roll calls gave intelligent prisoners such as Nicholas time to case the place.

Each guard tower had two SS soldiers and a big, ugly Spandau machine gun with an ominous-looking perforated barrel. The guards acted trigger-happy. At night, the big searchlights in the towers crisscrossed the entire area with their beams. On top of that, special squads of SS patrolled the camp streets and alleys after curfew. They had machine pistols and dogs. The old-timers said that they were just thugs in SS uniform who notched their belts for every prisoner they killed; that they were so bored on a long, cold snowy winter's night that if a face appeared at a barracks window after seven o'clock, they blasted first and asked questions second.

A fenced-in section at the camp's main entrance looked as if it might have possibilities. New prisoners were held there while they were processed. Sometimes, when an incoming batch arrived late at night, the Germans waited until the next day to start the paperwork and left the prisoners penned up overnight in the fenced area.

It didn't look heavily guarded.

If you could make it to the fenced-in area before the curfew and hide there until night, it might be easier to sneak behind the main, barbed-wire fence where there were several small buildings. One was a hut where they stored straw for the mattresses. You could hide under the straw and stay warm until you were ready to make a break. The fenced-in section was located almost directly under one of the guard towers; you'd be in the tower's blind spot....

Sleep was difficult. Part of the problem was bed bugs and the stink of overflowing crap barrels. The other part was thinking about how to get out. You couldn't turn off your mind.

The fenced-in area: It could work *if* you could cover up your footprints in the snow. Otherwise they'd track you from your block directly to the straw-storage hut, and you'd be a dead man.

What about the sewer? There was a sewer manhole located in an alley between the long blocks of huts and out of the line-of-sight of the guard towers.

As the days of December 1943 dwindled, Royal Lieu's barracks crowded with new arrivals. A hundred one day. A hundred-and-fifty the next. Two hundred-and-fifty the day after.

Roll calls took longer and longer. Tension ballooned. Who would be on the next shipment out? When would it be called? Who would stay behind?

In the dormitories, the prisoners huddled in whispering cliques and conspiracies. They did it more to bolster morale than to escape; the Germans seemed to have thought of everything.

Nicholas' size and *macho* personality made him a magnet for his despairing comrades. He stood almost a head taller than most of the Frenchmen clustered around him, seeking solace in the authoritative calm that his presence propagated.

He moved with a swagger that served notice he could take care of himself in a fight. And when someone would tell him that he looked like the famous Brown Bomber, American heavyweight champion Joe Louis, he would grinningly accept the compliment and began bragging about his own bouts in the ring.

It gave his bunkmates something to think about. So did the story of his getting out of a warm bed with a blonde in the middle of the night only to get arrested: The rumor going around was a lot more lurid than the facts warranted. But what the hell! If it gave the poor bastards a laugh, what was the difference?

He talked a lot but revealed very little. This provoked his acquaintances to high-flying speculation that he neither confirmed nor denied.

He carried himself with the panache expected of an American, and because he was the only one of that nationality in Compiegne, he had stood out from the very beginning.

In terms of personality and sheer drawing power he had a rival in a big, beefy Frenchman with a velvet tongue who bragged about the whore-house in Paris he had for German officers. The brothelkeeper, who moved easily among the French prisoners, had worked a deal to have food parcels smuggled in past the gate guards — as long as the guards got their share. And prisoners who had sought his perfumed goods on the outside now yearned for his culinary delicacies on the inside — cold lobster, smoked salmon, sausages, hams, chocolates, cigarettes, coffee, brandy and wine.

It was just another reminder that money talks; that money always talks no matter what the circumstances. In a camp where there was usu-ally a complete turnover about every few weeks, the brothel baron had been around for months. It mutely testified that he had enough money or food — or both — to keep on buying those Germans who selected the prisoners for shipment to the concentration camps.

If he had the gate guards on the take, maybe he could arrange for a letter to be smuggled out to Gardemann. The thought must have oc-curred to Nicholas.

If Major Gardemann or Colonel Schmidt, of whatever he was cur-rently calling himself, knew the mess his Haitian friend was in, he'd spring him in twenty-four hours just to keep him from letting the cat — the black cat — out of the bag. He would definitely want him to keep his incriminating information to himself, otherwise he risked banish-ment to a concentration camp for the sin of "race-defilement," as Hitler termed it.

The Germans and their honor. To protect it, Nicholas had gambled that Gardemann would give him anything he asked for. And he had: A car. Gasoline. An *ausweis.* Money.

If Nicholas *had* conned the whoremaster into getting the letter to Gardemann past the gate guards, one can imagine him awakening every morning, expecting to be told of his release courtesy of the influential major/colonel. But as New Year's Day 1944 dawned over Royal Lieu, it still had not happened. The camp bulged with new bodies and stank abominably. The water supply had dropped to a dribble. Prisoners held tin cans under eaves troughs to drink melting snow.

The camp's facilities stretched to the limit. It could take no more bodies, which meant an out-shipment, surely a mammoth one, was days — if not hours — away.

Morale had hit rock bottom. Hopelessness infected the prisoners as a disease. One can visualize Nicholas with his ear cocked for the public-address system, waiting for the sound of his name to be called and his deliverance at the hands of Gardemann.

But mid-January came and no word from him.

The shipments started. At roll call the numbers fired off, striking men in front of him, behind him, on the left, on the right.

It was better not to watch them pack. A buddy would slip them a can or two of food and a few words of encouragement. They'd shuffle out of the barracks like kicked dogs, little rucksacks on their backs, trying not to look back at the buddy waving. Wisecracks on their lips that fooled nobody.

It was now really hitting close to home for Nicholas. All the empty bunks. Including the whoremaster's.

Long past curfew, Nicholas watched the predatory searchlight beams flit across the dormitory wall. Outside, heavy boots crunched snow as the SS patrol clumped by with their whining dogs.

The smell was more bearable; with half the men gone, the buckets didn't slop over as often. The bitching and arguing had abated. Still he couldn't sleep. Too much on his mind.

They said that a fellow made his own luck. If he did, he didn't make it lying flat on his back. He was fully dressed when he eased himself out of his bunk, reached under it and brought out several cans of food. He stuffed them into his pockets, then sneaked out of the half-empty barracks and started walking....

Just being out there, defying the SS and their goddamned searchlights, worked wonders for his ego.

He walked for a long time undetected, until the barracks buildings were behind him, and he found himself in a wide-open area covered with snow. Then ahead he glimpsed more barracks buildings, and he felt the blood tingle in his veins. He halted by the first barracks, checked the food in his pockets again and rapped softly on a door, whispering a soft greeting.

The door inched opened a fraction, and the essence of female assailed his nostrils.

The women prisoners of Royal Lieu hadn't seen a male — let alone a black Adonis with a velvet tongue — in months. They smuggled him inside, giggling nervously, hugging him and relieving him of his gifts. Smothered by their welcome, he slowly thawed his frigid body against theirs.

"I heard that one of our prisoners (Nicholas) had gone to the women's camp during the night," said Robert Gandar, a French medical student, who knew of Nicholas at that time but had not yet met him. "All the camp heard about it. It was something fantastic."

25 January 1944: As the first names and numbers were bellowed, terror shrank each man's belly.

An hour later, when more than a thousand names had been called, the tension was endurable; no longer did a prisoner have to wonder when. He knew and could resign himself to quiet desperation.

Few could keep down their miserable breakfasts of stale bread covered with margarine and coffee. Latrines were overcrowded. In the dormitories they tied string around their cheap, battered suitcases and stuffed precious personal items into pilfered mattress covers.

The stricken prisoners emptied out of the parade ground. The prosperous ones wore skiing outfits and heavy fur boots reminiscent of campers on a hike. It was the last time that clothes would separate the privileged from the poor.

The line-up for the trucks curved sinuously through the fenced-off enclosure and past a shack where truculent SS guards checked identities and records.

At the Gare de l'Est station in Paris the train was already at the platform when they clambered off the trucks. German soldiers slid back the doors of boxcars bearing stenciled notices of their carrying capacity — "Forty Men, Eight Horses" — and ordered them to climb aboard until each was crammed with 120 men. Into their midst they slid a large metal tub along the floor. Then they slammed the doors shut and locked them on the outside with a lead seal.

Inside the boxcars light slanted through slatted windows latticed with barbed wire. Bodies stood packed tightly. Even before the train moved they cursed and elbowed one another as bigger, tougher prisoners fought to corner the space. The bickering, pushing and shoving inside the boxcar grew worse.

Every prisoner who survived the infamous deportation journey from France to Germany has a different story to tell, but collectively they make up a ghastly experience of overcrowding, freezing in winter, near asphyxiation in the heat of summer, hunger, thirst, primitive sanitation facilities, floors slippery with human waste, extreme psychological stress and ultimately the accumulation of corpses.

The plot was invariably the same; only the characters and the uniqueness of their personal horrors changed. It was a selection process that only the toughest minds and bodies survived. Whatever composure the deportees possessed when the train pulled out of the station had usually degenerated into bedlam and chaos within 24 hours — unless a strong leader emerged within each packed-to-the-gills boxcar to mediate and regulate the frantic mass-struggles for food, breathing space, fresh air and basic bodily functions. Where no such power figure emerged, boxcars would emerge at their destination with their cargoes frozen stiff, bodies hideously intertwined in the contortions of their death agonies and layered in their own excrement.

In Nicholas' boxcar the hum of conversation, the shuffling of feet and the rustling of bodies gradually waned, abandoning each man to his private fears.

The Gare de l'Est's familiar sounds resonated through the boxcar's wooden walls. The impatient whistling of trains, the clatter of thousands of footfalls in the great amphitheater of the station, the rapid-fire French of harried railway conductors.

Outside, life was going on. Inside, it was the beginning of the end.

At 1 p.m., the boxcar jerked. Buffers clanked, and the deportation train glided out of the station....

Paris lay far behind, and except for the clacking of the wheels on the tracks, silence gripped the deportees like the cold. From time to time some of them, catching sight of railway men at little rural stations, tossed notes out through the slats.

It was the desperate hope of sailors doomed at sea.

The freezing European night had shrouded the long train, and Paris was more than a hundred miles behind. In the crammed boxcar the staccato sound of wheels on rails clacked painfully through their skulls. The tub lapped close to the rim, sloshing over on those closest to it whenever the wheels jarred on an ill-fitting rail joint. In the airless space the stench thickened. Prisoners vomited, unavoidably splashing their neighbors. Tempers flared....

A lifetime later the train screeched to a halt. What now? Nervous conversation rattled like nails scattered on a tin roof. Voices hushed as clicking sounds came from keys twisting in locks. The boxcar's doors scraped open. Frigid air blasted through the rectangular opening.

"Out of the way! Out of the way!" shouted helmeted German shadows.

The prisoners shrank in abject fear.

The soldiers ordered two prisoners to lift the brimming urine tub onto the platform, where a row of empty tubs waited as replacements.

A flashlight beam stabbed the boxcar's dark interior. An officious voice ordered all to crowd to the back half of the boxcar. An SS officer, in gloves and topcoat, vaulted inside. "Back!" he snarled to weaker ones slow to comply. "To the rear! To the rear!"

Behind the flashlight glare the prisoners vaguely made out the dreaded high-crowned, peaked-cap silhouette. When they were crammed back as far as possible, the officer and an NCO climbed into the boxcar and began a head count. As the officer called out the count, the NCO pulled a prisoner from the crowded back section of the boxcar to the less crowded front half.

When the count was completed, the officer jumped down onto the platform and reported to a senior officer that all *stucke* were present and accounted for.

Stucke is German for the head of a cow. Henceforth to the Nazis they were no longer human beings.

The boxcar doors slammed shut again, and the train rattled eastward into the European heartland. The air soon thickened again. The tub soon brimmed again. And by this time those who got spattered didn't seem to care....

In the early hours of the morning screeching brakes jolted the deportees awake. The train halted. Puffs of steam shrilled from the engine. Then silence. Footfalls on the cement. The click of bolts. Doors scraping open. Icy air blasts.

"Friends," came a solicitous female voice, "we are the Swiss Red Cross. We have coffee and food for you. You may get out onto the platform and stretch your legs."

The vapid yellowish light of the station illuminated a platform crowded with deportees who had emerged from the boxcars. They huddled in isolated clumps, hunch-backed and hollow-eyed, blinking and twitching at the slightest innocent sound. The Red Cross women moved quietly among them, offering steaming cups of coffee and sandwiches.

The prisoners in Nicholas' boxcar stepped apprehensively down onto the platform.

The Swiss Red Cross women were permitted to dispense light refreshments to deportees strictly as a courtesy of the German government. They were under orders not to engage in any substantive conversations with them. And if they broke the rules, they did so at the peril of never being permitted to succor deportees again. So they were extremely guarded in their relations with them, confining their exchanges to the barest amenities.

This would have been Nicholas' problem when he tried — as surely he did — to interrogate them. But as always, when it came to women, he never took no for an answer.

One way or another he would have found out that their stop was the town of Treves, close to Luxembourg, a technically neutral country whose border was a mere 15 kilometers away. He would have discovered that, although there were few German uniforms in evidence on the platform, beyond the glare of the lights the station was surrounded by soldiers to prevent escapes.

But as to the train's final destination, he would have learned that the Red Cross women as ignorant as he was.

Fifteen kilometers or fifteen hundred. What difference would it make to a black man on the lam in all-white Europe?

Deeper into the Fatherland whistled the train, puffing more strenuously as it snaked across the pine-tree-studded Harz Mountains terrain of north central Germany.

By this time older and weaker prisoners had collapsed on a floor slick with human waste, left to be trampled on by the younger and stronger trying desperately to stay alive in their oxygen-starved enclosure. Prisoners battled waves of nausea and the dread of throwing up on those packed around them.

The Haitian sun arced high in the sky. Burros brayed. Dogs barked. Up in the hills Creole-speaking peasants cooked their pathetic little suppers over charcoal fires. In the suburbs elite families invoked Christian grace before meals in Parisian French, sat down to meals on tablecloths, with cups and saucers that matched, and knives and forks bearing Sheffield or Solingen imprints.

But so often, now that he was in his teens and big for his age, Jean Marcel would be late for dinner. The beach was too broad and too white, the girl on his blanket too slender, too beckoning.

Jean Marcel, you are late again! Where have you been? What have you been doing? We've told you again and again: We don't want you associating with that girl! She is not from a good family.

He was also getting in trouble with Headmaster Tippenhauer at his Catholic school.

Jean Marcel, if you have time for girls, you have time for your schoolwork. You will never be the man your father is if you don't pass your examinations.

But Tippenhauer's remonstrances had had the opposite effect: He assaulted his headmaster, got expelled from school and quit attending Sunday mass at the cathedral with his family.

Oh, Jean Marcel, what in God's holy name is happening to you? What are we going to do with you now?

Grinding parental demands. Drinking. Running with gangs. Back-alley brawling. Beating up policemen. Impending arrest. Raging to get away from it all. To escape to somewhere different. Anywhere.

Exile in the neighboring island of Martinique, on parole to an uncle he hardly knew, and slave work in a local hospital. Minutely watching everything the doctors did, thinking he might like to do the same some day.

Then Paris! The thrill of discovering the magnificent City of Light.

The gendarme with the white baton always at Rue du Harve and Boulevard Haussman. The parapet at the Pont des Arts as the barges float by. The writers, the artists, the musicians, the movie people populating the Deux Magots, the Cafe de Flore, the Brasserie Lipp. Sipping a wine outdoors with a newly found painter friend. Across the street the girls of the Grande Chaumiere beckoning, hoping for an offer to paint them in the nude.

Then running into Gardemann again after all those years. ... Did he ever get the letter? The one smuggled out of Compiegne. What if he'd received it but wasn't going to lift a finger, figuring his troubles were over at last, now that Nicholas — the only one who could squeal on him — was on a one-way trip to Germany, from whence he would never return?

The train rolled to a stop. Steam hissed. Boxcar doors scraped open. Guards poked rifle butts into the stuporous mass of humanity. *Aufstehen! Aufstehen!* On your feet! On your feet! *Heraus! Heraus!* Get moving! Get moving!'

The station was dimly lit. Guards, peevish from their rousting from warm bunks to receive another cargo of *stucke*, restrained vicious-looking dogs on leashes. In background shadows SS officers caucused in chummy klatsches. The prisoners eased themselves stiffly onto the platform, fear blanking out the life from their faces. Awful as the boxcars had been, they constituted the known, and they balked at leaving. Ahead loomed the unknown.

On these shipments from Compiegne, as many as ninety-five corpses were known to have been laid neatly side-by-side on the station platform of Weimar.

The town was the birthplace of Nietzsche, a renegade Catholic priest with whose philosophies Nicholas had been so taken as a rebellious teen-ager. *The world is divided into slaves and masters....*

It was January 29, 1944, as Nicholas stood on the platform, one of a thousand slaves waiting meekly for their German masters to herd them away to their fate at Buchenwald, the dreaded concentration camp near Weimar.

But first the roll call. It was high noon when the SS roll-call leader finally satisfied himself that all *stucke* were present and accounted for. They were marched off in a column-of-fives to waiting trucks. Stumbling docilely toward the vehicles, they jerked spastically when SS barked commands at them.

Nicholas and a half dozen prisoners found themselves separated from the main body of prisoners and prodded aboard a truck, which they had all to themselves He noticed that the other trucks were packed, with prisoners teetering on the tailgates, but the truck he rode in was almost empty. When its tailgate clanked shut, two SS men with machine pistols rode in the back with them, but only one SS rode tailgate on the other trucks.

The latest Compiegne transport traveled narrow, winding streets hemmed in by steep-gabled houses whose roofs lay heaped with snow. Gradually the town receded, and the shivering, anguished deportees rolled through country clumped with majestic, snow-laden fir trees.

Nicholas might have been captivated by the Christmas-postcard beauty pressing in on all sides. But not if he had known that he and the prisoners in his truck had been secretly tagged NN. It explained why two guards were riding shotgun instead of one.

Persons tagged NN administratively became non-persons. All official traces of their existence, such a birth and marriage records, were erased. They disappeared into the "night and fog" of Hitler's decree.[1] Yet they subsisted stubbornly in the limbo of concentration camps, forever dogged by the lethal footnote to their names that put them one step ahead of execution.

Every SS camp guard enjoyed a license to submit NNs to the utmost in brutality and deprivation.

Christmas 1943 approached, reminding Vildebart Nicolas that he hadn't seen or heard from his brother in months. Vildebart was ill and in the hospital, so he sent his wife Andree across Paris to the apartment in the Eiffel Tower area to check on Johnny.

On a cold, dreary December day in 1943 she arrived there to discover new tenants occupying the luxurious quarters on the fifth floor. The family was apologetic. *No, Madame, we know nothing whatsoever of a Monsieur Jean Marcel Nicholas. We have never heard of him. Sorry, but we cannot help you.*

Andree quizzed the concierge. He told her that Johnny had been picked up about a month previously.

Many a French woman, terrorized by the mere mention of a Gestapo arrest, would have gone home, content to leave well enough alone. But not Andree. A small but determined white woman, she presented her

---

1 See Appendix, p. 301.

self at Gestapo headquarters in the Rue des Saussaises and made inquiries.

She was informed that they had never heard of any Johnny Nicholas, or any Jean Marcel Nicolas for that matter. The names meant nothing to them. She explained that her brother-in-law was a tall, medium-colored Negro and that it was impossible for them not to have noticed him. In lock step with Paragraph III of the N&N decree, they insisted that they had no record of any such man. They conceded that there had been arrests on November 23 in the Eiffel Tower area but denied that any of them had involved a Negro.

Andree and Vildebart were worried and mystified. They would have been stunned to discover that Johnny had been tagged an NN. But they would have understood why they were getting such conflicting information.

CHAPTER FIVE
BUCHENWALD

From the top of the tower a searchlight's narrow beam probed the night, sweeping patiently back and forth across the camp, probing the shadowed emptiness between the buildings, then gliding on.

The beam momentarily bathed a chapel-like building with a tall steeple, but the "steeple" was really a chimney, as Nicholas and the other deportees would soon discover.

The truck skidded to a halt in the thick snow. A guard barked at his charges to get out. They stretched limbs stiffened during the freezing ride from the railroad station. The truck whined off, leaving them standing there, stamping the ground to start body heat flowing again. An SS noncommissioned officer ordered them in fractured French to form a column, then marched them off.

The snow muffled their steps. Their battered suitcases — the last remaining links with home and the familiar — swung by their sides.

Inside, the building blazed with light so bright that they squinted defensively or covered their eyes. The pungent odor of carbolic disinfectant burned nostrils and throats. Along one wall stood a row of gleaming, white washbasins. The only other furnishings were several long, wooden tables. The floor was brick and scrupulously clean. They slept on it — or tried to in the glaring light — until four o'clock in the morning, when the NCO stamped in and told them to be ready to move out in five minutes.

They waited in formation for him for an hour. When he finally arrived he marched them across to the chapel-like building, where he lined them up.

From atop the huge curved archway of the main gate a battery of searchlights blazed their beams on the newest arrivals.

The thin, pencil beams wandered off, illuminating a vast, parade-ground area carpeted with fresh snow. Beyond that stretched endless rows of barracks separated by broad, symmetrical walkways.

From the first rows of barracks emerged men in bizarre costumes. In their crimson trousers and green vests, beating on drums and blowing horns, they looked like circus performers. They hurried along double-time, forming a perfect formation in the vast assembly area facing the huge main gate.

Looking beyond the costumed musicians, Nicholas now saw hundreds of figures flood onto the assembly area, waves upon waves of them, until the snow was black with bodies packed tightly in perfect squares.

The aisles between the squares were blocked here and there with motionless figures lying on the frozen ground.

The morning roll call at Buchenwald concentration camp had begun.

The prisoner horde resembled skeletons in rags. Their blue-striped uniforms appeared vulcanized in rubbery grime. Beneath their stubbly faces their skin pulled taut against their cheekbones. They wore their shapeless caps pulled low over their faces and ears as if they were drowned in shame.

Although the snow muted their movements, the freezing air carried the hum of their whispering, moaning, coughing, wheezing. The gate-house searchlight beams flitted capriciously over their tortured ranks, pausing occasionally to satisfy the curiosity of operators warm in the gatehouse tower. In brilliant cones the light bathed old men with feet swathed in paper and tied with string, young men with heads wrapped in pus-soaked bandages, indeterminate men with the pallor of death about them. Nicholas noticed how the prisoners' skin stretched across their cheekbones like parchment, how their toothless mouths gaped, how sunken were their staring eyes.

Intermittently the searchlight beams bathed better-clothed men in clean stripes and toting clubs. They roamed the aisles between the ranks and columns, snarling and cursing, beating the rapidly freezing men into tighter, more perfect formations.

Nicholas watched aghast.

Mutzen auf! The command crashed across the public-address system and amplified a thousand times, shattering his eardrums.

Instantly 35,000 men removed their caps as if puppets on a string. *"Mutzen ab!"*

With the same impeccable precision, the puppets replaced their caps.

The roll call began. It would not end until every single name had been accounted for. Regardless of time, weather, life or death, the roll call ground on and on as individual prisoners shivered and died in the cold.

Dozens of times the SS roll-call leaders mispronounced names. A prisoner could be present, but if he didn't hear his name correctly, he didn't answer; he was therefore listed as missing and assured of a brutal beating when the guards eventually located him.

Sometimes a prisoner couldn't answer: He had died during the ordeal, which often lasted three hours. It wasn't unusual for the SS records office to fall behind in its massive paperwork. As a result, names of men who were dead or who had been transferred to other camps would be screamed meaninglessly and endlessly over the loudspeakers. To fill the blanks on their clipboards the tenacious roll call leaders would launch a second roll call, using prisoner numbers instead of names.

Time meant nothing to them: A roll call could take six hours — and even longer when prisoner functionaries, who were always appointed for political reasons, never for their intelligence, simply didn't know how to count.

During these horrific ordeals, prisoners often collapsed and hit the granite-like compacted snow with a brittle snap. As if in a carefully rehearsed military drill, prisoners around the collapsed man picked up his body and passed it along hand-to-hand until it was finally laid on a sidewalk by the barracks.

To the *lagerschutz* — club-wielding prisoners appointed as security police — the gaps in the ranks constituted disciplinary offenses. They milled into the formation with clubs swinging, hammering the living into the spaces left by the dead.

Nicholas, mesmerized by the spectacle, had lost all track of time. He didn't know if it was one hour later or two or three when the public-address system boomed again.

"Mutzen auf!"

Again he saw the caps come off in amazing unison.

"Mutzen ab!"

Again they were replaced with equal precision.

But not good enough to satisfy the chief roll call leader. Standing on a raised platform, his greatcoat buttoned up to the neck, his hands heavily gloved against the brutal cold, he screamed the pair of commands a half-dozen times before he finally dismissed the formation.

Instantly the mass of humanity disintegrated into separate human beings haunted by individual fears and ills, hobbling stiffly back to their quarters, driven by the flailing clubs of the *lagerschutz. Aufstehen! Aufstehen!* On your feet! Get in there, they snarled.

Nicholas heard an SS shout an order at him and his comrades to march back to the washroom where they had spent the night. En route they passed the chapel-like building, and he watched incredulously to see the morning's dead being off-loaded from handcarts and laid against its walls.

Back in the washroom, a *kapo* — a prisoner put in a position of authority — ordered Nicholas to strip. He put his clothes on the hanger the *kapo* gave him, dropped his watch, wallet and other valuables in the bag he was handed, and packed everything into his suitcase. He tied the suitcase with a length of cord provided, wrote his name and address on a label and stuck it on his suitcase.

The *kapo* ordered him into an adjoining room from whose ceiling hung a dozen electric clippers. Another *kapo* grabbed a pair and began shearing Nicholas' head, face, armpits and crotch.

The clippers were blunt. He nicked and cut Nicholas repeatedly, but didn't give a damn.

The cuts burned fiercely after they ordered him to jump into a huge creosote bath. The *kapo* pushed his head beneath the tarry surface, then told him to get out and motioned him toward a shower. He was deluged first with ice-cold water, then scalding water.

He searched for a towel. There weren't any. Prisoners stood naked, praying for their own body heat to evaporate the scummy liquid.

Prisoner-attendants moved in with hand pumps and sprayed him all over with another chemical that stung salt in his cuts. It left him coated with a chalky dust.

He glimpsed his reflection in a mirror in a stainless-steel frame. Under other circumstances his new-found whiteness might have triggered a chuckle. Not this time.

The washing and delousing completed, Nicholas and his naked comrades were herded out of the washroom, through a subterranean passage, up a flight of stairs and into a long room with several rows of counters. At each counter he picked up a different item of clothing — a shirt, a pair of blue-and-white-striped pants and matching jacket, a cap, a pair of socks and eight pairs of wooden clogs. There was no time to get a proper fit: Prisoner-attendants behind the counters flung the clothes at the new arrivals double-timing through the line.

At the last counter an SS guard ordered them in German and bad French to line up by fives. As he yelled Nicholas' name, he handed him two triangles of red cloth and two rectangles of white cloth; also a needle and thread to sew them to his uniform.

Colors differentiated class in Nazi Germany's concentration-camp system. Green was for convicted criminals, yellow for Jews, pink for homosexuals, black for gypsies, red for political prisoners and prisoners of war. Political prisoners wore the red triangle with the point down; POWs with the point up.

The rectangle of white cloth, with the prisoner's number stenciled, was worn on the left breast below the colored triangle. The triangle-rectangle combination was repeated on the right trouser leg.

Nicholas, Johnny, officially identified in camp records as Prisoner No. 44451, Boston, U.S.A., sewed on his red triangles.

In the indescribably brutal society of a concentration camp, any newcomer, regardless of how rich, powerful, influential, sophisticated or resourceful he had been on the outside, was a mere babe in swaddling clothes. When the SS Labor Service officer shouted: "Skilled workers one step forward!" any veteran concentrationary could have whispered to Nicholas to step forward whether he had a skill or not and try to bluff it. Survival hung on a simple rule-of-thumb: Men who worked indoors lived longer than men who worked outdoors. Skilled workers, more often than not, worked indoors, therefore they lived longer. Indoors, the chances of survival were poor; outdoors they were remote.

The reward for Nicholas' ignorance was assignment to Buchenwald's dreaded rock-quarry detail.

On January 29, 1944, he was with the detail when it fell out after roll call and marched out through the camp's huge main gate and into the magnificent, pine-covered countryside of Thuringia now mantled in snow. The near-zero temperature penetrated his thin, cotton uniform, and everything that he had been through must have seemed too devastating not to be a nightmare. Yet he could not deny that he was in a long column of marchers, five abreast, picks and shovels over their shoulders, armed SS guards riding herd on them, all sinuously winding out into nowhere, each man hiding his thoughts, hoarding memories of home and family to sustain his will to stay alive.

Eventually the column ascended the slopes of the Ettersburg. They stood for a moment, their breath clouding the predawn air; the older, weaker men near exhaustion, the younger men panting vigorously, dreading the order to start digging.

Aufstehen! shouted the SS man in charge of the detail.

Picks and shovels resumed attacking the cavernous bite begun by legions of prisoners so many years previously and continued without surcease. Their tools gnawed into stubborn granite. They swung with enthusiasm; it rushed anemic blood through their bodies and kept the cold at bay — except at the hands, feet, tips of the nose and earlobes.

It was dig or die, for Thuringia in winter was the Siberia of the Third Reich. Had not Nature innocently been their policeman, there were SS guards all around with rifles and vicious Alsatian wolfhounds.

And *kapos*, too. Functioning as "trustees" in a civil prison, they wielded some authority. But in Buchenwald, whose prisoner government was Green, that is, made up of criminals, any prisoner chosen to be a *kapo*, or prisoner-foremen, was just another criminal.

Kapos often rivaled and sometimes surpassed the SS guards in callousness and brutality. It was how they kept their jobs, how they earned and perpetuated better food and less bestial treatment for themselves. Often, merely to justify their presence and authority, they actively sought out prisoners to harangue, kick, hammer and beat into working faster.

Only when a *kapo* strutted further down the mountain slope, or had his predatory curiosity aroused by something further up-slope, could the workers at the top level risk talking.

What was so special about the higher levels?

Prisoners at that altitude enjoyed an excellent vantage point. They could track the movements of the SS detail leader or the prisoner foreman when they wandered off, and this knowledge allowed the prisoners to decide when it was safe for them to lean back on their shovels.

The question for Nicholas and any other rookie interested in enjoying the privilege was: How do I get up there?

The old-timers would warn them: Unless you're a Ruskie or Pole, forget it. You wouldn't last long; they run things up there. If you're not one of them, which all of them up there are, and you get assigned to their detail, they will kill you.

Not all the quarry detail prisoners swung picks and shovels, Nicholas soon discovered. Somebody had to pick up broken rock and load it into large, wooden carts. Somebody had to push the carts up and down the slope, from one level to another, making pick-ups.

They did it with no more in their shrunken bellies than a slice of bread and a pint of watery soup. On the uphill, the cart threatened to roll back and crush them. On the downhill, they had to brace to keep the cart from careening down the slope and dragging them behind it.

Between pick swings the old-timer told in a low voice of how some SS sadists amused themselves. Instead of doing the merciful thing and shooting a prisoner through the head, they forced him to push a tremendously overloaded cart uphill. Under a hail of kicks, blows and threats the doomed men would try the impossible, only to have the cart roll over them.

The advice was obvious: Don't get assigned cart detail.

You never can tell how strong a man is when he's trying not to die, said the veterans. He can push and push for a long time, but that makes the SS impatient; they want their fun now. They get tired of waiting and just push him off the top level. Look for yourself; it's a long way to drop.

Nicholas and the new deportees in the quarry detail listened raptly to the wisdom as if their lives depended on it. And it literally did.

The greatest danger, they learned, was the boredom of the German guards. You can't expect the black-uniformed sadists to languish in the freezing wind and fog and blizzard and not long to be back in their warm barracks. They're obsessed with the belief that's exactly where they would be were it not for filthy, lice-infested *stucke* from every country in Occupied Europe ready to escape at the slightest invitation.

To break the monotony, some SS stood on the top level, picked up rocks as big as they could lift and dropped them on innocent prisoners working on the second level. If they missed their targets, other SS laughed them to ridicule them. This forced the embarrassed SS to draw their pistols and pick off two or three innocents on the level below them just to prove their marksmanship.

Aged prisoners afforded the jaded SS their greatest diversion. They'd order a tottering grandfather to climb one of the young, slender pines that dotted the mountain slope. *Mach schnell!* they'd command. When they got the old fellow up there, three or four of them would shake the tree violently until he toppled out of it to his death.

But there are worse places in this hellhole than the quarry, the veterans of Buchenwald muttered, so don't complain.

There are? queried the newcomers incredulously. Like where?

The SS vegetable garden, they were told.

Tended by prisoners on punishment detail, it existed in a continuous state of expansion. Tons of plowed-up rocks had to be carted away. The garden was always being fertilized. Tons of human waste had to be hauled from the prisoners' gigantic sewage ditch. Prisoners, two at a time with a wooden carrying rack, were pressed into service as the beasts of burden for two weeks of punishment. It was deadly to move too slowly; but if they moved too fast under the ceaseless threats and curses of the guards, foremen and detail leaders, the human ordure slopped over the edge of the rack onto their uniforms. Washing facilities were almost nonexistent, so the garden detail stank like dungheaps. When they had served their two weeks, they were like lepers to all other prisoners.

Fourteen hours later it was pitch black. Soon it would be time for the long trek back to camp. The old-timers warned the newcomers to be on the look-out for suitable rocks.

Rocks? What for?

It was an old Buchenwald work ethic. Every prisoner had to carry a rock weighing at least five kilos back to camp. It was advisable to start looking for it a suitable rock as early in the day as possible because, in the last-minute rush, the only one left in sight could be 15 kilos. And if that was all a prisoner could find, that's what he had to carry — if he wanted to live to see tomorrow morning.

Illuminated only by the glow of the snow, the procession of exhausted, rock-toting prisoners wound its way back to camp. The only ones not carrying rocks were those pushing wheeled carts piled with the bodies of those who had worked their last quarry detail.

Carrying their rocks back to Buchenwald wasn't the end of the misery; there was still roll call. Hours of standing in roll call.

They held roll call at least twice a day. The established wisdom passed out by the veterans was: Stand absolutely still in the square you're assigned to. Don't talk. Don't cough. Don't even sneeze or you give the *lagerschutz* or their *kapos* an excuse to work you over with their clubs.

Sound off when your name is called. Be alert: The bastard won't pronounce it right, but if you don't answer, he lists you as missing. If you're missing, the goddamn roll call goes on and on, until they've accounted for you — dead or alive.

Don't put your hands in your pockets or turn up your collar against the wind. Keep your back straight. Do you smoke? If you do, don't pick up the odd butt you'll find lying around. If you've stashed away any extra food, don't have it on you at roll call.

If they catch you, it's the bock, a wooden rack set up next to the roll call leader. They stretch you over it so your ass sticks up. Five to 25 lashes with a horsewhip, sometimes a cane, then 50 to 150 deep-knee bends to strengthen the muscles. Then one of the medics paints your ass with iodine.

If the Roll Call Leader is not in the mood for bock, he'll tie your hands behind your back and toss the end of the rope over a tree limb. He'll hoist you up about six feet until your shoulder blades pop out of joint. He'll beat you in the face or kick you in the balls while you're strung up. It might last half an hour. Then again, it could be four.

That's what he'll do to *you*. That's not even talking about what they'll do to *me* and the rest of us. If one of us screws up, everybody gets it. No food for a day. Double-time all over the assembly area full of holes and gullies for an hour with every man lugging a big rock. The first to stagger or slow down gets a one-way ride to the ovens — that building you thought was a church.

The column of prisoners approached the sprawl of barracks buildings behind the high, barbed-wire fence with the 600 volts of electricity running through it and the 20-foot-high guard towers every 250 feet. "Straighten up there!" yelled the SS detail leader, starting to count cadence. *"Ein-zwei-drei-vier!"*

Had anyone ever escaped from Buchenwald?

Two, back in '38, said one old-timer. Turned up missing at roll call, so the bastards made every single man stand there for 19 hours until they could be accounted for. It was five degrees above zero that night. In the morning, they had 25 frozen to death. At noon, they had 70.

If there was a single piece of advice dispensed by the veterans most critical to survival, it was the wisdom of sticking to one's ethnic group,

The reason for this stemmed from Europe's historical prejudices that have convinced each ethnic group that it is superior to every other; that have divided Europeans and kept them continually at war with one another. Centuries of prejudices have bred a pandemic of biases, hatreds, stereotypes and caricatures that, in the dog-eat-dog, every-man-for-himself pressures of a concentration camp, incubated to the most virulent degree.

The only way you're going to last is by sticking with your countrymen, said the old-timers. You protect them, they protect you.

Just because we all hate the SS doesn't mean we all love one another. The Czechs can't stand the Poles. The Belgians hate the French. The Norwegians can't get along with the Danes. The English think they know it all.

The Socialists despise the Communists, but they both hate the Criminals, and the Criminals are against everybody.

It's a power struggle every hour of the day, seven days a week. You can keep your head down and your mouth shut and try to tough it out on your own, but you won't last a week. You'll be an outcast.

What about the POWs?

Very exclusive clubs, said the veterans. They rate themselves superior to every other class. The English POWs stick to themselves, Dutch to themselves. Poles to themselves.

Just remember: Nobody's a loner and lives. If you want to survive, you join somebody's group. It's the only hope that you have; that any of us have.

Being the only black in Buchenwald and the only American, Nicholas would have been extremely dubious about his chances. And even more so if he had known that, shortly before his arrival, several bruised and battered men in American uniforms had been brought into Buchenwald, tagged N-N and had been executed without delay.[1]

The awful torment of the evening roll call was over. The new deportees, frozen, drained and demoralized, hobbled into a barracks full of camp veterans. On crude, trestle tables illuminated by the glare of a single electric-light bulb, each man ate his single piece of bread slicked with margarine and his fingertip-sized piece of sausage.

Eat fast, warned the old-timers, otherwise you may not get to eat at all. Some drunken SS sergeant — maybe even your own barracks leader — is liable to stagger in and there'll be hell to pay. Maybe there's a button missing from your uniform. It could be your uniform's dirty, he'll say. That's a laugh; everyone's uniform is filthy. If he wants to nail you, there's a rule or regulation that lets him nail you. If there isn't, he'll make one up on the spot.

Maybe he doesn't like the way you look or the way you talk. Maybe it's just nothing. He'll kick over the tables — your supper with it. He'll kick over your locker, wreck your bed, make you run full speed around the barracks twenty times.

---

1 Nicholas escaped the fate of the N-N decree, although how remains yet another mystery.

The thin mat between Nicholas and his wooden bunk stank of human shit. So did the blanket over him. One can picture him shivering violently, yearning for the searing sun of home.

He wore only an undershirt. It was against regulations to wear shorts or trousers. If caught in them, it was the bock for the offender and an hour double-timing around the assembly area in shirts only for everybody else.

The barracks were jammed to twice capacity, but the aggregate body heat failed against daggers of icy air piercing every crack and crevice in the old stone building. Ice glazed the inside of the windows. Stiletto-like icicles hung from holes in the roof. Cold radiated from the mildewed stone walls and chilled the wooden bunks.

He had heard it was best to grab a bunk in the center of the barracks. That was where it was warmest. But if you had to go outside in the middle of the night to piss, your mat and blanket were liable be gone when you got back.

Worse, somebody might crawl into your bunk in your absence, and you'd have to beat the bastard with your fists. The ruckus would rouse the *stubendienst*, the barracks leader, who would come running and order the whole damn barracks outside for a one-hour drill in bare feet and undershirts.

Nicholas' thoughts spun wildly as he lay down on his wretched bunk on that first night. He was stunned by the numbing assaults on mind and body.

Nietzsche's cliché concerning masters and slaves must have mocked him. The little indolent, sun-splashed island whose dust he had so gleefully shaken from his shoes must now have seemed too incredibly wonderful.

CHAPTER SIX
PRISONER POLITICS

Almost none of the prisoners had ever seen a black man before.

The police whistles of the *lagerschutz* shrieked as usual that frigid January morning in 1944. They were only prisoners like everyone else, but their authority as the camp's security police had turned them corrupt and inhuman. They clumped down the floor of the barracks, screaming and swinging their bludgeons at the half-naked, emaciated prisoners in their reeking bunks, rousting them outside, across the snow and into the freezing washroom.

It was there that they saw him for the first time.

Prisoners had to wash down to the waist every morning. There was seldom any soap and the water was frigid. It piddled out of huge, perforated cylinders in streams resembling the ribs of an umbrella. For most, the daily encounter with the water was a lick and a promise — unless hammered under the freezing spray by the milling clubs of the *lagerschutz.*

But the black seemed to enjoy it. His tawny body didn't flinch as the astringent jets of water flayed him.

They glanced at him covertly. The sight of his rippling physique made them sickeningly conscious of their own hollow chests and shrunken frames. His zeal to clean himself showed them what animals they had become. It was fear of a beating, not pride, that drove them to the water.

But they saw that the black man embraced the ordeal voluntarily, scrubbing himself with his bare hands as briskly as if luxuriating in the steaming shower of some prewar public baths.

They automatically resented him.

Back in the barracks they hurriedly dressed in their ill-fitting uniforms bearing the color-coded triangles of identification.

A block letter in the middle of a triangle indicated a nationality — "D" for German (*Deutschland*), "P" for Poland, "F" for France, and so on.

Nichlolas wore a red POW triangle, its apex pointed upward to distinguish his patch from the down-pointing red triangle of political prisoners. The large "A" in the triangle's center identified him as an American.

In the latrine, the only place where prisoners could talk without being harassed by the *lagerschutz*, the rumors had already begun to spread.

Impossible. He cannot be an American. His French is too perfect. His German is flawless. Something stinks. He smells like a stool pigeon of the SS. We will keep sharp eye on the schwartze. Let him make the slightest wrong move and it'll be the end of him.

In concentration-camp society, a prisoner's greatest mental agonies included ignorance and doubt: ignorance of the elements that controlled his life; doubt about the trustworthiness of those in whom he was supposed to trust. A new prisoner usually languished in limbo until he became accepted in one of the social groups. Thereafter he would find himself pigeon-holed.

The great defect of pigeonholing lay in the fact that a man might wear the criminal's green triangle, but that didn't always mean he was untrustworthy or lacked honor. The moral standards of a few "criminals" were higher than those of some "Reds," the Communists.

The SS system classified prisoners according to what the Gestapo police record said about them, and that could be true or false. So veteran prisoners knew that the color of a triangle didn't necessarily reflect the real character or politics of its wearer; true colors only emerged with the passage of time — usually a very long time. Each prisoner wove himself in a web of anonymity to protect his family back home from possible repercussions by the Gestapo.

Thus even among themselves prisoners falsified surnames and fabricated former occupations and lives. It was the only protection they had against the spies and informers that the German camp administration continually planted among them to learn what was *really* brewing behind the barbed wire.

Although the prisoners were under continual day-and-night surveillance from the ugly guard towers, they were allowed to rule themselves: They had their own government.

It was not a democracy; it was an unending struggle between the three most powerful groups — the Communists, the anti-Communists and the convicted criminals. Whichever of the three factions wielded the most power in a particular camp was the faction that organized, directed and ruled every phase of prisoner life in the camp. And from this ruling class the German captors co-opted a prisoner whom they believed would faithfully execute their every bidding.

The SS kommandant anointed this chosen prisoner *lagereldtester, or* president of the prisoner government. He, in turn, nominated prisoners of his own "color" to head the various branches of his government: Kitchen, mess halls, hospital, shops, and the crucially-important Labor Allocation Office, which exerted the most powerful leverage of all because it assigned prisoners to jobs that might either kill them or keep them alive.

Through the *lagereldester* and his cabinet of *kapos*, the SS kommandant's orders were executed.

The role of *lagereldtester* was privileged but highly dangerous. His tenure was an endless conspiracy to blunt the harshness of the SS kommandant's orders yet make it appear as if they were being carried out to the letter. It was a continuing masquerade calculated to reduce the murder and brutality and inhumanity — a masquerade that could be uncovered by a kommandant's "plant" within the prisoner ranks.

This was why the inmates of Buchenwald would wait and watch the black newcomer from a safe distance.

In the cavernous mess hall the miserable men clutched their hunks of bread. The most senior of the seven prisoners at each bare, plank table sliced the bread. He used a crude wood-and-string balance scale to weigh out equal portions of the oval-shaped loaf.

The men's anger, fermenting on their hate for the SS guards and their gnawing hunger, bubbled near the surface. Fingers stiff from the long night's chill snatched the morsels. Fights broke out regularly over unequal food distribution. The disputants would snarl and claw like hyenas scrabbling over a carcass — until the *lagerschutz* clubbed them bloody.

Nicholas watched like a spectator at a horror movie, aware but detached.

Then came the yellowish-brown soup flecked with gobs of floating grease. They slurped obscenely, clutching their precious bread in their talons, glowering at the Negro, whose self-control, by comparison, reduced them to swine grubbing in the trough.

Three minutes to roll call! Three minutes to roll call!

The dreaded alarm of the *lagerschutz* detonated the customary, controlled panic. Hunks of bread were rammed inside jackets as the mess hall choked with bodies flooding toward the doors and out onto the camp streets. They stamped their feet in the frozen snow as they formed up block by block in columns five abreast and staggered along the street toward the vast, open roll-call area.

Veteran prisoners eyed Nicholas with intense curiosity. The word was that blacks couldn't take the cold, yet this one held himself obnoxiously erect. They chuckled mirthlessly. *The schwartze won't last long.* He was ignoring the first rule of survival: Keep a low profile. Drawing attention to yourself was a deadly game. His blackness alone set him apart. You lived by lapsing into invisibility, by becoming as a snowflake in a blizzard to those who held the power of life and death over you.

They didn't know any Negroes, but European conventional wisdom at that time held that blacks didn't have a white's intelligence. This one would pay for his ignorance with a noose around his black neck one Sunday morning — the day set aside for hangings.

It was night. The outside work details had dragged themselves in exhausted from their pick-and-shovel projects many miles distant from the camp. The sickening evening meal had been gulped down. It was an hour before lights out. Nicholas and a lone *lagerschutz* struggled through the deep snow toward the western edge of the camp. The wind sliced through them, rounding the shoulders and humping the back of the camp policeman. But the black man walked tall, his arms swinging ludicrously by his sides. Except for an occasional handcart loaded with bodies and pushed by pairs of sickly inmates toward the crematorium, the streets were deserted.

The success of the Nazi concentration-camp system depended in great measure on the principle of indirect rule on which the German SS founded their camps. In everyday practice it was unusual for an SS officer to become directly involved with prisoners; the council of prisoners had that responsibility of translating SS commands and making sure they were obeyed.

Buchenwald, one of the oldest of the concentration camps, had been established in 1937 as a holding tank for the leaders of political parties that had opposed Hitler. From the outset, its prisoner council had been dominated by German Communists. They directly controlled the lives of every prisoner in the camp. The Communists were disciplined Germans powered by an inflexible political ideology and absolutely ruthless in enforcing their will among the prisoners.

It was the prisoner council — not the SS kommandant — who appointed *its* choices to fill myriad levels of supervisors, functionaries and foremen in the elaborate prisoner hierarchy. These key jobs were desperately sought after because they usually brought with them better food, clothing and working conditions.

With these irresistible perquisites at their disposal, the half-dozen men constituting the typical prisoner council held immense power over the lives of the prisoners under them.

The prisoner council men selected the names of those who would work in the dreaded outdoor details and were destined to die, and who would work in the warmth of the prisoner kitchen or the prisoner hospital, and were likely to live. In this subtly selective way, without having to engage in overt means, they liquidated prisoners not disposed to the Communist cause and enhanced the survival prospects of those who were.

They routinely detailed prisoners as clerks for the SS administration or as lackeys — such a floor sweepers, latrine cleaners or waiters in the SS mess hall — to perform mundane tasks in the areas of the camp reserved for the SS kommandant and his administration. These apparently innocuous prisoners served the double function of spies for the prisoner council, keeping them informed of everything they saw or overheard in the SS section of the camp. Through a network of such lackeys the prisoner council covertly stayed abreast of all but the SS kommandant's most secret plans and activities.

Considering the prisoner council's all-encompassing power and its passion for preserving its turf, it is difficult to conceive that the rumors being whispered around about the "black American pilot" would not have aroused its inquisitiveness. Every prisoner knew that the kommandant kept a stable of spies. And if Nicholas was one of them, and if he were to report unfavorably to the kommandant, the Communist governing councilors could find themselves thrown out of office and back among the rank-and-file again to face the horrors of everyday prisoner life.

Before that catastrophic contingency occurred, they would kill him.

But it wouldn't look like murder. They would trick him into coming into the prisoner-hospital, where he would be forcibly restrained while one of the prisoner-doctors administered a lethal hypodermic injection. Then, by juggling paperwork and a little bacterial sleight-of-hand, they could persuade the SS — if they even bothered to ask — that the victim had died from natural causes or disease.

Iron-disciplined as the Communist councilors were, however, they were usually fair and judicious. Before they invoked the final solution they would secretly summon suspect prisoners for interrogation.

The Buchenwald prisoner government convened in a large stone, windowless building close to the barbed wire perimeter of the camp. Officially it was designed as a canteen where prisoners could buy a few personal items. But it was a sham. It concealed a warehouse full of provisions and clothes used by the prisoner government as bribes for currying favor and maintaining Communist control.

The prisoner-councilors, conscious of their position, never permitted a prisoner to approach them without an order and an escort. The prisoner was always escorted by the *lagerschutz*. This functionary pulled on a weight hanging from a chain by the door. The sudden movement usually set a pack of dogs inside to yelping. A peephole slid open. A face growled admittance, the *lagerschutz* left, the door opened and the prisoner entered.

A *kapo* led the prisoner through a corridor of crates, boxes and bags of untouched supplies stacked well above the level of dimly lit bulbs. The shadows hid a screened pen filled with dogs and their fetid odors.

The prisoner emerged from the semi-darkness into a brightly lit, modern office that would have been a credit to the Kruppwerke. Metal filing cabinets along the walls. An expensive rug on the floor. Artistically designed lamps on desks heavy with files and ledgers.

The *kapo* escorted the prisoner to yet another room — a blend of modern living room and traditional *bierstube*. The sweet, heavy aroma of cigar smoke cloyed the nostrils. The prisoner's eyes focused on a long conference table busy with bottles, glasses and tidbits.

The six men who huddled there sported immaculately clean, well-pressed prison stripes. Each wore a black armband on his right sleeve and red triangles surprinted with "D" (for *Deutschland*).

The cabinet of Buchenwald's prisoner government was in session. Less than five minutes' walk from degradation and death, humiliation and suffering, filth and bestiality, fat and fleshy prisoner-councilors held court in pomp and plenty.

One of them was a figure familiar to all prisoners, a figure so self-assured as to walk the streets of the camp dressed in a heavy, fur-lined jacket and a plump Doberman thoroughbred on a leash.

The ugly, two-inch-wide, scalp-deep track that the *haarschneider's* clippers swathed down the center of each prisoner's head was absent in these men. They wore their hair fashionably long and lustrous with "Brilliantine."

It is entirely consistent with the circumstances that Nicholas would have been summoned to appear before the prisoner council.

You are wondering why we have sent for you ... the Comrades report that you have been asking many questions....

We wish to inform you that our government is dedicated to fairness and justice for all prisoners. We extend our influence to all comrades to protect them from the hated SS — regardless of nationality. We felt that you should know this.

It is our policy to meet all prominent new prisoners personally. You fall into that category. Some of us have been here since the camp was started, and we have never seen an American inmate before.

A veteran inmate would have immediately noted the serial numbers of his interrogators: Most of the current population of the camp wore five-digit numbers. These men of the prisoner council sported three-digit numbers. It was obvious from their comportment that they wore their badges of longevity proudly.

The litter of food and drink before them explained how they had survived and prospered.

They would have wanted to know if, as the records that their lackey-spy in the SS kommandant's office had reported, he was really a U.S. Air Force pilot, shot down over France.

Yes, he was.

Where had he been shot down?

Military regulations would have prohibited him disclosing anything more than his name, rank, serial number and date of birth.

Several of his inquisitors wore red-and-white cloth bullseye targets sewn on the backs of their jackets. It was the symbol that the SS made a prisoner wear if he was suspected of planning to escape: It drew attention to him. But even as recent an arrival as Nicholas would have wondered how many years had gone by since these sleek, pomaded prisoners had pondered escape.

It was not uncommon for an interrogatee to be offered food to soften him up. A snap of the fingers often produced a tray laden with beer, kidney beans, sausages and white bread.

As ravenous as Nicholas would be it is difficult, knowing his temperament, to visualize him accepting the patent bribe. It is more likely that he would have been disgusted by the plumpness and complacency amid so much misery that he would have eaten nothing and told them less.

For your own protection, Comrade, you must persuade us that you are what you say you are and can be trusted.

The flip side of the food question, however, was that maybe it was better to eat in their contemptible presence than carry it back to his block, where he could be jumped by roving criminal bands who routinely assaulted and robbed the rare men fortunate enough to get parcels from home.

If your fellow prisoners mistrust you ... if they think you are an informant for the kommandant, then they've been known to take matters into their own hands.... You will begin by telling us the name of your unit, the type of aircraft you were flying and your target when you were shot down.

Concentration-camp unity didn't seem to go far beyond a common hate for the SS. There were those who considered themselves infinitely better than others and entitled to hoard the privileges of the camp. And then there were parasites who got fat off others.

Where were you held before coming here? Fresnes? St. Valerian? Compiegne?

Certainly your prison record before coming here can be no great American military secret.

They could go to hell.

We have discussed your situation with one of our comrades who is very familiar with your military system. He tells us that your air force has trained Negroes as fighter pilots. But he hasn't heard of any Negro bomber pilots. How do you explain that?

They were accustomed to prisoners fawning over them, pleading for their favors, kneeling at their feet and begging them. Not to stony silence.

This Comrade says that if you are what you claim to be, you would have been flying a Mustang P-51, a Lightning P-38, or a Thunderbolt P-47. He assures us that these aircraft have been shot down and their details are well known to the German air force. You would not be revealing any military secrets if you agreed to describe for us the type you were flying.

Back in the warehouse shelves sagged under sacks of flour, canned food and preserves, winter jackets, gloves, caps and shoes while hundreds limped the snow-covered, stone-hard roll-call ground with nothing better than paper and cardboard wrapped around their frozen feet.

Some of the Comrades say that you are one of those colonials seen all the time in Paris. An entertainer, an actor, perhaps a prizefighter. More likely an abortionist or some kind of racketeer. That when the war started, you began trafficking in the black market. That the Gestapo caught you and threatened to shoot you unless you agreed to work for them. You agreed, and they sent you here to betray us.... What do you have to say?

He likely responded that he had already told them everything they needed to know. It would have been a predictable Nicholas rejoinder in the face of authority. He would have delighted in leaving his interrogators, so puffed up with their self-importance, dangling.

On Sunday, morning roll call was much later than usual: Buchenwald's kommandant required daylight for the show he put on every week. It began as usual: Gaudy-dressed musicians with their trumpets, flutes and drums dancing out into the snow; waves of prisoners bursting from their barracks in the background and forming into an immaculately symmetrical block, then the music fading.

Only the premonitory rolling of drums continued. Then they, too, faded.

"Mutzen ab! " crashed the loudspeaker.

The murmuring of the voices died on the breeze. Caps instantly removed and brought smartly against their wearers' right legs. A squad of SS marched into the assembly area convoying 15 men — three lines of five — in their midst. They halted just to the left of the huge main-gate entrance, immediately in front of a crude wooden structure.

It had a crossbeam with five dangling nooses.

The guards placed a small block of wood between each man's lips and tied it in position using wire knotted at the back of the condemned man's head. They tied their hands behind their backs, then ordered them to step forward and take their positions below the nooses. Prisoners arbitrarily pulled from the assembly were ordered to place the nooses around the necks of the condemned men.

Seconds later the step on which the men were standing was jerked from under them. The bodies writhed and twisted, swayed like lazy pendulums.

It was the same for the second row ... and the third. And when it was over, the loudspeakers exploded again: "*Mutzen auf!*"

Torn from his moorings in the civilized world, a prisoner's body and soul were doomed to extinction unless he sank new roots in the shifting sands of camp society. Each man had to scavenge for himself. Some, totally devastated by the initial assault, lapsed into a walking state of unconsciousness. They were known as "zombies"; bodies whose minds had transformed life, pain, misery and death into one form of insanity as a defense against another kind of insanity.

Other men, with extreme deliberation, consigned their true natures to the deep freeze and turned animal in order to stay alive. They case-hardened their humanity, numbed themselves against the stimuli of love, horror, grief, pity and concern.

And yet a few prisoners, usually men of great moral and often religious conviction, shouldered the burden of their humanity day after day, month after month, year after year, consciously rejecting any device that would make their awful subsistence less wretched.

Which type of prisoner would Nichols become — provided that he lived long enough? That must have tugged heavily at his mind.

CHAPTER SEVEN
HAITI

The big black body came flying over the stone wall.

The frenzied mob ripped into it the instant it hit the ground, hacking off the arms, legs and head and shrieking excitedly as the gory torso twitched on the dusty street. Some of the women, dancing around like spastics, soaked their bandanas in the blood squirting from the arteries in the neck stump. Their men folk, jabbering crazily in Creole, knotted a rope around the bloody mass and began hauling it through the streets.

Long into the night the drunken, rum-soaked mobs did their shuffling, orgiastic *chairo pie* dance through the streets of Port-au-Prince, following the feet, hands, head and genitals of their 25th president on the points of swords, spears and bayonets.

The relics of President Guillaume Sam were gruesome symbols of a new order for the tiny Caribbean island of Haiti. But it was to be an order that none expected.

From the beginning of that same year, 1915, when Sam met his death, the Atlantic Squadron of the U.S. Navy had been monitoring the growing turbulence on the island. From the bridge of his flagship, the USS *Washington*, Rear Admiral William B. Caperton had been scanning the beautiful, verdant island daily with his binoculars, wondering how bad things might become. From the cram course he'd taken on the complexities of Caribbean history, he knew just how violent Haitians could be: In the 111 years since 1804, when their national hero, Dessalines, had butchered all 70,000 French whites on the island and won independence for its blacks, they had used up 26 presidents — all but one of whom they'd ousted with violence and blood-letting, a new president every four years on the average.

Haiti's sorry attempts at self-government and record of repeated assassinations had been a source of derision by her North American neighbors who, although close by, shunned Haiti as a lawless nation of cutthroats.

When World War I erupted in Europe in 1914, the events in Haiti hit closer to home for the haughty Americans. The Germans had long tried to extend their influence in the Caribbean. They had business interests and citizens in Haiti. What if the Germans, on the pretext of protecting rights they deemed now threatened by the overthrow of President Sam, were to occupy the island? True, the U.S. also had citizens and property there. But Americans worried that Haiti controlled the approaches to the Panama Canal. If Haiti were taken over by the Germans, Kaiser Wilhelm could grab control of the Canal.

Word of President Sam's macabre wake reached Admiral Caperton on July 14, 1915. In the officers' wardroom, with his staff assembled, he shook his head at the news — and ordered 330 marines and bluejackets to go ashore the following day.

There was no harbor at Port-au-Prince. Just a stunning, white curve of beach blinding in the tropical sunlight, and in the center a great clutter of ticky-tacky, building-block houses in pinks, yellows, grays, browns and blues. Amid the haphazard architecture the twin cupolas of a white cathedral gleamed, with a towering wall of deep-green mountains as a backdrop.

A mile from the beach the smell of exotic tropical flowers clashed with the stink of human and animal waste lapping the gunwales of the landing boats and caused some marines to gag. Here and there the inflated carcasses of dead animals floated in the bay like obscene, bloated water bags.

The prows of the boats furrowed into the slime-covered sand and the Americans hopped nimbly over the side onto Haitian soil.

Under the bellowing harangue of barrel-chested gunnery sergeants to "spread out," they swarmed up the gentle slope of sand in their wide-brimmed Boy Scout hats, breeches and leggings with their 1904 Springfield rifles at port, waiting to blast the first *cacos* they set eyes on.

The *cacos* were Haiti's hereditary hill bandits who robbed, pillaged, raped and burned as a way of life. Almost all of the island's presidents had come to power by enlisting the support of these mercenaries. They owed allegiance to whomever paid the most. And when a revolution had been won, they found it hard to call a halt, continuing for weeks to occupy the cities and terrorize the population.

The tall, loose-limbed Americans moved cautiously up the trails from the beach that gradually broadened out to become the streets of the city. They stepped over heaps of garbage and around huge potholes. They held their noses because of the open sewage idly floating seaward down the ditches where sidewalks should have been. As they moved further into town they twisted and turned through cardboard shacks and tin shanties, tromping everywhere on the hollow shells of rotting mangoes and oranges with their clumsy field boots. From inside the primitive dwellings, glistening black faces peered out frightened, round-eyed.

Veteran NCOs who had seen the slums of Peru, the *favelas* of Brazil and the sampan housing of Hong Kong muttered that they had never seen worse.

Moving up out of the *basse ville*, the lower part of the town, the marines found the stench leavened with the sweet scent of frangipani, magnolias and gardenias wafted by the breeze from the steep hills above them. The section of Port-au-Prince where business and commerce were transacted reminded them of abandoned gold-mining towns of the American West. Unpainted two-story wooden buildings bleached to the gray sheen of driftwood by the sun's burnished glare, sagging perilously out of plumb. Buckled verandas and balconies supported by knock-kneed, toed-in columns. Mangy, emaciated dogs scrabbling after offal in the gutters.

In the 98-degree heat the Americans sweltered under their broad-brimmed hats. Their khaki shirts were soaked with large islands of sweat.

The silence, occasionally punctuated by the sonorous rolling of voodoo drums in the hills, was eerie.

In twos and threes the frightened inhabitants crept out from behind the buildings into the blinding sun. Coal-black women in voluminous Mother Hubbard-style dresses and brilliantly colored bandanas, hauling produce or firewood on crude shoulder racks with wide-eyed little urchins clinging to their skirts. The kids were half-naked in filthy rags. Many had no clothes at all. Timorously they padded up to the tall, fearsome-looking American *blancs*.

By the end of the day the U.S. Marines were being welcomed openly by the poor blacks of Port-au-Prince, who didn't seem to know who was fighting whom in their revolution-wracked country. No longer would the *cacos* invade homes and drag off fathers and sons to serve in their armies. With the arrival of the Americans, the women could once again go to the Iron Market safely and bargain for food and fruit. No longer would their daughters be in danger from the rapacious hill bandits.

Almost none of the U.S. invaders knew French. Even to those marines who did, the soft, liquid sounds of welcome in the Creole tongue would defy their understanding until they'd heard it spoken for several days. But the Americans knew joy and gratitude when they saw it written on the shiny, ebony faces — whether they understood Creole or not.

Other detachments of troops moved steadily upward to the higher levels of the city and up the slopes of the *mornes*, the foothills that grew up like a solid wall immediately behind the city. After the squalor they'd seen, they weren't ready for the lavish, Mediterranean-style villas with their expensive terraces, gardens of palm trees, poinsettias, breadfruit, *flamboya* and exotic Haitian roses. These were the homes of the city's aristocratic minority, the Haitians of mixed black and white blood who owned the country's coffee and sugar plantations and ran its business, commerce and government.

The mulattos were proud that they spoke true French and that they were people of learning, culture and sophistication. Many of them had lived in France and were educated there. They were the elite of Haiti comprising about five percent of the population. The other 95 percent lived in sordid squalor.

Their welcome to the U.S. Marines may not have been the wild, abandoned embrace of the dirt-poor peasants in the *basse ville*, yet it was no less genuine. Their coffee and sugar fields had been pillaged by the *cacos*. All work had come to a standstill. There was neither law nor order, and therefore no profits. They expressed their gratitude to the Americans in the superlative embroidery of their Parisian French and with the emotional restraints fostered by their Continental schooling.

Before long, however, the presence of the liberators would become *la misere*, an onerous, humiliating period to last 19 years, during which the proud, independent Haitian elite felt that the U.S. Marine Corps rode roughshod over their national prerogatives and made puppets of them. It may have been envy, but more likely resentment; resentment that they, the wealthy and learned, needed American troops to keep order and protect them.

Traditionally the light-skinned aristocrats held in contempt the dark-skinned peasants who worked for them. And the peasants despised the aristocrats. Yet both classes over the years were to unite in a hearty dislike of the Americans, who drafted the peasants into armies to build roads and bridges, upsetting their home and farm life and disrupting their ancient philosophy that decreed what wasn't done today could always be done tomorrow or the next day.

By the time the typical young marine had spent three years in the furnace of tropical Haiti he had taken all the insults he could stomach and was hearing voodoo drums in his sleep. He grew to despise the beautiful little Caribbean island because it loathed him. To him it had become just another goddamned banana republic.

It was May 1926. The Marines had been in Haiti 11 years.

At the gates to the cathedral where he had been baptized eight years previously, Jean Marcel Nicolas, who would one day Americanize his first name to Johnny and add an "h" to his last name, stood with his family and thousands of others who had come to witness the formal inauguration for a second four-year term of President Louis Borno.

For the second time in their generation the Haitians had gathered to behold the miracle of one of their presidents taking office in peace, at the legally appointed time, and as the result of an election conducted in accordance with the laws of the country. True, it had happened four years previously when Borno had succeeded President Sudre Dartiguenave — the first president under the American Occupation. But it was reassuring to see it happen again. Hopefully, thought Hilderic Nicolas and his wife Lucie, and thousands of parents like them, it meant that their troubled, tortured little island had come of age — that their vision of a viable black republic finally would come true. For that, at least, they could be thankful for the Yankee occupiers.

The thoughts of eight-year-old Haitian boys such as Jean were less profound. They were fascinated by the precision of the Honor Guard of Haitian gendarmes under the command of a U.S. Marine Corps captain.

Front and center of the khaki-clad battalion were the red-and-blue National Colors snapping in the breeze. The men were drawn up facing the huge cathedral, their Springfield rifles gleaming with fresh oil on the stocks, all sloped at exactly the same angle.

In the old days, Haitian presidents always took troops to church with them because the favorite tactic of revolutionaries was to strike when the president was deep in prayer. Any leader who failed to take this elementary precaution was liable to discover he'd been unseated when he emerged through the cathedral gates.

The dignitaries watched wide-eyed as ornate horse-drawn carriages glided up the wide, concrete driveway and deposited elegantly attired dignitaries at the bottom of steps leading up to the portico of the cathedral, an edifice modeled after the massive European houses of God. Droves of school children in their Sunday best flocked excitedly into the ceremonial area and were herded into place by harried teachers. A troop of Boy Scouts in shorts arrived and took their positions like miniature soldiers. Finally the roped-off sections on either side of the driveway were packed with the invited guests, and the hoarse sounds and shrieks of excitement lowered to a soft rumble of coughs and shuffling and whispers.

At last came the clatter of hooves. Suddenly a dozen majestic horsemen cantered up the driveway with their two columns guarding the presidential limousine. Jean and his friends watched enrapt as it glided to a halt and President Borno, in top hat and striped morning pants, stepped out into the shimmering morning. They watched as the horsemen climbed down off their spirited, prancing mounts and escorted the President up the stone steps.

Halfway up, Borno stopped, turned about to face the National Colors and removed his hat. In response the Colors were hoisted aloft in salute. The American captain bellowed "present arms!" The men in the battalion snapped their rifles to the vertical — and the brass band struck up *La Dessalinienne.*

As the final chords faded across the bay, the air exploded with the booming of a 21-gun salute at nearby Fort Nacional.

Those whose eyes were not on President Borno were on the American marine captain who had orchestrated the ceremony — a tall, stiffly erect figure with his gleaming, ceremonial saber held aloft as if posing for a recruitment poster.

That afternoon the most impressive public building in the West Indies, Haiti's Presidential Palace, was ablaze with bunting. On the steps the newly installed Chief of State arraigned himself in the company of his Honor Guard and his aide-de-camps in their spotless white uniforms. The guard and the aides were all that remained of the 1,200 or so generals that had been in the Haitian Army before the coming of the Americans. Under the comparatively sober auspices of the U.S. Marine Corps, those ex-generals who had survived to share the glory of President Borno's inauguration day had been reduced to the lowly rank of lieutenant or captain at the most. All raised their arms in salute as their President made his second review of his army that day.

As the troops paraded down the Champs de Mars, the street where President Sam's remains had twitched in the noonday sun eleven years previously, the martial strains of the band grew fainter. Finally the smiling new President and his aides turned around and entered the palace for the inauguration ceremony.

Jean was too young to realize that he and his family had been invited because of their status within the island's hierarchy, but it was an adventure not soon forgotten.

Once there had been only a single passport to that privileged caste-descent from a black-white union. When white Frenchmen in centuries past had lain with black women and become fathers, their mulatto children often inherited their money, their land and the benefits of education.

As a result, the ruling class in Haiti ultimately was made up of a small, light-skinned minority of educated landowners who considered themselves French, not African or Haitian. And those they ruled over were the African Haitians, the dirt-poor and illiterate peasants whose blood lines were pure, whose backs were strong and who toiled for a pittance in the plantations of the upper crust.

Jean's parents, however, had not been born in Haiti. They had come from the French island of Guadeloupe. Thus they were French citizens — he a light-skinned man, she much darker. His color gave him access to the elite. As for *Madame*: Her brother, Fortune Bogat, was a budding businessman who had a white wife from New York. These recommendations offset any disadvantage her darker skin tones might have posed in becoming part of Port-au-Prince's aristocracy. And, in addition to his desirable complexion, Hilderic Nicolas could add the high prestige of his job: He spoke excellent English and held the important post of Secretary at the British Embassy.

The Nicolas family climbed the marble staircase to a spacious salon. Every few feet along the salon's walls were wide, sweeping windows that opened onto spacious balconies, allowing the reception chamber to fill with the honeyed fragrance of the tropical air. Huge tapestries hung on the walls from an unreachable ceiling. Jean must have been overcome by the feeling of grace, elegance and dignity of the room. Along every wall thick-legged mahogany tables were draped with gleaming, spotlessly white linen tablecloths and loaded down under great pyramids of sandwiches, cakes and sweetmeats.

In a discreet, out-of-the-way corner an American-style cocktail bar did a brisk business with beautiful Haitian ladies and handsome men. Women with skins the color of copper, gold and lemon. Men in uniform or in immaculate white-linen suits. Foreign dignitaries. Bemedaled American Marine officers. Englishmen *de rigeur* in striped morning pants and spats. Excitable, frock-coated Frenchmen.

Glasses of Aux Cayes, Jeremie and *Anse-a-Veau* clicked in endless toasting. The great chamber reverberated with bass male laughter and the tinkle of amused women.

Males whose heads were easily turned by the sight of female beauty noted the chic of the *griffe, quarteronne* and *metisse* ladies around them. The skin tones of the *mulatresse* and the luxuriant hair of the *maraboute*. Draped in the latest creations of Worth and Paquin, gleaming with jewelry masterpieces bought on the Rue de la Paix in Paris. Tall, erect, sensuously graceful. Long shapely hands and feet. Faces that a sculptor dreams of.

They wore luxurious gowns of expensive silks, chiffons, georgettes and chic Parisian hats and gloves. Expensive perfumes lingered subtly on magnolia-petal skins. Soft, straight, nut-brown hair. Masses of fluffy, wavy black hair. Full red lips, alluringly pouted.

Most of the men were tall, inclined to thinness. Many with the craggy, eagle features that distinguished Haiti's business and government figures. Tall, slim quadroons with tawny, dusky-yellow skins and the glowing eyes of cats. Swarthy mulattos with crinkling, flaxen hair and pale gray eyes. Copper-colored giants with straight, jet-black hair, all sipping thimble-sized glasses of the famed but rare 100-year-old Presidential Rum,

Louis Borno was a stately man in his mid-50's of medium height with gray-brown eyes and an aquiline nose. He looked every inch the potentate as he stood at the head of the receiving line. In his coloring he could easily have been mistaken as a native of the south of France. At the British Embassy Hilderic Nicolas had heard it whispered that while Borno was a gifted international lawyer with the makings of a statesman, he was too admiring of the doctrines of Benito Mussolini, the Italian fascist, for British tastes.

Nicolas and the British wondered just how Borno, in his second term, might build upon what the Americans had accomplished for him in his first term. Because of the marines the *cacos* could no longer burn and pillage at will: The American-trained-and-officered *gendarmerie* had seen to that. They had restored law and order, security of person and property. Prior to the U.S. occupation the tiny black nation hadn't known such stability for 100 years.

Under Borno, too, the Americans had built all-weather roads. Cleaned up the streets and harbors. Constructed modern docks. Introduced modern sanitation and sewage-disposal systems. Eliminated yellow fever. Reduced the rate of malaria. Reformed the prison system. Installed telephones and electricity.

Hilderic Nicolas and his brother-in-law, Fortune Bogat, greatly admired the Americans, and little Jean Marcel easily assimilated their sentiments. But privately, most of Haiti's *elite* barely tolerated the Americans and despised the occupying Marines. The *elite's* wealth, and the privileges that wealth afforded them, had always isolated them from the peasant masses, and that is how they liked it. The *elite* resented the fact that the U.S. Marines were actually helping to educate the overwhelmingly ignorant peasant class; that could prove dangerous in the long run.

As a Frenchman, Hilderic Nicolas could appraise the American accomplishments dispassionately as did his British employers: Monumental achievements of incalculable value in preparing the island for self-government one day. Yet he was also able to understand how his class could feel emasculated in the face of the huge, efficient American steamroller.

In the Haitian Club and in the city's private salons, the mulatto aristocrats threw up their hands in theatrical Gallic gestures of disgust at the way in which the Americans had vulgarized Haitian education. The Yankees were obsessed with vocational schools at the expense of the college-preparatory education. *Sacre bleu!* Their sons, destined to be doctors and teachers and lawyers, were being pressured to become farmers!

Hilderic Nicolas knew, however, that his caste really resented something more profound. The Americans, by funneling money into the building of trade and agricultural schools, were creating a system without precedent in Haitian society: a middle class of artisans and skilled workers. The stoic, uncomplaining, illiterate black African peasant who could see no further than a life in the cane and sugar fields, the one on whose broad back the privileges of the ruling class were assured, could now escape by becoming a member of the bourgeoisie.

At the Institute of St. Louis de Gonzague, where Jean went to school, the dilemma of Haiti's upper-crust parents was echoed by their children. The kids were fiercely proud that the Presidential Palace was a copy of the Petit Palais on the Champs d'Elysees in Paris. They talked proudly about the military perfection of the *Garde d'Haiti*, which had been trained and officered by the Americans. They didn't always appreciate being reminded that it was the *Yanquis* who had built the Presidential Palace after Haitians had burned down the original structure in one of their many revolutions.

When angry words led to blows at the big, white three-story academy in Port-au-Prince, the good Brothers of Christian Instruction could be counted on to intervene on the side of the Americans: The Institute of St. Louis de Gonzague, like all private schools in the country, was continuing in operation at the sufferance of the Marine Corps. If the Brothers, an order of French Catholics, weren't careful, they might find themselves tutoring farmers instead of the country's future professional men and government leaders.

After more than a decade of U.S. occupation, most members of Haitian nobility had resigned themselves to the humiliating belief that the *blancs* were in their little nation to stay and regarded them as unable to tie their own shoelaces. So the Haitian *elite* tended to tolerate their occupiers with contempt veiled thinly behind French graces and good manners.

Jean was 10 years old in 1928 when his father sent him to boarding school in France. Even at that early age the American Marines had cornered the market on his heart and imagination. The conquest would radically influence the course of his life.

He made the long ocean voyage with his brother Vildebart, who was four years his senior. Vildebart was already attending school in France. He had come home for a vacation and was returning to commence a new term.

For Lucie Nicolas, saying goodbye to her youngest son, a handsome boy inclined to plumpness, big for his age, with an agile mind, a loving heart, generous to a fault, was almost more than she could bear. It was less tearful for Hilderic, who tended to be a silent and undemonstrative man. His older sister, 14-year-old Carmen, was devastated. They watched until the ship was a smudge on the cobalt horizon, realizing that the next time they saw their "baby" he would be a young man.

When it disappeared, an era had ended for the Nicolas family.

Their French-style home was never emptier than on that night. Carmen doted on her little brother as only an older sister can. And he idolized her. Now he was gone. Amid the constellation of religious pictures on the wall were photos of her two brothers — smiling, confident, full of promise. *Madame* Nicolas contemplated the picture of Jean, in his velveteen suit with the knee pants, posing by an ornate chair in a photographer's salon. She could not banish from her thoughts the frightening dream that she had had shortly before Jean's birth. Nor the strange man in the dream and what he had foretold about the fate of her new baby.

Her tears came freely. *Madame*, whose Christianity had never completely broken her associations with voodoo, had never told her husband of the dream — and never would.

Lucie Dalicy Nicolas had always consulted dreams for consolation and guidance during the crises in her life. She also believed in the supremacy of wild herbs and plants, of voodoo remedies over the prescriptions of the University of Haiti's doctors. On countless occasions, when her children or those of relatives were ill and failed to respond to the treatments of physicians trained in Western medicine, she had successfully used voodoo potions.

While Hilderic Nicolas was relieved that the children had been cured, he was agitated whenever his wife played doctor: In an island where voodoo is the dominant religion, he, a professional Frenchman, forever extolling the supremacy of Western culture, anguished that his *elite* friends and associates would suspect his wife of associating with *boccors* — the practitioners of voodoo's healing arts.

Not only would it have been very un-French; it could have prejudiced his employment by the British.

Hilderic, facile in several languages, considered Creole a peasant tongue and therefore beneath him. *Francais* was the language of *his* home, he was proud to say, as were most of the island's *elite*.

If Hilderic Nicolas considered Creole with scorn, he was even more prejudiced against voodoo. Yet he was as powerless as any other *elite* parent against what some experts say is a socio-cultural reality of Haiti; namely that whether parents approved or not, some Creole and some vestige of voodoo unavoidably rubbed off on their children.

This phenomenon was due to the fact that the several servants employed in the typical *elite* home spoke only Creole, not French. To interact with the servants, at least one parent *had* to speak Creole — however poorly or unenthusiastically they may have done so. Also, every *elite* home engaged one or more nannies for their children. These nannies were invariably Creole-speaking peasant women who communicated with their charges in their natural tongue. Most *elite* children, therefore, grew up understanding Creole. But they would not — because of the linguistic prejudice — use it readily in the company of their peers.

Jean would have grown up understanding Creole and speaking it — until he discovered that it was not considered *de rigueur* for a member of the *elite* to do so. As a young teenager he would have spoken it when he began sampling the night life of Port-au-Prince: The bustling outdoor markets, the tacky cafes, the back-alley gambling dens and sleazy bordellos, where Creole's liquid melange of French and West African argot flowed as easily on the tongue as good wine.

Wherever Creole flowed, some taint of voodoo could not be far behind.

It was not only Hilderic Nicolas who was uneasy over his wife's connections with voodoo herbalists; her brother, Fortune Bogat, was also concerned. After years of struggle Fortune was finally getting a foothold in the Haitian business community of the early 1930s. Rumors of his sister's dalliance with voodoo medicines were the last thing he wanted making the rounds of his sophisticated *elite* customers.

For Uncle Fortune, getting established was easier than for most of his competitors. He actually liked the Americans; they had jump-started his little island's non-existent economy. And, of course, he had married an American.

Uncle Fortune had allied with private U.S. interests in ventures such as sugar, railroads and communications, ultimately becoming General Motors' exclusive representative on the island.

In Haiti, even more so than in the U.S., a successful business career depended on maintaining the right social connections. It could seriously embarrass him among the Americans, who, in a kind of knee-jerk cultural reflex, equated *all* voodoo with "black magic." No, to have the *blancs* know him as Bogat, brother of the *boccor*, could be the kiss of death to his ambitious business aspirations.

As for *Madame* Nicolas: No matter how she might shock the neighbors, she would continue to use voodoo remedies yet make sure that she and the rest of her household appeared regularly every Sunday for mass at the cathedral in Port-au-Prince.

Only Madame had had the dream. Only *she* had met the strange man who had troubled her sleep that ominous night — and continued to do so. She had had the dream several months before Jean's birth, in the autumn 1918.

The stranger told her that the quickening in her womb was a boy and that she must name him Jean. And dutifully she had taken him to the cathedral on Armistice Day 1918 and had him christened Jean Marcel.

That part of the dream she revealed to Hilderic — but not the part that still frightened her through all the years that had passed since then. The stranger had warned her that Jean would leave the island one day and that she would never see him again.

Johnny's mother, Lucie Dalicy Nicolas, who worried that when her son left home she would never see him again. Although Catholic, she also practiced certain tenets of voodoo, common in Haiti. (Authors' Photo)

Carmen Nicolas, Johnny's big sister, was an adoring sibling. When he left home as a 10-year-old to go to boarding school in France, he saw snow for the first time and wrote her he'd bring some back for her. (Authors' Photo)

Johnny (left) and brother Vildebart pose as students at the Ariistide Brand Academy in St. Nazaire, France, during the late 1920s. When his headstrong younger brother got it trouble, Vildebart had to intervene. (Nicolas Family Photo)

Hilderic Nicolas (left) and his wife Lucie and daughter Carmen, circa the early 1920s. Hilderic was a secretary in the British Embassy in Port-au-Prince, giving him status in the island's elite. (Nicolas Family Photo)

Johnny Nicolas at age 10 showing his scholastic medals earned while attending boarding school in St. Nazaire, France, in 1928. (Nicolas Family Photo)

Harry Tippenhauer, principal of the academy where Johnny attended high school in Port-au-Prince, said the youth was a quick study especially in science but a free spirit who lacked discipline. (Authors' Photo)

Leslie Bogat (left), Johnny's cousin, and his sister Carmen on the porch of the Nicolas home in Port-au-Prince. Leslie was the son of Fortune Bogat, a leader in Haiti's commercial community. (Authors' photo)

Leslie (left) and Fortune Bogat, Johnny's uncle, go over family scrapbook in Port-au-Prince. Fortune was General Motors' only dealer in Haiti. Like Johnny, he was rebellious as a youth and concluded early-on that Haiti was much too small to contain his hell-raising nephew. (Authors' Photo)

CHAPTER EIGHT
COMING OF AGE

At the boarding school in St. Nazaire the European winter leached the bones of the two Haitian boys. Aged 10 and 12, they wallowed in home-sickness for their tropical island as bitter winds blew the astringent spume of the roiling North Atlantic into every crevice of the coastal city, inflating them with gloom.

But there was more than the abrasive climate of Brittany feeding their deepening misery.

In vast dormitory, with its white-sheeted, black-iron beds, alien smells and impersonal students, the brothers kneeled on the polished floor each night just as Madame Nicolas had taught them. Prayer was their most intimate link with home. They looked forward to it. Yet on their knees they were most vulnerable to the hazing of upperclassmen.

"On the first night at the college," Vildebart recalled many years lat-er, "we both wanted to pray before going to bed, and the older boarders came and laughed at us, and Johnny got mad ... He was a tough guy ... this guy wanted to boss Johnny, and Johnny got mad. Johnny did not fear anybody once he became enraged. The boy slapped Johnny, and Johnny took after him; he would start fighting without regard to size."

Vildebart, wincing from the sting of the taunts and jeers was afraid — but not for himself: Jean was highly emotional and couldn't take it for long. It would do no good to tell him that every new boy had to go through it; that it was part of boarding-school life. He knew that Jean was disarmingly big and strong for his age and could seriously hurt his tormentors if pushed too far.

With aching hearts and far from home, they painfully discovered that this was not the France depicted so nobly by their Francophile father and in the books he had chosen for them. Their classmates were a far cry from the brave heroes they had fantasized about whenever the French

Brothers of Christian Instruction at the School of St. Louis de Gonzague in Port-au-Prince had told their tales of La Belle France.

The brothers threw themselves into the school's classical regimen of mathematics, science and languages to drown out the hurt inside. Vildebart, being the older and more disciplined, made the transition. Jean didn't; his bubble had been too cruelly burst. He became another victim of the innocent beastliness of the boarding-school system. Beneath the pugnacious stance he had developed to fend off the hazing, he yearned for his mother's arms, his father's presence, familiar food, his own bed....

He awakened one morning to the familiar tolling of the first bell. A dormitory full of yawning, groaning, stretching boys in their nightshirts grumbled their way out of bed. Jean crossed to the window — and gasped. Snow!

The first snow of the winter. The first he'd ever seen. Hundreds of times he'd read about it. Seen pictures of it. And now he was about to get his first feel of the magical stuff.

The washing, the dressing, the bed-making, the polishing of his rectangle of dormitory floor that morning seemed to take forever. He hardly touched his breakfast because of nervous excitement. He raced outside to romp and revel in the glamorous, tingly, powdery stuff.

He thought of his sister Carmen and his promise at the dockside: She'd never seen snow either, and he'd told her that the first time he saw some, he'd scoop up a boxful and mail it to her.

Marvelous as was their first thrill of snow that day, their thoughts that night were, as usual, never far away from poinsettia season back home. Flowers as tall as trees, scarlet blossoms the girth of dinner plates. They had visions of all the wondrous trees and flowers that the students of the Aristide Briande Academy had never seen. Bougainvillea. Breadfruit. Frangipani. *Crotons.*

Jean especially missed home, Vildebart said. The warm, hazy Haitian mornings. The breeze from the hills carrying the smell of coffee roasting in thousands of peasant *cailles*, the pungent aroma of burning charcoal. The throbbing of the drums somewhere in the towering hills, confounding one's sense of direction. The dank, greenhouse smells assailing the nostrils on stepping out of the house after a heavy rainfall.

What French boy could know the lilting song of the *marchandes*, the peasant women in their colorful bandanas, their baskets of wares balanced perfectly on their heads, padding to the Iron Market in their bare feet? Ramrod straight. Hips swiveling, and their high-pitched call, telling the world of their wares. Leaving behind them on a hot, dusty afternoon a lingering trail of soft Creole, liquid as if it were a scent, not a language. Their laughter at some private joke as soft as the water caressing a beach. Or some of the wealthier ones riding donkeys side-saddle, their baskets heaped with mangoes and bananas. Calabashes the size of cannonballs. The hollow clop-clop of *le shine*, the shoeshine boys, hammering their brushes on the rungs of their foot rests, trying to drum up business.

And at night, as the two brothers knelt in prayer amid the foreign smell of French polish and stiff, laundered sheets, they imagined the sudden fall of evening over Port-au-Prince. It was as if someone pulled down a blind. The kiss of velvet night on the face. The croaking of the *crapauds.*

In time Jean emerged from the exile of homesickness. The excellence that the French teachers demanded left him little time for moping. What he couldn't shake, however, was the reputation he'd gained for being an unlikely young brawler. Like the "top gun" in an American Western, he had innocently set up himself as the tough hombre to beat. Vildebart worked to steer him clear of trouble, but they weren't continually together because they were in different classes. So Vildebart wasn't always around when Jean ran into trouble. Given Jean's quick temper and boarding school ethics, however, a serious punch-up or worse was the proverbial accident waiting to happen.

It happened when a 17-year-old senior confronted him, said Vildebart. "He wanted Jean to join in some horseplay that the school did not approve of. The other boy, who was taller and much older, slapped him two times. Jean jumped back, took a knife out of his pocket and threw it at the older boy."

Luckily for both, the blade hit the senior in the hand, nicking a finger. The school honor council held a hearing, and Jean was found blameless.

But that wasn't the end of it. The minor injury to Jean's adversary, however, turned out to be a major wound to Jean's reputation. In the sacrosanct code of this boarding school for young French gentlemen, the Haitian student acquitted himself admirably living up to his classmates' stereotype of the "black savage."

"He retained a certain bitterness afterwards," Vildebart said, "but the experience made him more mature. From then on Jean could be considered an adult, and he acted that way."

Until his arrival in France, Jean had been more French in his feelings than Haitian; France was steeped in more glories and heroes for an imaginative boy to look up to than little Haiti. As the son of a Guadeloupe-born Frenchman, he had inherited his father's Franchophile heart in the cradle. In the Nicolas home, *La Belle France* was the incarnation of *La Marseillaise*, the majesty of the *Arc de Triomphe*, the sadness of the Tomb of the Unknown Soldier, the glory of the Eiffel Tower.

But at the Aristide Briande Academy he had discovered that Frenchmen — certainly young French gentlemen — were no better than his comrades back in Port-au-Prince. If anything, they were a lot worse. He had seen *La Belle* in her housecoat, without make-up and with curlers in her hair.

In Haiti he looked down from the upper rungs of the social ladder. In France he was looked down on as a black colonial with a wicked temper and a knife to match.

He might brag of his island endlessly ablaze in sunshine, but his boasts proclaimed his private feelings that France had snubbed him. And too often the Haitian achievements that he cited came from the technological charity of the Americans.

In his heart he must have felt himself a boy without a country.

His mother could read between the lines of his brave letters home. Behind his proud recitations of excellent grades in math, science, history, English and German she could feel the struggle. After several terms she and her husband transferred their sons to the College de Garcon in Grasse.

Twenty miles from Nice, Grasse was bathed by the Mediterranean and warmed by sunshine rivaling Haiti's. It seemed ideal for a pair of homesick Haitian youths — provided they could endure the winter of another boarding-school initiation.

Here, at the College de Garcon, Jean was much happier. But Vildebart, whose health had suffered in the flinty winters of northern France, wasn't responding to the glorious new climate. After only a term at Grasse, Hilderic Nicolas decided to bring his sons home.

Carmen didn't recognize him when he stepped onto the dock at Port-au-Prince: The plump, baby-faced 10-year-old that she had said goodbye to had come home a muscular, poised young man of 13 who looked, talked and behaved much older.

In the lush tropical surroundings of home, Jean slowly began to thaw St. Nazaire out of his heart; on his home soil his native generosity and spontaneity began to flower again. The wonder of seeing old friends and exploring old haunts made him radiate. He appeared unbelievably happy to be with his own color again. To belong again.

Hilderic Nicolas was also happy. Privately, though, as any solicitous parent, he may have wondered just how long Jean's exuberance would last. Many a Haitian returned from Paris only to lead a life of discontent. As long as they stayed at home they could go on seeing their verdant isle as the jewel in the necklace of the Antilles. But viewed from the City of Light, they had to knuckle down to the reality that their homeland was among the poorest nations on earth.

For the 127 years of its existence the sun had beaten down on its green beauty, incubating in its landed gentry an indifference to its abounding poverty. Haitian aristocrats could look out from their back-verandas and not see the native *cailes* 75 meters away — or their dirt-poor occupants. A sprinkling of *elite* would continue their lives of privilege and pleasure while the men folk of those who waited on their tables toiled their lives away in the sugar and coffee plantations of the few.

The peasants would gossip in their Creole vernacular by day and at night slip off to a cockfight. Or steal away into the mountains for their *tafia* and *clairin* wine and their mystical voodoo ceremonies. For them, today was the same as yesterday; tomorrow just another today.

And they were content for it to remain that way. What else could one expect from a people who lived by the Creole adage: *Moun fet pou mouri* (people are born to die)?

Hilderic Nicolas could remember when there hadn't been a single all-weather road in the country. Now there were 500 miles of new roads, courtesy of the U.S. Marine Corps.

And yet for all the good the Americans brought, he knew they had caused a lot of problems. Among the peasants, where the idea of formal marriage was almost unknown, a man had several wives. It was the *placee* system that made prostitution unnecessary. Yet the Americans had encouraged brothels along with their roads and their sanitation and their educational system. Almost 150 had sprung up in Port-au-Prince to cater to them.

Yes, it was disgusting, muttered the island's *elite*.

As for the educational system: They surely didn't want *their* sons becoming farmers.

Back home again, Jean was enrolled at the Harry Tippenhauer Academy, a private Catholic school with a reputation for high scholastic standards and firm discipline. Whenever he could sneak away from class, he broadened his education by slipping down to the *basse ville* to watch the American marines.

They were quartered inside the Presidential Palace grounds in a large barracks area. The big, leather-faced men marched in perfect precision, doing spectacular displays with their rifles as if they were a circus troupe.

They were always so unbelievably neat, with razor-sharp creases in their pants and shirts that fit perfectly. They even ironed creases in the sleeves — creases that ran vertically up the front, through the centerline of the breast pockets, over the shoulders and down the back. And their shoes shone like mirrors.

These *blancs* talked and acted as if they were God's gift to the world and America was a paradise.

They fractured English with pronunciations that made Jean's father wince. It was worse when they tried speaking French or Creole.

Haitian children found the huge breakwater the American Marines had built to load and unload their ships the most fascinating place to visit. The sheer mass of the supplies and equipment staggered them. The country of its origin, they were convinced, had to be the most prosperous nation on earth. Forest-green Ford trucks plied back and forth with more cargo in one day than most Haitians had seen in their entire lifetime. As the vehicles rumbled away, dozens of street urchins dangled delightedly from their tailgates.

Another youthful diversion was watching the young *Garde d'Haiti* cadets training at the Caserne Dartiguenave under their Marine instructors. The presence of several light-skinned cadets implied that other *elite* families, besides Jean and the rest of the Nicolas family, agreed the Americans weren't so bad after all. The majority of the trainees had coal-black skins. Peasants from the interior, Jean's discriminating father might have said, with no learning, no culture, no sophistication.

The trouble with the Americans, thought many of Haiti's *elite*, was that they attempted to carry the eminently reasonable principle of democracy a little too far; that they had lost their sense of class. They considered it perfectly proper to mesh the light-skinned cadets and their black peasant counterparts together to enjoy the same pay and privileges and share the same barracks — and ultimately to officer Haiti's police and army together.

What would not have been lost on bystanders as observant as Jean was that when the hoarse-voiced Marine sergeant drilled them in their khaki tunics and breeches, leggings, heavy boots and wide-brimmed hats, the difference in skin tone didn't affect their precision.

Close-order drill and uniforms were not the sole attractions. The Marines had introduced boxing into the training of the young officers-to-be. Boxing and self-defense were in the curriculum, and during the training sessions hordes of Haitians, young and old, clustered at the protective chain-link fence, watching in awe and admiration.

The Americans had brought music too, by helping found and fund the Presidential Band.

The military musicians grouped under the canopy of a huge sablier tree commanding one corner of the Marine parade ground. They sat on chairs and placed their music on metal stands. In the center stood an ancient little Haitian, impeccable in a white suit, on a raised platform — M. Occide Jeanty, director.

Sunday morning, before the sun had climbed too high, afforded Haitians the best experience. *Elite* attendees were most familiar with the classical works. Young Haitians of Jean's temperament preferred the occasional jazz melodies that Jeanty had borrowed from the Americans.

The Americans! Always THE AMERICANS! If it wasn't the deluge of their supplies, it was the excellence of their equipment. If it wasn't the fine cut and quality of their uniforms, it was the marvel of their jazz. If it wasn't this, it was that.

Sheer North American abundance and extravagance inflicted more than a few *elite* Haitians with a burdensome inferiority complex. Yet they could take pride in their ancestors' epic and blood-soaked struggle against French colonial masters, establishing the world's first independent black republic. It was a story drummed into Jean at the Tippenhauer Academy in Port-au-Prince.

Harry Tippenhauer, a black headmaster with German blood in his veins, was an engineering professor at the University of Haiti. On the side he operated the two largest private schools in Haiti. He remembered Jean's nimble wit, quick mind and intellectual curiosity about everything.

"He would help anyone in the class and completely forget himself," he recalled. "All the time he was ready to help, and with such a good mood that you just couldn't stop him. He was a special boy; warm and affectionate — very much so. If there was a friend who was in danger, he would give his life, and you couldn't stop him from doing it. He had an impulse, an inside will for doing things.

"His brother Vildebart had been head of *his* class. Jean couldn't be head of *his* class because he was following too many other pursuits. He had special subjects that he liked. He was wonderful in French. He was very fond of French history, and he was very good in science. An active student like Jean wouldn't stick to being head of the class for all subjects. He does exactly what he likes.

"There was no difficulty in teaching Jean. Sometimes, however, when he had something in his mind, when he was following an idea, it was rather hard to get all his attention in a subject if it was not really what *he* wanted to do.

"I taught mathematics. Jean was good in math, but Vildebart was much better. Vildebart was what we call in French a *puchet*, someone who has the will to study, do things correctly and succeed, while Jean, with his intelligence, was so smart that he didn't have to kill himself at a lesson to get it. He was almost — but not entirely — the opposite of his brother. He was just special.

"He could have been a top man as far as social work was concerned. His goal was to be the best. He wanted to become a leader."

Had Jean had ever posed disciplinary problems?

"With me, he obeyed," Tippenhauer said. "He was very respectful."

The headmaster revealed a very special place in his heart for his former student, and this forgives him for his charitable lapse of memory. On one occasion Jean's behavior had triggered what, by all accounts, must have been the most embarrassing classroom incident of Tippenhauer's entire tenure.

When interviewed in 1972, Tippenhauer, who still enjoyed the powerful physique of a fullback, had disciplined Jean by caning him across the buttocks in front of the rest of the class. Jean, whose sudden teen-age growth spurt had put him on a height-weight equal to the bull-necked Tippenhauer, had accepted the punishment stoically. When it was over, however, he wrested the cane from Tippenhauer' grasp, forced *him* across the desk and reciprocated.

"Jean was a very generous boy," said his mother, Lucie Nicolas. "He was almost always a good child in school." One of his early yearnings was "to go on a boat, to be a sailor, to travel," she said. And one of his early character traits was his tenacity. "If he said *yes* or *no*, he meant it, no matter what his parents would try to do to change his mind."

It was Madame Nicolas who revealed how Jean had caned Tippen-hauer, concluding: "And that is why he was expelled from the academy."

Long before his expulsion, however, Jean was already drawing audiences with his repertoire of exploits in French boarding schools and other venues. By the end of his first term at the Tippenhauer school he had made many friends. He preferred crowds of other 14-year-olds rather than one or two close comrades. Taller, heavier and stronger than the others, he invariably occupied the center of attention.

At 15, his unique identity began taking root. He was now spending more and more free time outside the Nicolas home at 106 Rue des Caserne, which was near the center of Port-au-Prince. During the long summer vacation of 1933, he grew increasingly restless and spent progressively longer hours away from home. Sometimes it was close to night before his anxious parents would see him again, striding into the courtyard, smiling his wide, infectious grin and proclaiming ravenous hunger.

Friends recall his spending vast amounts of time and pocket money at the Rex Theater, watching American movies. He doted on gangster films and those featuring black American jazz artists and boxers. After a movie he and the *elite* pack he ran with rendezvoused at upscale bistros to relive the exploits of John Dillinger, mimic the Mills Brothers or try out the latest gangster lingo or jazz *patois* they'd picked up at the Rex that afternoon.

Jean had a parrot's ear for dialects and languages. He spoke French at home — and Creole, when his father, who despised the peasant *patois*, wasn't around. German and English he studied in school. He picked up Spanish from his contacts with the prostitutes who came across from the Spanish-speaking Dominican Republic to ply their trade on the Haitian side of the border. And he tried his hand at American English, which he learned by hanging around the Marines and from watching American movies.

But, as his fastidious father liked to remind him, his son's acquired Yankee drawl would never pass muster at the British Embassy.

As the youth grew older, downed his first belt of hard liquor and began sampling the flesh dens patronized by the marines, he delighted in striking up conversations with them, pretending *he* was an American. It excited and challenged him to see how far he could push his impersonation.

Among the Haitian *elite* young set of the mid-3os, when athletics was a *cause celebre* in Port-au-Prince, newsreels of Joe Louis, the light-skinned heavyweight champion from Detroit, regularly drew huge crowds to the Rex. They inspired 16-year-old Jean himself to get into the ring. By this time he was more than six feet tall and handled himself like a heavyweight. Pierre Gabrielle, one of his closest boyhood friends, and eventually one of Haiti's leading sports promoters, became his manager. He did well in amateur tournaments, Gabrielle remembered years later.

Boxing's chief compensation came from its ego boost: Jean developed a stable of daughters of high society who came to the gymnasium to see the muscles ripple under his taut skin and to marvel at the litheness of his muscular body. Unfortunately his ring career came to a shameful close when, before an important bout, manager Gabrielle mistakenly rubbed him down with "Sloan's Liniment" instead of oil. It set Jean afire — but he gamely went a full round before allowing Gabrielle to throw in the towel.

The *belles* of the *elite* played coquette with him whether he won or lost: Although Hilderic Nicolas was not wealthy, he was nevertheless distinguished in Port-au-Prince. And this meant that to the designing mothers of the *elite*, Jean shaped up as excellent marriage material.

His disguise was perfect.

Like the typical young gallant of his set, he was quick to recite poetry and dole out flattery and flowers to his conquests. He worked hard at polishing the witty phrase and the penetrating observation. Yet unlike his friends, who unblushingly publicized their boudoir battles, he kept his to himself. While they endlessly reiterated past conquests; he prattled on about his future designs.

At 16, after three years at home in the beautiful island he once thought he'd never want to leave, he was ominously restless and impatient to go again. He often told friends that his ambition was to rove to the ends of the earth. "Haiti was too quiet, too small for Jean," Gabrielle remembered. "He was always wanting something new, something more exciting."

He wanted to become "very rich," said Vildebart. "He liked money not for its own sake but for the things he could do with it. 'I liberate myself with money,' he said. 'Without it, I don't live.'"

Dancing helped him vent some pubescent steam. He cut a familiar figure at Saturday night dances at the best nightspots. The Club Bellevue, the Club Cercle, the Port-au-Princien and the Trocadero were his favorites.

The Trocadero was in Bizoton, an hour's drive west along the curve of the bay. Its vast vine-and-rose-entangled veranda extended to the water's edge, where palm trees nodded in the soft tropical breeze. On a typical Saturday evening Port-au-Prince's beautiful people — and those who aspired to be — glided across the mirror-polish of its dance floor, while gay, multicolored Chinese lanterns festooned from the ceiling cast whirling shadows around the room.

Hunting was hot at the Troc. The best-looking *sang-meles* in the local Bluebook showed up to be seen. Their complexions ran from ebony and coffee to amber and cream. And as these beauties, in their diaphanous Parisian gowns, tangoed and rhumbaed sensuously, waltzed gracefully or reveled in the merengue, white-suited musicians played spiritedly, rivulets of perspiration trickling down their faces.

Jean zeroed in on the lighter skins. The idea of a white woman — especially white Americans *a la* the voluptuous gun molls in the gangster movies — crowned the summit of his fantasy life. At the Troc it was possible to see a beauty or two with blonde hair and Nordic features. But he knew that they were still *de coleur*.

On the down side, the nightclub circuit drew from the same refined, genteel, educated and worldly membership that had surrounded him all his life. Inevitably the glamour and excitement of the Saturday dances faded, and he turned to prowling solo for more daring diversions.

Down on the waterfront the nightlife lasted until dawn.

In the vast open market, the *Marche en Haut*, sleeping men, women and children lay with their pigs and *bouriques* burdened with vegetables, hugging their wares in their sleep for fear they'd be stolen. Along the Rue Nacional scores of tiny, yellow lights gleamed. They were the stalls of the *marchandes viandes*, the teeming city's all-night restaurants. Restaurants? Nothing but boxes on the bare ground, smoking oil lamps, barefooted woman glistening in the shadows. There'd be a stack of *rapidou* cakes, the native sugar, and a few slices of coarse cassava bread selling for a centime or two.

It would have been a snack Jean had never eaten in an exotic world he had never tasted before.

For ordinary, everyday voodoo-practicing Haitians, the Rue du Fr. Dehoux exerted an other-worldly enticement, not only because the street skirted the city cemetery; at night it offered a running stumble through a jungle of rickety gambling concessions, roulette wheels and dice games illuminated by decorated lanterns.

For sons of the *elite* such as Jean, the garish nether world of Rue du Fr. Dehoux offered discoveries and adventures alien to Christian homes.

Most of the gamblers were dirt-poor men in rags and bare feet stubbornly trying to change their luck. Changing one's luck constitutes a major preoccupation of voodoo believers. The spirits of voodoo are believed to assist the believer in identifying the most important aspects of his character and help him hold on to this vision of himself when life gets tough. Voodoo is a religion of survival. It counsels the believer in what to do to insure his survival.

For believers, *chans* (chance) is no matter of chance; one must actively work at enhancing good luck, fending off bad luck. It is a full-time, life-long vocation. It would come in handy later.

Port-au-Prince nights are oppressively hot, their calmness disarming. A powerful storm may mutely gestate above a roof of clouds, sealing in the aroma of wood smoke and roasting coffee wafting across the city from the Open Market. Overhead, great black bats flit like ghostly kites. The scents of *tafia* and *clairin*, the poor man's wines, cling to the darkness.

A pubescent young *elite* in his wandering rite of passage could find the mystery and the gloom, the smells and textures, electrifying and stultifying at the same time.

He might wander west to the poor quarter, the Croix des Bossales. He might recall from his history class that thousands of African slaves had stood there in chains, waiting to be auctioned. Just behind them oozed the putrid marsh into which the bodies of dead slaves had been pushed. And deeper in the same sinkhole, he might have heard, rotted the corpses of all the losers in Haiti's countless revolutions.

Jean's roving frequently took him to the *Quartier*, where prostitution ran amok. Deeper in sprawled the Frontier, the seedier section reserved for women of Spanish extraction, known as the *Dominicaines*.

Clients risked being mugged in the Frontier's shadowy, tortuous lanes where raven-haired Spaniards batted false eyelashes and pouted blood-red mouths from the windows of flimsy, drab and gray-bleached dwellings. The *Quartier* offered an obstacle course of tottering verandas, rotting steps, dislocated porch pillars, termites glutting the open sockets.

Jean spied beckoning women in plumage ablaze against the drab sheen of their fallen-down shacks. Gowns of silk and satin. Scarlet, purple, flame, sulfur ...

At La Paloma Blanca, a rambling villa on the Marquisand Road, *Madame* corseted her *Dominicaines* to heighten their bosoms and exaggerate their hips.

The American marines liked them that way, Jean learned. But why, he might have wondered, didn't they object to their legs, which were as thin as pouter pigeons'. And why were the older *Dominicaines* so popular when so many young ones were willing to please?

A token dance, then the *blancs* would be led off the dance floor by the hand and up an ornate, curving stairway once the pride of some colonial slave owner.

He first noticed her on a later exploration in the Frontier. She was beautiful; so magnificent that he lost his courage and fled to the Crystal Palace, a busy bordello outside the city limits.

There tall, lithe Dominican girls rhumbaed on a tiny floor with their men-for-the-night. He stood at the door watching. Light streamed from the salon through open jalousies, and he could see that they were wearing little or nothing at all beneath their long, flared skirts.

The word on the boulevard was that the Spaniards had to be truly superior performers if they could sell what many Haitian women were willing — even eager — to give away.

Jean sat at his table on the edge of the dance floor, drank rum and watched the mating ritual go on around him. Occasionally an adventuresome *Dominicaine*, indifferent to her partner, brushed past him suggestively with a swish of her long, taffeta skirts. But he was consumed by the sensational lady on the veranda whose beauty had frightened him.

His self-confidence braced by a rum overload, he quit the Crystal Palace and made his way unsteadily back to the district of the narrow streets and sagging porches.

She wasn't on the veranda where he expected her to be. She was inside, entertaining a marine — and several other marines waiting their turn. Crushed and humiliated, he stumbled away from the broken-down house and through the shadowed lanes to a tavern in order to quench his misery in the potent *clairin*. All it did was pump up his anger.

He staggered back to the Frontier, crashed into her boudoir, grabbed the marine and began beating him savagely. Two other marines rushed to their friend's defense, but Jean's rage was enough to throw all three across the tottering porch and into the street.

The fracas landed him on the "Most Wanted" list unofficially circulated among Marine Corps enlisted men in Port-au-Prince.

It was impossible to hide his cuts, bumps and bruises from his parents. Shocked at the new twist in their son's adolescence, they turned, as always in such crises, to Uncle Fortune.

"He liked to live splendidly," said Fortune. "He was a show-off, you see. Definitely a hell-raiser, but he didn't drink excessively. He gave you the impression of a guy who was very thoughtful about what he was doing.

"I definitely know he liked life. He was a *bon vivant*. He wasn't stingy; he was always ready to give you what he had.

"He was very bright and got good marks in his examinations. You would be explaining something to him, and before you were finished, he knew what it was you were talking about.

"He was a good talker. He had an adventurous type of mind. He was rather polite in talking to people. But ever since he was a child he'd had a very strong character. When he wanted to do something, he would do it. He wasn't afraid to start a fight with anybody.

"Haiti was too quiet, too small for him. Besides, he and Vildebart were too different in character to get along very well together. And he and his father didn't get along well either."

Fortune laid it on the line for Hilderic and Lucie Nicolas: If Jean kept it up, it was merely a matter of time, regardless of how big, strong and fearless he was, before the police would find him face down and floating in the gutter.

"I wouldn't have liked to see him stay in Haiti," Fortune said, "for he certainly would have gotten into trouble."

CHAPTER NINE
SEMPER FI

President Franklin D. Roosevelt granted the distraught Nicolas family an unexpected reprieve from their troubles when he announced that the U.S. occupation of Haiti would end in 1934.

Uncle Fortune wiped his brow in relief. He realized that a lot of Jean's "growing pains" could be traced to the Americans and the youth's obsession with everything about them; his dress, speech and mannerisms proclaimed it loud and clear. Maybe, he thought, Jean will forget all this acting-out nonsense after they've gone and revert to his once-loveable self. He knew that that was what Hilderic and Lucie prayed for.

Yet Fortune's feelings about the imminent departure of the *blancs* were mixed. He had made many friends among them. Because of them, his business had prospered. On the other hand, he couldn't help feeling pleased to see his sister and her husband smile once again.

Now, he told them, if they could just keep the boy on a tight rein for a few months until the actual U.S. withdrawal.

True to form, Jean couldn't stay infuriated with the *blancs* forever. How could he? They'd entertained him for hours drilling at the Presidential Palace. Unloading their cargoes down at the docks. Their mannerisms amused him. Their profanity made him laugh. Their slang intrigued him. It would be strange not to see their familiar white faces. Not to hear the "Hup ... tup ... threep ... fourp!" as they strode down the Champs de Mar. They made the town important. They filled it with a sense of action. A sense of something happening.

The new American president, in a dramatic goodwill gesture, invited Haitian President Stenio Vincent for a state visit to Washington. He accepted, and U.S.-Haitian relations began to heal. During its 1934 maneuvers the American fleet anchored in Port-au-Prince, and the city's high society thronged aboard the USS *Saratoga* for a gala reception.

In July, President Roosevelt visited Haiti. Port-au-Prince went wild releasing its pent-up feelings in the most lavish festival in the city's history. The battleships USS *Franklin Delano Roosevelt* and *Houston* anchored off Cape Haitien. A model of the airplane in which Lindbergh had flown the Atlantic was woven in brilliant flowers and proudly exhibited downtown. The American president, saving the good wine until the last, made the momentous announcement that his forces would leave the island two months earlier than scheduled. And, as a farewell gesture, he made a free gift to Haiti of all Marine Corps buildings and equipment on the island!

Nineteen years of political humiliation for the islanders had come to an end.

On the eve of the departure that August of 1934, more Americans fraternized with more Haitians — and *vice versa* — and clinked more glasses together than in all of the occupation years. When the last American vessel weighed anchor and its foghorn boomed a sonorous farewell, tens of thousands of delirious Haitians cheered frenetically.

Jean, out of his rapidly declining sense of duty to his parents, showed up at the formal diplomatic-corps parties and celebrations where the Hilderic Nicolas and family were expected to put in an appearance. But he was present in body only. The youth who once had had so much to say distanced himself in elaborate silence. If he spoke at all, it would be to correct his identity. He was not Jean Marcel Nicolas, he would point out, but Johnny Nicholas.

On these occasions his father's remonstrations were met with more silence. Silence, it seemed, allowed Jean to rebel without openly defying parental authority.

Tippenhauer, another major authority figure in his life, was the target of a different tactic of rebellion. In class Jean had taken to the wisdom of St. Thomas Aquinas and St. Augustine. He was now touting the dialectic of philosopher Wilhelm Friederich Nietzsche, and the big headmaster, sensing a volcano smoldering in a student for whom he had great affection, didn't know which way to turn.

In the Haiti of those days, where the greatest compliment one could pay an *elite* was to mistake him for a Frenchman, Jean couldn't have chosen a more repugnant champion: Nietzsche was a German. Germans and French had been enemies for centuries. He was also an intensely anti-Christian ex-Catholic priest.

It was not only embarrassing, but disruptive to the good order of the Tippenhauer academy for Jean to declare Christianity in error for propping up the weak and preserving the unhealthy. They should be allowed to die off, he argued, parroting the Nietzschean dialectic. Then society would contain only the best of the species.

Within Port-au-Prince's small *elite* enclave, where almost everyone was a relative of everyone else, the Nietzsche scandal would have been impossible to hide. Jean's parents would have been mortified.

Uncle Fortune rubbed his craggy features heavily. As Haiti's premier businessmen, he had many influential friends tucked away in high places. There was a lot that he could do — and had done. For example, it hadn't been that long ago that he had engineered a miracle on Jean's behalf by persuading Tippenhauer, still aggrieved over having his rearend caned by Jean, to grant his recalcitrant nephew his Bacchaulaureate Part I and Part II — even though the expelled youth had not completed the necessary schooling. But the Nietzsche insanity: That was definitely out of his league. The Nicolas's would be the laughing stock of the Sunday congregation at the cathedral. Never mind what His Excellency, the bishop, was likely to say.

What, he wondered, in the name of God, were they to do with the boy?

Uncle Fortune, then in his late 3os, was the only adult who could get through to Jean. They were two of a kind, he would explain many years later. In his young days Fortune too had dazzled the ladies, consumed his quota of rum and raised plenty of hell. He knew the polar pulls of puberty and duty on hot-blooded youth. He deeply empathized with Jean.

And they were both ardent admirers of the departed marines, which made them even more *sympatico*.

No sooner, however, would Uncle Fortune extinguish one fire than Jean would touch off another. With the marines no longer available to clash with at the Frontier, he had begun antagonizing his comrades by stealing their girlfriends.

He didn't have to steal, said his friends. He had what it took to win almost any young woman in the city. He made love in any language, they chuckled, preferably Creole.

Next, he extended his activities to include married woman. The lady and her chaperone were dropped off in front of the Rex Theater by a considerate fiancée or indulgent husband, who then drove off to his office or to a luncheon appointment at the Haitian Club. *Madame/madamoiselle* and chaperone bought their tickets and took their seats in the dark interior. Jean, already in a nearby seat, always made sure a gangster movie was playing and he always arranged for a side door to remain unlocked. At some point in the movie the lady excused herself from her chaperone and exited the Rex by the side door, where "Johnny" awaited her....

A couple of hours later she returned through the same side entrance in time for the final scenes, then duly exited with her escort. During the short walk from the cinema to the waiting car, *madam/madamoiselle* would extract the essential details of the film's plot from her chaperone — just in case. And the naïve spouse/beau would drive them back to Bois Verna, Kenscoff or another of the city's upscale suburbs, none the wiser.

Jean's plot was always the same; only the women and the playbill changed. But now it wasn't vengeful U.S. Marines he was dodging; it was jealous buddies and cuckolded husbands.

It had gotten so bad, recalled Uncle Fortune, that whenever he and Jean entered a tavern, "before he sat down he'd always check for the other exits. He was always prepared for what was going to happen."

About the time Fortune and Jean's parents thought that there was no new embarrassment with which the youth could shock them, he proved them wrong.

Sitting on their verandas about five o'clock one summer evening, recalled Madame Nicolas, she and her family, like the rest of Port-au-Prince, was perspiring heavily, praying for seven o'clock, when cool breezes would blow down from the mountains towering behind them, bringing blessed relief. As they glanced toward the hills they saw inky black clouds curling around the hilltops and drifting down the valleys toward the town. Yet their veranda was bathed in brilliant sunshine.

It was always that way before a violent storm, she said.

The temperature in Haiti begins to climb from a daily average of 90 degrees in April to around 92 degrees in May. By June it has reached 95. Unlike the United States, where a 95-degree day can be followed by a 90-degree day, the heat in Haiti seldom varies during the summer. Within a degree or two a typical July will register 98 degrees day after day, week after week; and August is an unyielding repetition of July.

This results in a tremendous heat mass over the island in summer. The seasonal shifting of the winds brings a humidity that makes the heat even harder to bear. It is the time of incredibly heavy rains.

Within minutes fat raindrops splattered the Nicolas courtyard, leaving spots as big as silver dollars. Port-au-Princiens knew that up in the hills the dark clouds had unleashed a deluge and that soon the dusty little hillside trails would become raging torrents.

Within 15 minutes the gutters on the side of the road by the Nicolas house churned and hissed with ochre-colored water a foot deep. The burnished sun had paled to a sickly grey. Blinding flashes of lightning burned through the haze. Staggering explosions of thunder assaulted the eardrums and rocked the earth. An icy wind swept down the mountainside like an avenging scythe, whipping pliant palms almost to the ground. Massive mango trees and oaks groaned under the punishment.

Outside, the road was a raging torrent three feet deep, sweeping toward the sea stones, rocks, branches, tree trunks and everything else that got in the way.

A cataclysmic eruption of thunder and lightning — then silence. The cobwebs of fog retreated up the valleys, and once again — until tomorrow about the same time — the city would revert to its usual, scented, steaming self.

Port-au-Princiens feared the daily summer rainstorms even though they had become used to them, Madame Nicolas explained. The authorities had constructed a special canal system, the Bois de Chene, to quickly drain the city after the deluges.

Late that night, when the air was once again calm and the mountain breeze cool and sweet, the Nicolas family learned that in the poor section of town, several families had been swept into the raging Bois de Chene and almost drowned: A heroic young man had dived in and saved them.

It was their errant son, they later learned. "He was always trying to do things for people," said Madame Nicolas, "especially when they were scared."

During his 17th and 18th years Jean seemed to his parents to be calmer, less stressed. Maybe Fortune's Dutch-uncle talks scared some sense into him. Maybe he finally realized the serious implications of his father's deteriorating health.

Since his expulsion from high school, time had hung heavily on his hands, but he was spending progressively less of it in his parents' company. Home had become a pit stop, a place to eat and sleep while living a clandestine life elsewhere.

Uncle Fortune did some sleuthing. He telephoned friends and business colleagues who, in turn, quizzed sons who had been Jean's classmates. What had *they* heard?

They painted a picture of a troubled nephew. Some had heard that he was earning money tutoring language classes in one of the city's private schools. Others said he'd been seen in biology classes at the University of Haiti. Strangest of all, especially for one so verbal, so talkative, some reported him reticent and elusive, caught up in vague and mysterious pursuits that seemed to have set a pattern for the rest of his life.

It may have been during this secretive period of his life that Jean, who knew Major Gardemann only distantly as someone whom his father, Hilderic, brought home on occasions, developed a personal relationship with the German diplomat.

After the departure of the Americans, the *gendarmes* of the *Garde d'Haiti* remained the highly professional corps trained by the U.S. Marines. The peasant-class constables and black officers continued full of fanatic zeal for enforcing the law without fear or favor, whether the lawbreaker be palest *elite* or duskiest peasant.

Jean knew this but chose to ignore it.

It was 1936, and he was 18. Curious about a crowd gathering around a disturbance in a Port-au-Prince street, he muscled in to find out what was happening. Gendarmes already on the scene ordered the crowd to disperse. Jean, too proud to take orders from someone he considered an exalted peasant fresh from the *caille*, defiantly refused. The *gendarme* grabbed him, and Jean's entire future was altered in an instant.

Port-au-Prince police always paraded with rifles. While on street duty, however, they carried only revolvers. They seldom used these weapons because they had a much more persuasive implement — the *cocomacaque*. A stick about three feet long and two inches in diameter, the *cocomacaque* was the pride of its owner, who usually coated it with oil to enhance its ripe-banana color. The wood rivaled the hardness of iron — especially at the huge, knotted business end.

Jean tackled the policeman so fast that the man had no time to wield his *comomacque*, and knocked him down. The other *gendarmes* immediately piled on Jean, wrestled him to the pavement and handcuffed him.

When Uncle Fortune got the news, he hit the ceiling — then raced downtown to bail him out.

En route to police headquarters — a two-story frame building across from the National Palace, he remembered the fate in store for anybody arrested *before* the American Occupation. It had always meant a beating.

In those days beatings came in three grades. The sergeant might instruct the guard: *"Refleche-le petit-petit,"* which meant he wanted the prisoner "refreshed" a little. If he wanted a good hiding administered, he would say: *"Refleche-le mais pas levez orgueil."* (Refresh him — but don't arouse his pride.) And if he wanted the unfortunate prisoner beaten to death, the command was: *"Fai pie le per die terre."* (Make his feet leave the earth.)

As Uncle Fortune ascended the rickety steps to the red-and-yellow police headquarters building, he prayed that Port-au-Prince's *gendarmes* had remembered their American discipline and had not reverted to old instincts. Inside the police chief's office, he pulled off the *tour de force* of his trouble-shooting career by literally snatching the arrogant, unremorseful Jean from a potential prison sentence and rescuing the good name of his family.

The harried Fortune delivered his errant nephew back into the custody of his frazzled parents and issued an angry ultimatum: Jean had to clear out of Haiti — no ands, ifs or buts; and he, Fortune would gladly pay the fare. If Jean balked at the proposition, then he'd be strictly on his own from there on. Uncle Fortune simply had had enough.

It took a while to get an agreement and make the necessary arrangements because Hilderic, in declining health for some time, died the following year, in 1937. His passing seemed to help bend Jean toward his uncle's ultimatum.

Fortune's plan was to enlist Jean in the French navy, but there was problem: The recruiting vessel wasn't scheduled to make its usual twice-a-year stop at the French island of Martinique for another six months. With six months to kill, his nephew could plunge Haiti into another revolution, he thought. Somehow the lad had to be conned into temporary cold storage somewhere. So Fortune drafted him off to the custody of another uncle, Pierre Chauvel Gabrielle, who lived 700 miles away on the island of Guadeloupe, until the recruiting ship arrived.

Fortune realized that it could only be a very temporary expedient: If Haiti was too small for Jean, Guadeloupe, a scattering of breadcrumb-sized islands in the eastern Caribbean, didn't stand a chance — unless they could get the youth something more to do with his time than drinking, gambling and womanizing, and punching out the local *gendarmerie*.

A temporary job somewhere. That was it. But sweating in a sugar cane field or rum distillery, the kinds of jobs held by the locals on Guadeloupe, were out: Sons of the Haitian *elite* were conditioned from birth for much higher callings. So Uncle Fortune, ever the improviser and string-puller, and Uncle Pierre conspired to set Jean up working at a local hospital.

When family and friends, waving sadly from the Port-au-Prince dock, had shrunk doll-size in his perspective, Jean went below decks and gazed through a porthole. The sun, a mammoth coral ball, slipped down into a sea of sapphire and night fell, dark and mysterious. As the velvet night smoothed his cheeks, the phosphorescent Caribbean twinkled beneath him. The seagulls' scream pitched higher.

Through the encroaching darkness shone the myriad peasants' fires dotting the *mornes* towering behind the city. The white of the cathedral's twin cupolas gleamed through the gloom — the cathedral where he had been baptized almost 19 years earlier.

There, as an eight-year-old, he had had his first close look at one of the fiercesome *blancs* — a stocky Marine Corps captain with a gleaming saber, in charge of the Haitian *gendarmes'* Honor Guard; and he'd become forever hypnotized by the might and manners of the Americans.

From the dock *Madame* Nicolas, Carmen and Uncle Fortune waved.

Carmen's tears knew no bounds; she had doted on Jean ever since he had been a baby. *Madame* also wept, but her tears flowed with a bitter wisdom that was far beyond her daughter's understanding; she was remembering the stranger in her dream and the dire warning that he had uttered.

Throughout her life dreams and divinations exerted a powerful influence on *Madame*. All the major events in her life, she said, had been presaged in her dreams, and she had always shared these foretellings with her husband and others. But this dream, the one in which the strange man in the burial grounds had spoken to her, she had kept hidden in her deepest heart because of the indescribable terror that it boded.

As for Fortune: He watched the vessel disappear in the darkness and sighed with profound relief. He was the happiest uncle in all of Haiti, even though he knew he'd miss his spirited nephew.

CHAPTER TEN
AMERICAN PLANES!

On August 27, 1943, a top-secret truck convoy code-named "Transport South" drove out of Buchenwald and, after a 60-mile trip, pulled up in a broad, flat, tree-studded field at the base of the Kohnstein Mountain, a 500-foot high hill in the Harz Mountains of north-central Germany. The commander of the detachment, SS Major Barnewald, got out and watched his 40 SS troops supervise the unloading of 107 prisoners — mostly Poles, Russians and a few Germans.

What the prisoners and their guards immediately noted were two grotesque-looking, 38-foot-diameter excavations defiling the beautiful grassy, tree-studded slope of the mountain. These gaping orifices, called Main Tunnel "A" and Main Tunnel "B," would come to symbolize a monstrous but little-known crime against humanity that history would call Camp Dora, a Buchenwald subcamp.

A second Buchenwald contingent of 1,223 prisoners arrived on September 2. It was comprised mostly of Poles, Russians and French — and one Englishman, Cecil Jay, a carpenter by trade.

Jay didn't know Nicholas at Buchenwald. They would meet nine months later at Dora, become friends, and Jay would play a key role in the black man's life.

"The fields [at the foot of the Kohnstein] were full of beet," Jay remembered. "As we came into the fields, we saw a few small tents made out of plywood. These tents were in front of the tunnels, in the fields and woods. As we arrived, we were put in the tents straight away, and after the first night we were taken into the tunnels.

"Our orders were to build a temporary kitchen [for the SS guards], then a sick bay, and also a large shed for the dead people who, they told us, would come in a few weeks. So we knew what was going to happen.

[123]

"The first beds were built eight days after I arrived. The first [sick] prisoners were put in these beds; the rest [slept] on the stones [on the tunnel floor] until beds were made.

Jay and his 10-man crew began erecting prefabricated wooden buildings. Over the following months these would eventually mushroom into a large, conventional camp of hundreds of barracks, offices, warehouses, storage facilities, garages and other specialized buildings.

As for the rest of the Buchenwald contingent: The SS marched them into Main Tunnel "A," which, they would discover, was interconnected by 23 smaller-bore cross-tunnels with Main Tunnel B. Once inside Tunnel "A," the Buchenwald deportees were tossed picks, shovels and jackhammers and ordered to begin widening and expanding the tunnel maze. They worked around the clock in 12-hour shifts, then collapsed onto the rubbled floor of several pre-existing tunnels set aside as dormitories. For the next seven to ten months, until regular barracks were built outside, they — and some 10,000 to come after them — ate, slept, lived and died in these tunnels under unforgivably inhuman conditions.

Back in Buchenwald, it was winter 1943-44, as savage a season as Siberia ever served up, and the word "Dora" meant nothing to the thousand-man regiments of slaves trudging in the dark through the refrigerator of Thuringia. Nicholas trudged with them, sometimes shouldering a pick, sometimes a shovel, but always skidding and slipping, tired and weary in all-consuming physical and mental numbness.

He, like they, walked a treadmill, a cycle without beginning, without end. Sometimes digging in the rock quarry. Sometimes grading the railroad embankment. Sometimes clearing drainage ditches and water mains.

All in the freezing cold.

At night he staggered back to the camp at Buchenwald; he, like them, always toting the mandatory rock or trundling ahead their pushcarts of dead.

Three months had passed since the arrival of the dark-skinned "American Air Force flyer." Despite the 24-hour-day obsession of prisoners with their own survival, they couldn't help but notice him strut around, chest out, chin in, back straight.

Who did he think he was?

Old-timers wondered why the stupid *schwartze* kept drawing attention to himself that way. They'd had one or two Americans in the past, but never a Negro before. Certainly not one who could talk to the English, French and German prisoners in their own languages.

Big bastard, too; the kind you'd want on your side if a gang of Greens grabbed you in an alley.

What's he doing in Block 48? Why not in the block with all the other POWs? Is he a POW or isn't he? Could be a stoolie for the Commies or the Crims. Then we'll just have to arrange a little accident for him.

Better sure than sorry, right?

Every old-timer knew having Commies at the top was better than having Greens. The Greens had been in control for a while, and instead of *pretending* to play along with the SS, as the Commies did, they'd worked hand-in-glove with the bastards, willingly carrying out the Nazis' most repressive and brutal programs for their own greed and personal profit.

Sure, the Reds were tough as nails and favored their own over everybody else. But it was their militant organization and iron discipline that managed to end-run around the SS and save numberless lives. Not just Commie lives either, but prisoners of every stripe.

The Commies had stoolies everywhere, tampering with records, fiddling with food requisitions, manipulating manpower drafts, writing phony requisitions for medical supplies. There was no trick they wouldn't try — at least once. And when one backfired, the trickster paid for it in the crematorium.

It didn't take Nicholas long to realize that he was playing in a new league. This wasn't some rumble in a Port-au-Prince back alley between teen-agers who couldn't hold their first taste of hard liquor. It wasn't even the night streets of Montmarte, where a hoodlum would slit your throat as quick as he'd look at you, or downtown Paris, where a Resistance fighter with booze on his breath and a grudge in his gut gunned you down in the street.

Buchenwald wasn't live-and-learn; it was learn-or-die. You could be a sophisticate who had trawled the boulevards for the best in food, wine and women. You could know your way around the cafes, the salons and the brothels. You could flip from trading *argot* with a pimp to *Hochdeutcsh* with a Nazi officer. But you had to be smart enough to slam your ego into neutral, keep your big mouth shut and your ears unplugged.

Nicholas would have to find out which cook would slip him an extra hunk of bread. Which clerk would whisper advance warning of an outside detail to avoid or inside detail to try to wangle into. Which prisoner-medic in the hospital would spare half of a sulfa tablet for an infected injury.

Just as important, he would have to find out what these people demanded in return.

Lagereldtesters ... lagerschutz ... stubendients ... kapos: How ironic to discover that even slaves separate themselves into slaves and masters.

Some of these "masters" sported spotless stripes under heavy jackets with fur collars to shield them from the freezing wind. Some strutted the camp's muddy streets with pomaded hair and well-groomed dogs on leashes, passing stick-figures hobbling in the opposite direction, pushing wheelbarrows of frozen corpses to the building that looked like a house of the Lord.

At Buchenwald the organization chart in the SS headquarters barracks provided a rectangle bearing the words "PRISONERS' MAIL". What made the lie more compelling was the fact that each prisoner was actually issued a printed card with little columns for recording incoming mail (*posteingang*) and outgoing mail (*postausgang*), month by month. It was, of course, an institutional illusion; a throwback to the German obsession for having a place for everything and everything it its place.

Some Buchenwald prisoners were regular targets of parcels of food and personal-comfort items sent from loving families via the International Red Cross. But few of the targets were ever hit: The in-coming mail was systematically plundered by venal SS men. And if a parcel ever reached the actual prisoner for whom it was aimed, by the time he got it, there'd be little left but crumbs, wrapping paper and string.

Consequently no record of their receipt ever appeared in the incoming box provided on the prisoner's mail card.

Likewise, the outgoing box was another cruel hoax because it was a crime for a prisoner to possess writing materials, never mind write a letter. And if the prohibition was cast in concrete for rank-and-file inmates, it was doubly so for a black, *untermenschen* and N-N; which is why it is amazing that Nicholas managed to smuggle a postcard out.

His achievement demonstrates that even though he was, at this time, a callow lower classman in the Buchenwald Academy, he was learning fast. He was, in the words of his brother Vildebart, "always making things happen."

In due course a Paris postman delivered the postcard to Vildebart's apartment on the Rue de Charonne. The stamp, bearing Hitler's likeness, was postmarked Buchenwald, March 1, 1944. The message, penciled in crabbed letters, was written in faultless German:

> *I am well. I can receive some parcels. Write me in German. You can send me fresh or cooked vegetables as often as you wish. Send me some shaving soap and a toothbrush. I hope your wife is in good health. I would also be grateful for some tobacco.*
> *Best wishes, John*

The message, which had a Block No. 48 return address, was the only one they ever received from him. *I can receive some parcels ... as often as you wish.* The statement implies that, even at this probationary stage, he had already made his first move in beating the system.

Austehn! Autstehn! "Outside! Outside!" roared the barracks orderly, the *stubendienst.*

While the hollow hulks stirred in their hard bunks, a tremendous crash shattered the silence. The exhaustion-drugged prisoners, reacting to what they could only assume was some new form of SS harassment, leaped onto the stone floor and threw their hands up to protect themselves.

A magnificent, sparkling chandelier of ice, forming malevolently in the peak of the roof throughout the long winter, had fallen on the floor between the center-aisle bunks, snapped its splendid, yard-long, crystal spikes, skittering them in all directions. Overnight the thaw had loosened winter's grip, causing it to plummet to its destruction.

It would have killed a man had it fallen on him, yet it signaled life. Spring was aborning, and the invisible leaden weight on every prisoners' shoulders eased a gram.

It was a Sunday in March. As a concession to the Lord's Day, roll call was always held later. Standing in the vast, mucky assembly area, with the lemon sun's feeble rays warming haggard faces and chapped lips, seemed next to godliness.

The assembly area had been threshed to filthy slush by winter's millions of footprints. The *lagerschutz* held their clubs ready to beat anyone who marred the symmetry of the roll-call formation. The roll call leader of Block 48 was SS Master Sergeant Erhard Brauny, 33, handsome and blue-eyed, who, but for his short stature, idealized the Aryan so eulogized by Hitler. Brauny, pompous at a podium on a raised platform, snapped off the names over the public-address system.

The sunlight worked its magic. Great continents of cottony clouds drifted lazily through the blue amphitheater of the sky. No spikes of cold pierced the feet. No frost scalded lips and eyebrows. They had clung by their fingernails through a winter's horror, and now the faint stirrings of spring infused hope in every heart.

The sound of Allied bombers began as a faint droning, gradually swelling until their sonorous thunder reverberated in the ground beneath their feet. Some of the more daring new prisoners, while standing rigidly at attention, eyes front, risked peeking at the ordered swarm of silvery flecks in the wild blue yonder.

The camp veterans had long ago become used to them. The Americans, they knew, had flown over the camp so many times and never dropped their bombs. The splendid sight of the quartet of white contrails streaming far behind each high-flying speck was always exhilarating and awe-inspiring but hardly worth risking Brauny's woeful anger.

How did they know that they were American planes? They were well aware, as were all Germans at this juncture of the war, that the Americans bombed only in daylight, the British only at night.

Brauny, the fastidious roll call leader, obviously highly irritated with the competition from above, continued to roar out the names. He would pause intermittently, glance sourly skyward, return to his clipboard and resume roaring.

Fernand Rambaud, a Frenchman, remembered that Nicholas shouted "American planes!" at the top of his voice: "They're American planes!"

It was the first time that Nicholas had ever seen them, although the veterans had learned long ago that U.S. bombers not infrequently flew directly over Buchenwald on their way to targets deeper in Germany.

The hearts of Rambaud and the other prisoners froze: The naive American had committed the cardinal crime of speaking without first being ordered to do so by the roll call leader. They steeled themselves for some dreadful punishment to be called down not only upon the black man but, as was the custom when one prisoner violated a camp rule, upon *all* prisoners.

The public-address system exploded with Brauny's command that Nicholas be brought front and center.

Rambaud watched as the *lagerschutz* and his *kapos* pounced on Nicholas and frog-marched him toward the podium, pounding him with their clubs. When they reached the roll-call platform, they released him.

Rambaud remembered Nicholas standing very tall, very erect, looking directly at the SS sergeant, whose penchant for on-the-spot shooting of prisoners who irritated him was part of Buchenwald legend.

The prisoner didn't exist who did not tremble at the thought of detonating Brauny's incendiary wrath. The mass formation gulped in unison as they watched Nicholas out of the corners of their eyes. What was he trying to do? And Brauny? Was he ill? A healthy Brauny would already have pulled the trigger, and four prisoners would already have been plucked from the ranks as the black American's pallbearers.

By this time the huge echelon of American heavy bombers in precise formation — they would have been either four-engine B-17 Flying Fortresses or B-24 Liberators — was directly overhead. The collective sound of the engines was so thunderous that Rambaud and most of the prisoners couldn't hear — even over the PA system — what Brauny was saying to Nicholas or what Nicholas was saying in response. But the contortion in the little SS roll call leader's livid face and the pistol that he cocked and held against the black man's head were sign language enough.

He's done for now, thought Rambaud. As good as dead.

As the bombers' thunder waned, the prisoners braced themselves for the pistol's sharp crack and the collapse of the big black body by the podium....

By all the rules and precedents of Buchenwald life, this is what should have happened, but it never did. Instead, Brauny uncocked his pistol and lowered it.

Incredibly, whatever Nicholas had responded in his defense had stayed the murderous little SS sergeant's hand.

Until the appearance of the bombers, Nicholas had zealously hewed to concentration-camp wisdom: Keep a low profile. Never attract attention to yourself. Be faceless. Opinionless. Voiceless. Just *be* — and you might — just *might* — survive. But he had attracted attention and — without meaning to — had established an instant reputation for himself.

Supercharged versions of his exploits at Compiegne — especially the interlude at the woman's camp — had dogged him from the start at Buchenwald and conferred some mild celebration on him. But this was something very different. By his successful standoff against one of Buchenwald's more promising sadists, he had stripped himself of the last vestiges of whatever anonymity he had ever possessed.

Brauny slipped the pistol back into its holster.

The prisoners stared goggle-eyed in disbelief as Nicholas executed an about-face and marched smartly away from the podium. (Rambaud would later learn that Brauny promised personally to shoot Nicholas if American planes ever bombed Buchenwald.[1]) And even before the "American" returned to his place in the ranks, where he already towered over all around him, he had already been elevated to Superman status.

In their unceasing efforts to pump their power and influence throughout the camp's finest capillaries, the Communists had managed to steal parts and fabricate a primitive radio that they used secretly to monitor British newscasts. Information, they knew only too well, was power. Possession of news of the outside world and of the progress of the war gave them immense leverage. They skillfully leaked these newscasts around the camp — or withheld them — as they did with all their other gratuities, such as extra food, a better pair of shoes, and easier work details, indoors instead of outdoors, in order to further consolidate their power base.

Out in the rock quarry the morale of exhausted pick-and-shovel swingers depended almost as much on news of the outside world as it did on food and water. Prisoners who had lost all hope conjured new reasons for staying alive when, courtesy of the Communists, they were transfused with the momentous news of the impending Anglo-American invasion of German-occupied Europe.

When would it happen? The prisoners could only guess, but the prospect kept their lifeblood flowing when reality screamed for them to shrivel up and die.

On the slopes of the Etterswald, winter was conducting a masterful withdrawal, stubbornly dumping snow on the backs of the slaves in the

---

1 Bombs finally fell on August 24, 1944. Little damage was done to the camp; but the Mibau, a plant manufacturing radios and gyroscopes a quarter mile beyond the camp's perimeter fence, was damaged and 300 prisoners working in the plant were killed.

quarry, where Nicholas now toiled on the top level. After months of conning and wangling he had worked his way into the elite company of Polish POWs. With his knack for languages, he rapidly came to understand snatches of their conversations and to make himself understood in simple phrases.

Snow and ice made the climb to the mountaintop tough and dangerous, which explained why the SS and *kapos* policed the area as little as possible. So the Poles leaned back on their tools and posted lookouts to warn when guards were in the area.

Be grateful, the veteran Poles advised, that we've only a few miles to march to this hellhole every morning. Any further away and the SS donkeys would declare it a subcamp.

A subcamp, they learned, was formed when the SS determined that they could save time and money by building a smaller camp right on a work-project site. The rock quarry was bad, but at least they got to go back to Buchenwald at night. If they turned the quarry into a subcamp, they would have to live on site in tents on the slope of the godforsaken mountain.

A subcamp formed its own prisoner government, which was almost always linked umbilically to the main camp government that, in the case of Buchenwald, was Communist. So Buchenwald subcamp governments were usually dominated by Communists.

Buchenwald, Nicholas discovered, had 50-plus subcamps and twice that number of outside details — some as "outside" as the Rhine River and the English Channel.

No matter where a subcamp was located, Buchenwald's SS commander was the supreme authority over all of them. It mattered nothing to him whether a Criminal, Communist, Socialist or even a Nudist government translated his orders to the prisoners; all he cared about was: Will they carry out my orders to the letter? If they couldn't, he simply threw them out without hearing or ceremony, replaced them, and there wasn't a damn thing they could do about it. These privileged prisoners of the governing council were instantly plummeted to the abject status of ordinary prisoners, where they had to fight to survive.

No wonder, then, that the battle between Communists, Socialists, Criminals and the other political elements for domination of the prisoner government was fought so viciously.

In the main camp a long-term prisoner had usually survived that long because he had learned the politics and intrigue of the camp. But transfer him to a subcamp and instantly he was a neophyte again, lost and compass-less in a new maze of personalities, favors, loyalties, allegiances, tits-for-tats and *quid pro quos*, with a different chain of command to ferret out and a reconfigured labyrinth of intrigue to navigate.

Before the Buchenwald kommandant established a distant detail as a subcamp, regiments of prisoners were first trucked out — usually to some wilderness far from the prying eyes of curious civilians — to build barracks to house the SS personnel who would arrive later. Once the SS were housed, the prisoners were given the go-ahead to build barracks for themselves. While construction was going on, the prisoners subsisted in tents, freezing in winter, sweltering in summer. When the SS barracks were completed and the SS moved in, the site received subcamp status. And it didn't matter whether the prisoners had completed construction on their own barracks. If they hadn't, they had to live in tents. All that mattered to the Buchenwald kommandant was that his SS were comfortable and well fed.

Of Buchenwald's subcamps, none came to bear a name freighted with more fear and dread than "Dora."

What was going on at Dora?

All that the Poles on the Etterswald could tell Nicholas was that Dora was about 75 kilometers away. Some top-secret work, according the grapevine. Whatever was going on, they whispered nervously, it was sending back lice-ridden skeletons at the rate of 50 a week for cremation because it didn't have its own crematorium yet.

Back at the quarry in Buchenwald it was May 18, 1944 — a day of rejoicing for the Poles on the top level of the Etterswald. A BBC newscast, heard on the Communists' secret radio and whispered excitedly from prisoner to prisoner, reported that soldiers of the Free Polish Army, fighting alongside the American and British armies in Italy, had raised the Polish flag atop Monte Cassino. A Catholic monastery, it had been turned by the Germans into an impregnable fortress that for months had blocked the Allied advance up the Italian boot. But no longer.

As the Poles atop the Etterswald swung their picks and shovels, their hearts pounded less from physical exertion and more from the electrifying news.

But Nicholas, whose jaunty, informal style had broken down the characteristic reserve of many of the Poles, wasn't around to lead the cheering section: A week earlier, on Friday May 11, after roll call, Brauny had bellowed a command, shunting the black man aboard a truck bound for Dora.

CHAPTER ELEVEN

BOUND FOR DORA

In May 1944, when Nicholas and the latest shipment from Buchenwald were dumped off at the base of the Kohnstein, the formerly quiet fields of beet had been replaced with the ominous architecture of a subcamp. Ten tall guard towers with machine guns and searchlights rose equidistant along an eight-foot-high, electrified, barbed-wire fence encompassing the equivalent space of 110 football fields.

The fence line, which had the general shape of an inverted trapezoid, bounded the *haeftlingslager*, the prisoners' section of Dora. A guarded gate on the east end of the fence line gave access to the SS section of the camp, whose approximately 20 buildings clustered near the entrance to Main Tunnel B. (The SS didn't require barbed wire or guard towers around their section of the camp.)

The *haeftlingslager* at that time consisted of around 50 — it would rise to 75 — barracks, offices, warehouses, administration buildings, hospital and storage buildings, a kitchen, mess hall, canteen, roll-call field and gallows.

And on a gentle rise close by the hospital barracks sat Building No. 40, a facility without which no SS slave-labor camp could function adequately, a crematorium.

A quarter mile to the east gaped the south orifice of Tunnel B.

Mutzen auf! roared the assistant roll call leader. *Mutzen ab!*

Hardly had the caps snapped back on again when Master Sergeant Brauny walked across the grassy roll call field at the base of the Kohnstein Mountain, a clipboard under his arm. The sight of the little *feldwebel* must have wobbled Nicholas' Adam's apple. The only conceivable up side to getting assigned to Dora *had been* the certainty of getting out from under Brauny. Now even that perverse consolation was *kaput*: His nemesis was the new roll call leader at Dora!

Ausziehen!

It was the order to strip, shake their clothes and lay them at their feet to let sunlight delouse them.

Lice worried the SS incessantly; they carried typhus. In the confined recesses of the tunnels, lice rapidly turned into a typhus epidemic capable of wiping out the entire project, so the SS policed lice more ruthlessly than *haeftlinge*.

The prisoners stripped sluggishly, baring bleached, shrunken hides to the May morning sunshine.

Since its inception nine months previously, Dora had been getting by with one roll call per day. Brauny declared a return to the traditional two. Previously corpses were excused, but he announced introduction of the Buchenwald tradition: *All* prisoners must be present and accounted for at roll call, living *and* dead.

The sergeant also announced that SS *Obersturmfuehrer* (First Lieutenant) Karl Kahr, the camp's new medical officer, had instructed him to inform them that prisoners on sick call, when competently examined and found too sick to work, would now qualify for relief — slips of paper bearing Dr. Kahr's signature. Each slip gave the bearer permission to be off work for a half day, two slips for a whole day, and so on. The prisoner could rest in his bunk in the tunnels if that was where he lived; or in his barracks; or in the prisoners' canteen, where he was expected to sit at one of the tables, not lie down.

Brauny's scowling manner left no doubt that the *Herr Doktor's* radical departure from past practice greatly offended him. He made it clear that if shirkers and malingerers abused "convalescent" slips, as they were called, they would not live to do it a second time.

Brauny stepped back from the podium and turned it over to SS Sergeant Wilhelm Simon, the labor allocation officer.

Simon ordered all prisoners with technical or scientific training to step forward. He was — or *said* he was — looking for carpenters, electricians, plumbers, sheet metal workers, drill-press operators and other trades. He announced that volunteers would be given special training of the greatest value to them when the war was over.

But first, the roll call.

Brauny started calling off the names....

Four thousand naked newcomers recently from Buchenwald trembled in the early-morning mountain air. Their thin uniforms no longer covered bellies bloated by malnutrition. Buttocks shredded by whippings, eroded by starvation. Necks and backs knobbed with ripe purple carbuncles, pulsating. Torsos furrowed by whip and cable oozing pus. Crotch and armpit crops of yellow-headed boils where lice had grazed.

Each man's scrawny rib cage ballooned grotesquely when he barked the mandatory *Hier!* as his name was called.

Anziehen!

The desperate men gratefully struggled back into their stinking stripes.

All prisoners with technical or scientific training! Front and center! Simon shouted.

The cagey graduates of Buchenwald hesitated, wise in the risks of volunteering. The SS used tricks to weed out "shirkers and malingerers" seeking "soft" details. Was the volunteer call real or a ruse? Today, volunteering could mark an innocent man "morally unfit" for the privileges of a state-supported "custody camp" — as concentration camps were euphemistically termed — and scarcely worth the bullet expended on his execution. But come tomorrow and *not volunteering* could carry the identical indictment.

A prisoner never knew how the wind blew.

One risked a forward step. ...Another gambled. ...Two here. Three there.... Then more ... and more....

Nicholas stood his ground.

There were no more volunteers.

Mutzen ab!

Caps swung back on heads, and the volunteers marched off by fives, leaving Nicholas and the rest of the formation braced ramrod stiff, queasy with the fear that they'd been too shrewd for their own good.

Am I alive or dead? ... Am I awake or asleep, imprisoned in some ghoulish nightmare?

In the swirling dust, Nicholas coughed violently with every breath. Tremendous explosions collapsed his eardrums, drove daggers of pain into his brain, extinguished all but the flimsiest whispers of consciousness. Stumbling over jagged rocks that ripped his shins to shreds, eyelids drawn to fine slits against corrosive dust that abraded the eyeballs, he staggered along near-sightless in subterranean maze sculpted for a horror movie.

It was the ultimate bad dream of childhood — marooned in the belly of some biblical whale, sentenced to wander the torturous coils and evils of its mammoth entrails until Judgment Day.

Nicholas was not alone inside the bowels of the Kohnstein Mountain, some 500 feet below the summit. He was one in a vast army of human ants enlarging a vast system of tunnels to advance Germany's Most Top Secret weapon project of World War II.

German defeat hung in the balance; the work had to be done in the shortest possible time. The Weapon came first; the slave-workers were judged expendable.

They trudged with rocks in their arms or pushed loaded carts on metal tracks through a chaos of boulders to the outside. There they dumped their cruel cargoes on the mountain slope. They subsisted amid the incessant clatter of pneumatic drills boring holes for explosive charges. Every explosion reverberated through the mountain, dislodging ceiling boulders that buried them alive, crushed dozens to death and mutilated scores. Screams, cries, shouted oaths and stentorian commands clogged the claustrophobic atmosphere. Wretched men atop 30-foot-high scaffolds, their eyes filled with quartzite dust, blindly swung pick axes at the ceilings, missed and plunged screaming to their deaths.

Mach schnell! Mach schnell! Hurry up! Hurry up! roared the SS, ramming them with rifle butts. *Heraus! Heraus!* screamed the prisoner foremen, the Criminals, scourging them with lashes made of electrical cable.

If the prisoners ran too fast, they tripped and smashed themselves between the loads they carried and the boulders obstructing the tunnel floor. Because they couldn't see more than five paces in the swirling dust, the stronger were continually bumping into the weaker, slower-moving men. Prisoners with armloads of rock kept colliding, spattering blood and splintering bone, collapsing and never getting up.

Those who made it to the tunnel mouth with their rock-loaded bascules (small wheeled carts running on rails) found their hearts thumping wildly, their breath rasping, their knobby knees quivering uncontrollably as if they had just been plucked from the ice-cold sea. They schemed endlessly to malinger at the rock pile, gulping drafts of clean, mountain air. And all the time they squinted like frightened ferrets at the *kapo* in charge of the rock pile — and his sinister length of cable.

It was the last trip for the weakest. They slithered to their knees, doubled up, vomited their meager breakfast of greasy slop. They were immune to the stench of the puke in their crotches. They were beyond the blows of the rifle butts and the lashings raining down on them.

The stronger, like Nicholas, still lurched through the billowing rubble. The space between eyeballs and eyelids wore raw with grit. They opened their eyes only for an instant and then had to close them. Grit lodged in the backs of their throats, triggering them into paroxysms of coughing. The detonations intensified the perpetual dust storm, blotting out the vapid, yellowish lights strung along the center line of the ceiling. Without them as a guide, prisoners were temporarily blind, not knowing if they were heading for the exit or about to crash into the craggy wall of the tunnel.

There was neither air conditioning nor sanitation facilities and no drinking water. They got almost nothing to eat — a piece of bread and a rotten potato. They subsisted as little better than animals. They relieved themselves where they stood.

After 12 hours shifts changed.

The old shift staggered into four short, densely packed tunnels to eat and sleep. They were the first cross-tunnels (Nos. 43, 44, 45 and 46) located off the south entrance to Main Tunnel A. The haggard prisoners collapsed onto four-tiered, lice-ridden bunks, two and three sharing a single mattress still warm with the waste of the shift that had just vacated them. The walls, ceilings and floors of these dormitories — like the entire subterranean maze — were rough, unfinished surfaces of raw rock, perpetually cold and slick with dampness. There were no windows, no water, no sanitary facilities. The air prisoners breathed and re-breathed reeked with the fine dust spewed everywhere by the detonations. It scoured their lungs during their few hours of fractured sleep.

Trucks piled with corpses emerged every other day from the bowels of the mountain and whined off toward the crematorium in Buchenwald; Dora's crematorium had not yet been built.

"There were about 8,000 working in the tunnels when I was in Dora," said Jay, who slept in Cross-tunnel No. 46 and later No. 24. "If you didn't work properly, you were knocked to death, kicked to death. They didn't care what happened to you. If you were dying, they let you die.

"There were few bandages, no water. Nothing. They drank their own urine off the floor. They got typhus or diphtheria. Clothes and shoes of dying men were stolen off their bodies as they lay there. It was impossible to come to the aid of a dying prisoner. The SS would have punished you. It was absolute horror."

Thus ended a typical shift at Dora.

For Nicholas, as for every wretched man plunged into the inferno of Dora's tunnels, it must have constituted a baptism of evil — the most colossal assault on mind and body of his life; a literal foretaste of what the French Brothers had surely warned him of at the St. Louis de Gonzague Academy, when he was a teenager.

And, like every prisoner, he would have had to reach down within his ultimate soul to find the wherewithal to hold on when it would have been so easy to end the torment. Too easy. A simple *sheisskopf!* thrown at one of the helmeted SS would have been enough to win him a quick bullet and a fast trip to infinity.

Had he elected that alternative, Neitzsche, whom he had never forgotten since his puerile attempts to understand the German prince of nihilism, would have been in his corner. What more convincing evidence of the adage regarding slaves and masters? The proof screamed all around him, thumbing its nose at the ridiculous concepts of love of fellow man, chivvying him for his grandiloquent vow that he would never be a slave.

"This is what Hell must be like," thought Frenchman Jean Mialet, who slaved in the tunnel nightmare more than half a century ago.

Nicholas must have made a similar comparison. In his first day he had found out the hard way why Dora had earned its odious nickname — "The Hell of All Concentration Camps."

He would also have discovered that unless his luck changed, he'd be a dead man before too long. If a premature demolition charge, falling rock or predatory SS didn't nail him, starvation or disease would — unless he could figure a way to dodge such a fate.

Dora's slaves knew pain, exhaustion, beatings and starvation but not what they were supposed to be doing and why. If they had possessed that knowledge, they would have been even less willing — if that were possible — to work than they already were: They were aiding and abetting the most secret German military undertaking of World War II, a proj-

ect guaranteed by its designers to win the war for the Third Reich. So it
would have been pointless to inform them of that fact.

Such knowledge was reserved for a handful of key civilians and military men, including SS *Kommandant* Major Otto Fourschner, who held
the power of life and death over them all.

Fourschner's superiors had handed him a sprawling maze of tunnels
bored into the Kohnstein in prewar days for the exploration of mineral
resources. His assignment: to transform the giant complex into a vast,
modern underground factory.

It was to be the largest production facility in the world under a single
roof. Completely invulnerable to Allied attack from the air, its purpose
was chiefly to mass-produce Hitler's secret weapon, the world's first
guided ballistic missile. Called the V-2, it was the weapon on which Hitler gambled all of Germany's resources in a desperate last-ditch effort
to defeat the Anglo-Americans and win the war.

If the Kohnstein had been made of glass instead of gypsum and
quartzite, someone viewing from above would have noted the "ladder" deformed in a slender S-shape curve. The ladder's two "rails" are
38-feet-diameter borings designated Main Tunnels A and B 600 feet
apart. The ladder's "rungs," of which there are 23, are smaller-diameter
tunnels spanning the interconnecting distance of 600 feet between A
and B tunnels.

Tunnel B was 1 1/4 miles long and runs completely through the base
of the Kohnstein; tunnel A went only part way through.

Fourschner was ordered to (1) extend Main Tunnel A all the way
through the hill; (2) double the number of cross-tunnels from 23 to 46;
(3) enlarge the cross-tunnels to match the diameter of the main tunnels; (4) pave[1] the rough tunnel floors with concrete; and (5) move in
machinery and equipment to mass-produce V-1 and V-2 rockets.

The task was as straightforward as it was formidable. Under peacetime
conditions the removal of so vast a volume of earth would have presented

---

1 As early as December 1943, with the dust clouds of the enormous task
of enlargement and expansion still swirling, several tunnels had already been
paved with concrete. Manufacturing machinery and equipment sufficient to
complete four V-2s had been produced by hastily trained slave laborers working under specially imported German civilian engineers and technicians. From
the German standpoint this progress represented an unparalleled industrial
achievement less than four months after British bombers had plastered Peenemunde, the original site of V-rocket design and production.

no extraordinary difficulties to competent engineers. But in August 1943, when the Dora project got the green light from Adolf Hitler, the Anglo-Americans were inexorably drawing the noose of defeat around Germany's neck. The nation was in crisis, its industrial infrastructure reeling under the relentless assault of Allied bombers, and had begun gasping for air. Surplus equipment and manpower for the project didn't exist.

Waving these objections aside, Fourschner's superiors in the SS Construction Branch demanded that he, like a magician pulling a rabbit out of a hat, deliver this Kohnstein miracle *within a year* to permit V-2 production to begin immediately thereafter.

The major, a fanatic SS man who regarded non-German life as cannon fodder, drafted his work force not only from Buchenwald but from concentration camps all over German Occupied Europe. Among his unwilling slaves were Nicholas and Jay.

The two prisoners' paths never crossed until the late spring of 1944, when the phased transfer of the slaves from tunnels dormitories to permanent outside barracks had just begun. When they met, Nicholas had already survived several months in the ghastly subterranean environment, and Jay had endured it seven months. In all that time, however, he never noticed the black man there.

But that would not have been unusual: Thousands of prisoners were packed into the tunnel dormitories. Their faces were perpetually covered with dust, making it hard to distinguish one from another. They never showered or bathed — much less saw daylight — for months at a time.

Long before Jay ever struck up a conversation with Nicholas he had noticed a "nigger" — the term he used in his testimony before the Nordhausen tribunal — several times in the tunnels at roll-call. He was curious about the black's identity. As *kapo* of a carpentry construction crew, Jay wielded more influence than a rank-and-file prisoner, so he was able to make some inquiries. He learned that the black man was an American from Buchenwald who had behaved like an idiot during a roll call, when enemy bombers had flown overhead, and had almost gotten himself shot by *Feldwebel* Brauny. That was enough for Jay; he had no interest in idiots.

On subsequent roll calls, however, he kept glancing at the "American." Here was a golden chance, he thought, to pick up a little war news first hand from the other side of the Channel. What a luxury that would be!

Jay was a veteran of the German concentration-camp system; he had been a prisoner since 1939. He had learned that survival depended on giving all strangers a wide berth. Every stranger could be an enemy in disguise, an informer, a con man, a criminal; someone out to steal from you, trick you, manipulate and use you to his own advantage. In making the first move toward friendship with the "American," Jay was delayed for a long time by his congenitally embedded survival instincts. But finally he made the move.

At roll call in the open, grassy meadow area at the base of the Kohnstein, "I noticed this great big black fellow again," the Englishman recalled, "and I asked the *lagereldtester* who he was. He said he was an American from Buchenwald."

Jay, a tiny bird-like man, a London East Ender with an impenetrable Cockney accent, had served with the British Army occupying the German Rhineland after the end of World War I. When the British occupation ended, he stayed behind in Germany, married a *fraulein* and raised a family in Springe.

Even before the German invasion of Poland that led to the outbreak of World War II, Jay's two sons enlisted in the German armed forces. Despite this familial gesture of patriotism, when England declared war on Germany in September 1939, Jay was declared an enemy alien shortly afterwards and interned in Buchenwald.

He was one of Buchenwald's earliest tenants, which accounts for his relatively low serial number — 6496 — when compared to that of Nicholas — 44451.

Jay, then a prisoner for five years, finally decided to approach the Yank. It would be a blessed relief, he thought, to be able to talk to somebody in his own language again.

And talk they did .

Whether they actually understood each other is a matter of conjecture. Jay's accent was easily penetrable only by denizens of the exclusive London ghetto from which he hailed. As for Nicholas: His version of the King's English would have been equally formidable to the Cockney Londoner: a melange of British Diplomatic, Harry Tippenhauer Teutonic, Jimmy Cagney Gangster and Marine Corps Received Speech.

Jay maneuvered himself close to Nicholas at roll call and managed to exchange a few words. "He said he was completely fed up with the SS," Jay recalled, "and he asked me if I was able to get him some bread. Afterwards I spoke with [him] almost every evening."

Initially the most that Jay could coax out of him was small talk. Evidently, in his brief tenure in the subculture, the black man had rapidly soaked up the protective distrust of strangers. He had no intention of getting snagged in the tangled skein of Dora's ever-roiling power struggle.

Jay, recognizing that the shoe was on the other foot this time, realized he had to earn the "American's" confidence before they could *really* talk. "The sort of things we talked about were life in the camp and the work we did," Jay recalled. "He said the work he was doing was terrible. And he did tell me that his parents were pretty well off, and that if he could only write them a letter he would be all right."

Nicholas and Jay met accidentally and developed as close a relationship as was possible, given the deeply distrustful and suspicious nature of concentration-camp society. Was it another "accident" that took Nicholas to the next crucial fork in the road of his eventual deliverance? A rock, dislodged from the ceiling following a demolition blast in the tunnels, crushed his arm.

For the first time since he found himself outside the prisoner hospital, standing in the sick-call line.

For the miserable slaves of Dora the only limbo between the hell of the tunnels and the damnation of the roll-call field was the prisoner hospital. The name "hospital" was a cruel joke: This short, bottle-shaped, blind-end tunnel boasted four-tier wooden bunks, a few filthy blankets and little else. Leon Halkin, a Belgian, remembered it well.

"I go to the camp hospital with three fellow inmates who are suffering from dysentery," he said. "None of them will come back. We are forced into the same room where we already find Polish, Russians, Gypsies, Germans, French and a couple of Belgians. Altogether about 60 naked, emaciated, feverish people cramped together on bunks....

"Here they don't treat human beings, only numbers. No nursing, no food or drinks are provided. When the sick are taken into the room, they are naked. Then, still naked, they are put into a bed which is already occupied by another ailing prisoner."

Direct responsibility for the prisoner-hospital rested with the Head Prisoner-Doctor. In the course of the camp's evolution the post rotated among several prisoners. It was first occupied by Hessel Groeneveld, M.D., a 36-year-old Mennonite from Nijmegen, Holland, who had arrived with Jay, when the advance party from Buchenwald debarked that August in 1943.

In the coming 12 months Dr. Groeneveld would expand his staff of prisoner-doctors from two or three to around 40.

Just as prisoner "hospital" had to be taken with a pinch of salt, however, so had prisoner "doctor." Few prisoner-doctors performed with the Dutchman's skill because they weren't qualified physicians. Most of them had no medical training or qualifications. They were plumbers, schoolteachers, streetcar drivers, shopkeepers. A prisoner-doctor didn't have to be anything except be politically acceptable to the council of Communist prisoners who ran the prisoner-hospital, or *revier*, as it was universally called throughout the concentration-camp system.

Nicholas, of course, knew none of this as he awaited his turn in the long line of miserable sick standing in the line by the base of the Kohnstein hill. But he would have been watching and listening to everything that he witnessed in Dr. Groeneveld's pathetic hospital in the tunnel, storing it away for possible use.

The record doesn't reveal how many times that the black man returned for treatment. It is known that his injuries healed and that he returned to the abominable work in the tunnel. But his brief visit to the *revier* sparked in his fertile imagination an idea for getting out of his subterranean hell — provided a rock fall from the ceiling didn't kill him first.

He'd seen the prisoner-doctors at work in the *revier*. With his medical experience, he thought, *Hell, I could do that. There's nothing to it!*

Many who lived to tell the world of their experiences in Dora owe their survival in part to SS Lieutenant Kahr, a slim Austrian physician in his early 30s.

Concentration-camp prisoners did not, as a matter of the strictest protocol, address SS officers or NCOs without first being invited. It didn't matter if the prisoner was *lagereldtester* or *kapo*. The policy still held, and violators could be shot on the spot. But Kahr was different.

It was a common slight flung by Nazi Germans at Austrians that "aren't *real* Germans." The difference, however, went beyond that.

Kahr was far from the image of the stereotypical SS medical officer. In the massive archive of concentration-camp literature accumulated since the end of World War II, "SS doctor" is synonymous with quack, charlatan and dilettante; with respectable and even esteemed physicians who subverted the Hippocratic Oath with an oath to Adolf Hitler.

The term evokes visions of sociopaths using prisoners as human guinea pigs for medical experiments, and indeed documented cases of such atrocities exist. In Dr. Kahr's case, however, the weight of testimony in the Nordhausen War Crimes case and personal interviews with former Dora inmates prove him to have been the exception to the rule.

A graduate of the universities of Graz and Vienna, Kahr had been a freshly minted physician at the outbreak of the war. Keen to do his patriotic best for the Fatherland, he wouldn't settle for anything less than the most prestigious branch of the German armed forces — the *Waffen* SS. A superbly trained, superbly disciplined fighting machine, it had trampled the Polish Army into its home soil and romped through the French and English armies on the Western front in 1940. Nearly 30 years later, Kahr said: "You have to remember the times. It was exciting. Everyone wanted to be in the *Waffen* SS."

He served as a battalion combat surgeon in France, then on the Eastern Front, where he struggled in vain to staunch the flow of SS blood being soaked up by the limitless snowy Russian steppes

Before long the atrocious conduct of some of his own *Waffen* SS against innocent Russian men, women and children began to erode his noble notions of the black-uniformed corps that he had joined. What kind of Germans were *they*? He asked himself. What kind of a Germany was *he* fighting for?

Russian shell fragments pierced his head and left leg during an artillery duel. The wounds rescued him from debilitating doubt and regret and relegated him to a hospital back in Germany, where, he naively assumed, men in his country's uniform still conducted themselves decently.

Eventually his wounds healed, but not his severe limp. Headquarters stamped the jacket of his service record "Unfit for Combat" and posted him to the one assignment that *Waffen* (combat) SS men feared more than Russian infantry — duty in the SS Concentration Camp Branch, which *Waffen* troops believed was nothing but a dumping ground for malingerers, perverts, psychopaths and cowards.

Dr. Kahr arrived at Dora with the same prejudices.

It was his first experience as the medical officer of a concentration camp, and he was horrified, first as a human being, then as a physician. At the university he had been taught that the German medical profession was the envy of the modern world. In Dora he found the health care of the prisoners advanced little beyond the standards of the Middle

Ages. The savagery of war on the Russian front had not stripped him entirely of hope for the world, and he resolved to do what he could to improve the deplorable medical infrastructure.

During the war, "We had good times and we had bad times," Kahr said many years later. "When I was a physician with the troops in Russia and in France, it was a good time. My work in the concentration camp was the worst ... the worst time of my life. You could see so much misery, but you couldn't help.

"Conditions were very, very bad.[2] The problem was there wasn't enough food for the prisoners, and they were worked too hard. Their resistance was so low that the medicines and vaccines didn't work. They

---

2 Josef Ackermann, a German prisoner who worked as a clerk in the revier at Dora, testified regarding the state of prisoner-patients before the Nordhausen War Crimes tribunal. "The physical condition of most of the prisoners — one could almost say 90 percent of the prisoners — was so bad that ... the bones were showing. A large part of the prisoners were suffering on their legs, which was due to ... the bad shoes that [they] were wearing, and ... the long ... standing during the 12-hour work period. The bad physical condition ... may be judged from the fact that even though they didn't have any disease or ... were not actually ill, that they were so weak ... that they were unable to do any work.... Many of [them] on the way to and from work collapsed and died.

"Hundreds of prisoners came daily to the prisoners' dispensary for treatment, and during those occasions I was able to determine that the most of the prisoners had wooden shoes; that they were barefooted within these wooden shoes; that they had clothing which was absolutely insufficient for this cold time of the year. ... The shoes were kept on the foot in that the prisoner took a piece of rope or a piece of wire and bound it around his foot, otherwise he would have lost the shoes.... During the deepest winter and during the greatest cold I saw many prisoners who didn't have any ... stockings whatsoever....

"During the warmer ... as well as the cooler times of the year, in most cases they didn't have any underclothing whatsoever. They wore only a shirt ... They had a shirt, a pair of pants and a jacket ... their summer clothing was made out of twill and in winter it was a substitute material which was made of wooden threads. This material was even thinner — one could [see] through it, and it did not protect one from the cold.... There were some ... prisoners who were able to obtain a coat, but ... this coat was [also] of this porous wooden material, and he had to freeze if he had to stand on the roll call field for hours in the cold. If it went very quickly, the roll call was over inside of half an hour to three-quarters of an hour. But it could take as long as 2 1/2 and even three hours.

"The prisoners had to be counted individually. It was not only the prisoners who were standing on the roll call field, but every prisoner had to be accounted for, [even] if they were working some place else. If the prisoners were

had very little food for the prisoners. I hoped that in my position I would help improve it.

"I saw so much brutality I never believed that after the war I would be a physician again."

In Berlin, where Kahr reported for his new assignment after a nine-month hospital stay, the SS Chief of Medical Affairs, Dr. Lolling, warned him: "You are now going to come [sic] to a camp where very bad conditions reign. But I call your attention to the fact that the man in charge of administering the camp [Major Fourschner] is not very interested in improving the life of the prisoners."

The warning hadn't prepared Kahr for the shock he received when he limped through the tunnels on an inspection tour shortly after his after his arrival in February. Air choked with dust. The clamor assaulted the eardrums. Shriveled men coated in white, limestone dust squatting in the rubble to relieve themselves. Pissing in their hands to wash their faces. The rockfalls. The screams of agony. The stony indifference of the SS. The prisoners' bunks sprayed with liquid shit. Blankets mobile with lice. The cannibalistic ritual of the dead being stripped of their clothes and wooden clogs by their pallbearers.

He discovered that the prisoners wore their thin cotton uniforms year around; that they had no socks, and half them had no shoes.

Their food ration could barely keep their hearts beating: At 6 a.m. a half-liter of "coffee" — it was often warmed-up beet juice; one piece of bread; 20 grams of margarine. Clear turnip soup at noon. At 6 p.m. turnip salad and maybe a nibble of sausage.

Kahr couldn't believe that *Kommandant* Fourschner expected a prisoner to heft a pick and shovel or lug huge rocks clutched to his chest for 12 hours a day on 2000 calories. Fifteen hours a day if roll calls were counted. For details working at distant subcamps he learned that it could be nearly midnight before they marched back and were dismissed from roll call.

---

some place else, these figures had to be exact, and it often happened that the figures did not coincide....

"The post surgeon [Dr. Kahr] wrote repeatedly to the administration requesting that better clothing be issued to the prisoners. I [typed] these letters myself. The reply was in every case: 'We have nothing.'"

And three hours later it was *aufstehen! aufstehen!* again as the *lagerschutz* bludgeoned them out of their bunks to start another day.

They were dying at an average rate of 850 a month. Rates fluctuated, depending on an ever-rising prisoner population, but the monthly death toll never fell below 500 to 800.

By May 1944, when Nicholas arrived in Dora, the Austrian medical officer, despite the belligerent indifference of his kommandant, had wrought highly impressive improvements in the four months since his arrival. Out of chaos and congestion he had successfully organized an administration barracks, an internal-medicine ward (Barracks No. 17 and 17A), a surgical ward (No. 38), and a contagious-diseases ward and septic-operations ward (No. 38A).

Five barracks. He was shooting for *eight*.

For haeftlinge, Kahr? Eight barracks? You must be mad. Not when our own German civilian engineers and technicians here at Dora are crying out for housing!

The kommandant must have wondered why Kahr didn't follow the example of Dr. Plaza, the previous medical officer, whose solution to the camp's disaster in prisoner health care had been to bicycle into Nordhausen every evening and stone himself into a stupor.

No, concluded Kahr, there was no way that he could win. Win officially, that is. But unofficially? He began to play with the idea that what the kommandant didn't know couldn't hurt him.

The Austrian physician was also desperately short of surgical equipment and medicines. Operations had to be done without anesthetics or rubber gloves. All his attempts to requisition from higher headquarters were ignored. He had between 700 and 800 hospital beds total, but they were never empty long. Sometimes he had two or three patients in the same bed at the same time. No sheets. Just one straw sack and two blankets.

Edema, pleurisy and inflammation of the bowels had reached epidemic proportions. Malnutrition was a plague, the common cold a killer.

About 90 percent of the patients were so emaciated that their bones were showing. Many died from lack of adequate shoes and warm clothing — especially after standing for several hours on the roll-call field. Only in the surgical barracks did conditions remotely resemble those in a normal hospital. Its six separate rooms accommodated 120 beds.

Amazingly they weren't the typical, rough-hewn wooden bunks; somehow the Austrian physician had organized steel, hospital-style beds for his surgical patients. With mattresses, too.

But elsewhere?

In the contagious-diseases barracks 200 dying men competed for 250 sulfa tablets a day. In the internal medicine barracks 700 men typically lingered between life and death jammed into 350 beds. Many expired on the clean straw mattresses and white sheets that Kahr's resourcefulness had just begun to acquire.

At least four times a week he inspected conditions in the tunnels and observed the inhumanity of it.

Kahr wrestled the age-old dilemma of the lifeboat captain: His vessel is full and he daren't risk pulling any more victims from the water for fear of capsizing and losing everyone. For all his ingenuity and stubborn adherence to established medical wisdom, he must have felt as if he were bailing back the tide with a pitchfork.

Besides his daily battle with the kommandant, he faced the opposition of Brauny and Simon, the two SS sergeants who kept ripping up and throwing away his convalescent slips, driving prisoners with 104-degree temperatures into the tunnels. They were NCOs; he was a lieutenant. If it happened again, he had promised them a court-martial. The threat would restrain them for a while, but he knew they would find another pretext.

Any further appeals to kommandant were a waste of breath.

Major Fourschner had his office in the second cross-tunnel, where he shared space with various Mittelbau directors. He left his desk at the same time each morning to do a complete walk-through of the entire system. He always did it in full uniform, advertising his 110-percent identification with the *status quo*. (It was widely rumored that the gold ring he wore — it was embossed "USA" — had been slipped off the finger of a dead American pilot, but there was no record of another American POW at Dora.)

Nicholas had had enough experience in Buchenwald to know the dangers of approaching an SS officer without invitation. The horrors of the tunnels must have driven him very close to the edge for him to confront the doctor without permission.

"I think it was in September [1944]," Dr. Kahr said. "He came into the *revier*. He had some injuries — in the leg, I think — from working in the tunnels, and he said to me: 'I am a physician. Can I work here? I am not a political prisoner. I am an American prisoner of war.'"

Kahr was amazed at the black man's nerve. But instead of reacting in typical SS knee-jerk fashion and having him disciplined, he suppressed his initial impulse because he knew that he needed all the help he could get in the prisoner hospital. He checked Nicholas' registration at the SS headquarters office and noted that his card identified him as an American from Boston. Kahr intuitively doubted that the *schwartze* was a qualified physician, yet he decided to give the black the benefit of the doubt and try him out.

"He was the only Negro and the only American," Kahr said, "and I wondered what the prisoners would say about a Negro in there." He talked over his proposed assignment with some of the prisoners working in the *revier*. "They wanted the Negro," he said. "He was the only one in the camp, and apparently he was [already] a sensation with them."

Nicholas survived his try-out as a prisoner-doctor. Kahr discovered him to be "very good" at treating the wide range of ailments that routinely presented at sick call — cleaning infected wounds, dressing and suturing them, setting fractures, applying casts, prescribing simple medicines and salves.

"He was a very good man," Kahr recalled. "He was very friendly and always full of good humor. He had a good relationship with the prisoners. They liked him."

Nicholas duly surfaced in the dispensary barracks, where he was put him in charge of sick call. He had traded his filthy, begrimed and ragged stripes for a freshly laundered set — a very rare sight outside the prisoner hospital compound, and he sported a red *helf artz* band on his arm.

Deep within, where the real Johnny resided, he would have felt fantastic over his *coup*. And why not? He had engineered the impossible. A winning touchdown in the final quarter. Conned his fall from Hell into Heaven. That Old Lady Luck again. Clean uniforms every week, three squares a day. Inside work where you didn't freeze your ass off. Nothing more strenuous than pushing a pencil. And no more roll calls!

And the food! Oh, the food! Not the shit slung in the tunnels. The Comrades who ran the *revier* carried a big stick around the camp. Sooner or later every poor son of a bitch came there for some kind of help, right? Even the SS — for secret treatment for their VD rather than risk *Kommandant* Fourschner's wrath.

Yes, the Comrades had clout where it really counted. No wonder their cuisine ranked next only to what showed up on the tables of the SS. He still couldn't believe it: the most incredible soup once or twice a week. The prisoner-doctors didn't throw away all those rabbits they used in their "medical research."

No, his achievement was so mind-blowing that he would have been insufferable — even to himself. There was none of the mendicant monk about him.

A two-by-four on the head couldn't have stunned him more had he known that the Top Comrades who ran the *revier* were secretly conspiring to get rid of him — the permanent way if necessary.

The problem was political. It originated in an unwritten but binding "Constitution" under which every concentration camp functioned. The SS kommandant instructed the *lagereldtester*, the head prisoner, in detail in terms of the camp's specific mission. The Constitution left it almost exclusively up to the head prisoner and his council of governing prisoners to decide *how* to accomplish that mission.

The SS governing system, said Stephane Hessel, a former French prisoner, "creates intrigues among single groups, plays people of different nationalities, races, religions and professions against one another. At first, let them waste away in the most squalid and abysmal conditions of fifth, hunger and violence. Pick out the meanest, toughest and most brutal — they spread like worms in a moldy piece of cheese — and give them power over the others. Then let everything take its [natural] course."

The immense independence that this arrangement conferred on the *revier's* prisoner government extended to making key appointments. The prisoner-hospital was a key power-and-influence center, and the prisoner councilors, who, at Dora, were all Communists, scrupulously guarded job openings there. Invariably, to maintain their power base, when vacancies occurred, they filled them with fellow Comrades. For them the revier's plum posts and perks were reserved. So they heartily resented Nicholas — a POW and avowed anti-Communist — in their midst. The *revier's* ruling Comrades were blind and deaf to any other logic: Every prisoner tapped for the *revier* must be Red. The *schwartze* upset their color scheme.

Nicholas, however shrewd he may have been in navigating the back alleys of Port-au-Prince and the black market of Paris, was an innocent trapped within the devious designs of Communists and Criminals fanatically pledged to eliminate each other. The black man's eleventh-hour con of Kahr had backfired him into the lethal fire zone separating Reds and Greens.

A *revier's* government wielded power out of all proportion to the number of its staff. It used its *helf artz* to maintain the always-perilous balance of power between the conflicting political groups. Along with the immense legitimate good that they did under appalling conditions, they routinely practiced political selectivity, keeping alive "friendly" prisoners, lethally injecting "enemy" prisoners, troublemakers and elements incorrigibly obstructive to the Communist game plan.

But for all their power, the Communist councilors were not about to second-guess the direct order of an SS officer — even if he was a fragile, underweight lieutenant, retread and semi-invalid.

New to concentration-camp intrigue, Kahr was ignorant of all this politicking in the background. When he installed Nicholas as *helf artz* in charge of sick call, he did not know that he was in violation of any Constitution. He didn't know that his innocent appointment had put the black man in harm's way.

Nicholas was equally clueless about the dangers he was running into as the new *helf artz*. But Jay, his friend, the veteran concentrationary who may have paved his way, surely knew. So why didn't *he* warn him? Probably because Nicholas would only have laughed in his face.

Nicholas' dispensary occupied the east room of a three-room barracks. He had a crude desk, a chair and table. Behind his chair ascended a flight of shelves crowded with bottles and jars of ointments, salves and pills. A corner window allowed him to glance up the Kohnstein slope occasionally to a stone quarry where SS firing squads conducted executions.

It would have been a daily reminder of the flimsy thread from which his deliverance from almost certain death in the tunnels dangled.

To his east sprawled the SS section of the camp and, just an eighth of a mile beyond, he could see the giant orifices of Tunnel B and Tunnel A gaping obliquely at him from across the grassy field.

Dora's daily drove of sick, lame and dying curled in a long line up to the dispensary barracks door opening onto Nicholas' room. Every prisoner whom Nicholas admitted to the hospital or awarded a convalescent slip to meant one less prisoner in that day's labor force, and that antagonized NCOs Brauny and Simon, who were tasked with delivering every possible prisoner for work. For these two SS men, too many convalescent slips translated into too many tongue-lashings from *Kommandant* Fourschner over a deficient labor force.

A prisoner-clerk admitted the begrimed men six at a time. Nicholas examined them, questioned them, filled out the paperwork, cleaned their infected wounds and injuries, incised and drained their boils, bunions and carbuncles, painted them with iodine and bandaged them with paper strips.

He took the temperatures of those lacking visible symptoms and placated them with a pill, potion, palliative or salve — or the rare unguent of a convalescent slip. But 90 percent he sent back to work in the tunnels. The rest, typically the pneumonia, influenza, bronchitis, dysentery and advanced tuberculosis cases — or what he *thought* were those diseases after remembering all he had picked up from Coicou, Pape and the rest of his medical-school comrades in Paris — he hospitalized. Being new on the job, he couldn't admit patients to the hospital ward without first consulting the chief prisoner-doctor.

The room next to the dispensary boasted washbasins, bathtubs and toilets. It was the next stop for the hospitalized. Kahr had decreed a bath for every prisoner admitted, and Nicholas directed the bathing. If water — it was always cold — and soap were available, he and other prisoner-hospital staff scraped the filth from the scrawny, fevered bodies, which were then lodged temporarily in the barracks' third room, at the west end of the building, where Kahr had installed 10 beds.

The west room functioned as the dispensary's transition ward. Nicholas lodged his serious cases there until a senior prisoner doctor could examine them. If Nicholas' diagnosis was confirmed, the patient was placed on standby for transfer — when a vacancy occurred — to one of three other hospital barracks.

There was scarcely a man reporting to sick call who didn't suffer some form of chronic low-grade pain — even if they showed no overt disease symptoms. Aspirin was the only tablet that Nicholas had in abundance, and he dispensed them generously more as a gesture of goodwill than a remedy.

Almost all prisoners suffered some dysentery. For them he handed out dark-colored charcoal tablets. They were supposed to bind the contents of the bowel but seldom did, so their efficacy was more psychological than actual.

He saved his precious sulfa ration for prisoners with open wounds and for victims of the *bock*. Without sulfa, shredded buttocks incubated a runaway stew of infection, systemic blood poisoning and death.

Whether or not he had any medications left to offer, to all Nicholas dispensed the upbeat banter for which he was gradually gaining a reputation. He kibitzed easily with them in French and German, or in the crude Russian and Polish that he had picked up, or in English with the few prisoners who understood that tongue.

He made a point of learning prisoner's names and where in the tunnels or around the camp they worked. Each time they came back, he pried a little more into their work assignments and their lives back home.

He worked up an inventory of yarns, quips and one-liners and was at his most entertaining when it came to malicious gossip about the SS and their latest stupidities.

The *revier's* Comrades, who had been ordered to keep him at arm's length, couldn't help notice his rapport with the sick. As one sick call ran into another and still another, accounts of his facile bedside manner infected even the iron-disciplined Communist councilors who, less than a few weeks before, had been united in the decision to oust him or terminate him. What they were seeing before their incredulous eyes was a better sick-call *helf artz* than any Comrade who'd ever worn the red armband. So the Commies were rethinking their initial analysis of the interloper.

The best indication of how far they had come in their re-analysis was that they were unofficially sharing the war news with him. No, he hadn't yet been invited into the nightly klatsch that clustered around their secret radio and listened to the BBC. But he got most of it second hand: Comrades who were in the klatsch began passing little along little nuggets — especially involving American battlefield successes.[3]

Nicholas immediately started incorporating them in his consulting-room spiel.

Fantastic, Johnny, fantastic! … Are you're sure it's true, Johnny? Are you sure? Who told you, Johnny? Where'd you hear it, Johnny?

He would shoot them the enigmatic grin that was his trademark and deflect them with glib generalities and facile foolishness.

---

3 Nicolas' credibility soared when the BBC reported on June 6, 1944, that the Americans had landed in Normandy.

Behind the grin, however, he would have been wrestling his own private demons: In a world where hundreds qualified for every single sulfa tablet he had, whom should he give to? Whom should he deny? Who to live? Who to die?

His patients would never have guessed it because week after week he kept up his pills and patter. They did discover that even if they didn't get a pill, they were likely to come away with a glowing account of America the Beautiful and its inexhaustible men and material marching to liberate them.

"He was dynamic and convinced of final victory," remembered Jean Septfonds, a French prisoner.

The black man's stories of America were of a nation that he had never seen with his own eyes; a larger-than-life Home of the Brave framed in the lens of the jaunty, boastful, free-wheeling U.S. Marines who had enriched his childhood and the movies he saw at the Rex.

When Jean Berger, a prisoner from Angers, France, showed up at sick call, he pleaded with Nicholas to give him bandages and medicines for sick comrades back in the tunnel dormitories. Nicholas never failed his requests, Berger said.

Gabriel Boussinesq, another Frenchman, had worked himself to exhaustion after an unbroken 18-hour shift. He was scheduled for a second 18-hour shift when he staggered into sick call. If Nicholas hadn't given him some convalescent slips, his demise was certain.

In return for the slips, the grateful Frenchman, a nonsmoker, gave Nicholas a few cigarettes.

Tobacco functioned as currency in the camp: Boussinesq knew that the black man handed out cigarettes to patients when he had nothing else to give them. Jean Septfonds, a Frenchman who had worked in the tunnels, limped into the dispensary one morning with three huge *phlegmones* on his right leg. He'd fallen a year previously and pierced himself on rusty barbed wire. The infection had persisted, and he knew that the stubborn pus was leaching his life away. Nicholas excised the infection, swabbed it with the alcohol and bandaged it with paper. Septfonds remembered Nicholas pressing convalescent slips on him, affording him a few days of life-saving reprieve.

Each morning after the last sick-call prisoner cleared the dispensary, the *revier's* prisoner-doctors cooked their customary clandestine pot of soup. For several mornings Nicholas secretly set a can of it on the sill of the dispensary's rear window for Septfonds to pick up. The

Frenchman's *phlegmones* eventually healed, and he went back to work in the tunnels.

He survived the war and returned to his home in Auxerre. "If I had not gone to the *revier* and to Johnny," he said, "I would not have returned to France. [Because of Nicholas] I was very often able to slide secretly into the infirmary, and that way I was able to be saved. He rendered numerous medical services to everybody."

"Johnny Nicholas remains indelible in my memory, although it was a casual relationship," said Wincenty Hein, the Polish lawyer from Crakow, who had fought in his country's resistance movement.[4] As Prisoner Clerk in the *revier*, Hein was responsible for records and statistics. "It appears that he gave his place of birth as Boston and his occupation that of doctor.

"He was not given to small talk. His replies to questions regarding his birthplace and occupation were artificial, suggestive, hinting and aroused our curiosity. His answers were not tied together. There was no continuity to them. He didn't encourage conversation about those kinds of questions. When one tried to pin him down to specifics, he would claim poor memory.

"Of course, you must understand that, in the camps, conversations were a game in which neither party was completely honest. But they were a relief from the strain of camp life.

"It's difficult for me to pass judgment on his qualifications as a doctor or his occupation. I am well acquainted with the rules of the camp, and I will never forget the method of having to live in that environment.

---

4 Risking his life, Hein kept a secret diary during his sentence at Dora. His entry for May 13, 1944 records a transport of 600 prisoners from Buchenwald, bringing the total Dora population to 11,233. It notes the new arrivals generally as tradesmen, farmers, skilled workers, musicians, five doctors and one Russian engineer. They included Gypsies of Czech and German origin, Poles, Russians, Belgians, German criminals, Frenchmen and one American.

Page 7 of Hein's diary for this date includes the entry: *American/44451, Nicholas, John; 5-10-11; Boston, U.S.A.; doctor.*

After his release from Dora, Hein joined a U.S. war-crimes investigation team. As a former statistical clerk in the prisoner hospital, he was able to furnish American prosecutors with a mass of mortality and morbidity data invaluable to their case. After the trials he returned to Poland, where he privately published a statistical handbook on the treatment of sick and injured prisoners at Dora.

People were given assignments for which they had no background, and most likely Johnny fit into this classification.

"He would avoid the subject of his medical qualifications. He liked, in a childish manner, I thought, to boast of having achieved certain successes. He spoke quite often about incidents related to the [U.S.] air force.

"His recollections were monologues. And he would only talk about what *he* wanted to talk about. I recall once that he talked about the interrogation methods used by the Japanese secret police.

"He didn't wear the regular prison uniform, and this fact — plus the better food and other conditions that he enjoyed — made prisoners suspicious of him."

Eventually, said Hein, when their friendship matured, Nicholas confided that he was a U.S. air force officer and pilot on a secret mission for the Allies. "He remains in my memory rather pleasantly as a human being in the full warmth and meaning of the phrase. He was not an argumentative person, but warm and understanding."

The hopelessness of Nicholas' pathetic remedies for his patients and their crucial shortage could only have worsened any inner conflict that he may have felt over his incredible new lease on life: Who should get his precious sulfa and charcoal tablets, aspirin and paper bandages? Who shouldn't?

He must have wondered how long he could delude himself. A prisoner-doctor, if he was honest with himself, could not forever elude the fact that sick call was an elegantly choreographed charade; that as long as *he* knew it be a charade and *they* didn't, he was party to the cruelest fraud.

The larger, all-encompassing fraud, of course, was that there were no cures. There never had been. Even the best medical care in the world couldn't stave off the pernicious inroads of chronically poor rations, extreme cold, extreme heat, lack of sleep, exhaustion and malnutrition. All any prisoner-doctor could do today was try to hold back tomorrow.

And tomorrow was what Nicholas saw every time he looked through the corner window of the dispensary and beheld the corpses heaped randomly, patiently awaiting the crematorium.

Wincenty Hein, a Polish lawyer from Krakow (third from left), became acquainted with Johnny Nicholas at Camp Dora and was a key witness at the Nordhausen Trials. Here he's shown with American GIs after his liberation. (National Archives)

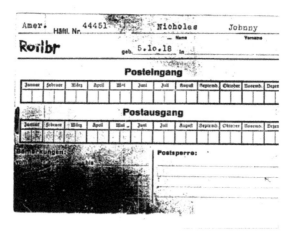

Camp Dora postal card identifies Johnny Nicholas as an American with Serial Number 44451. His birthday is wrong: He was born Oct.20, 1918. (National Archives)

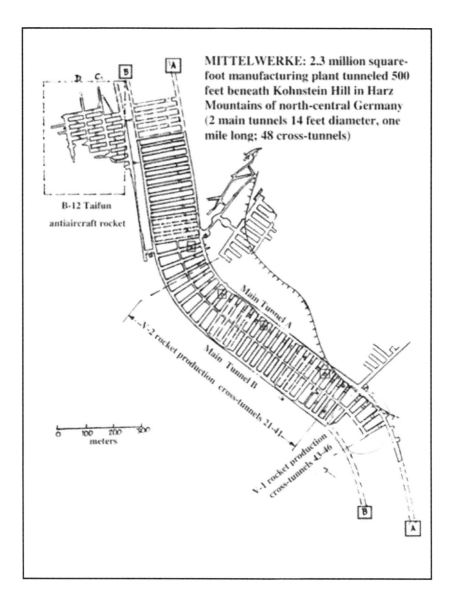

MITTELWERKE: 2.3 million square-foot manufacturing plant tunneled 500 feet beneath Kohnstein Hill in Harz Mountains of north-central Germany (2 main tunnels 14 feet diameter, one mile long; 48 cross-tunnels)

B-12 Taifun antiaircraft rocket

V-2 rocket production cross-tunnels 21-41

V-1 rocket production cross-tunnels 43-46

Main Tunnel A

Main Tunnel B

0 100 200 300 meters

Camp Dora was called the Mittelwerke (Middle Works) after construction was completed. The huge plant was built 500 feet under the Kohnstein Hill near Nordhausen. (National Archives)

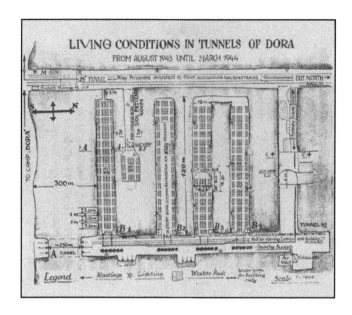

Living conditions were abominable during the first six months of tunnel construction. Official deaths among 10,000 slave laborers shown in Nazi records totaled 2,882, but others estimate it was 50% higher. (National Archives)

Entrance to Camp Dora/Mittelwerke tunnels was covered with camouflage netting to disguise its use. (National Archives)

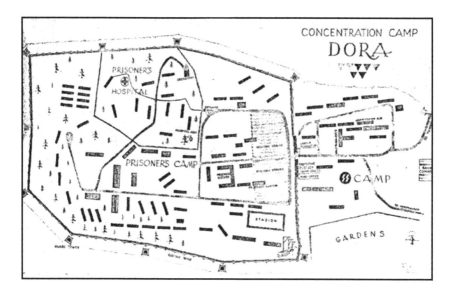

Prisoners and SS were kept distinctly separate after V-2 production lines were completed. Before that prisoners worked inside the dust-choked tunnels. (National Archives)

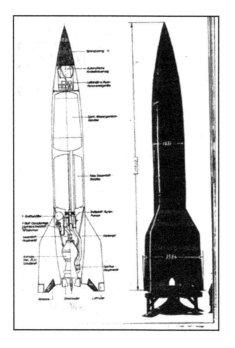

V-2 rockets stood 46 feet high and flew at the speed of sound. The forerunner V-1 rocket or "buzz bomb" was a Model T by comparison. The Nazis launched 5,823 V-1s and 1,054 V-2s, half falling in London. Casualties totaled 33,442. (National Archives)

V-2s moving down assembly line at Camp Dora.
Initial production was targeted at 3,000 but
only a third of that actually were fired. (National
Archives)

Post card written in German that Johnny Nicholas sent from Buchenwald
to his brother Vildebart in Paris in late 1943. Note likeness of Adolf Hitler
on stamp. (Vildebart Nicholas)

An American GI eyeballs V-2 rocket fins after U.S. troops liberated Camp Dora in April 1945. U.S. spirited away components and German rocket scientists, forming the basis for the U.S. space program and the landing on the moon in 1969. (U.S Army Photo)

CHAPTER TWELVE
KAMMLER'S ORDER

On August 27, 1943, less than six weeks after the last British bomb had exploded on Peenemunde, the first truck convoy of "Operation Transport South" whined up to the base of the Kohnstein and discharged Jay, the English carpenter, and the rest of the advance party from Buchenwald.

Colonel-engineer Kammler had worked his first miracle, and Hitler would shortly make him a general.

On the wall map of SS Construction Branch Headquarters in Berlin, "Closed Area B" — the terrain around the Kohnstein — was still an innocuous rectangle colored green. During that first snow of the winter of 1943-44, when *Lufwaffe* pilots flew over the Harz, it appeared to be the same pastoral, pine-forested Christmas-card idyll. But it was a horrific illusion. The malignancy of Camp Dora was metastasizing well beyond the hill itself. It would eventually be supported by a complex of 31 sub-camps[1] crammed with some 32,000 slave laborers, all within a convenient 20-mile radius.

Under the dome of the hill, located at map co-ordinates D 09-53-10, *Kommandant* Fourschner had wrought order out of the subterranean rubble. The jagged floors had been paved with concrete and walls smoothed. Electricity, illumination, air-conditioning and plumbing had been piped in. The cross-tunnels gleamed with well-oiled tools and dies, lathes, bench presses, drilling machines, borers, planers, stamp

---

1 Harzungen, Ellrich, Boelcke Kaserne, Kelbra, Klein Bodungen, Wieda, Blankenburg, Rossla, Osterode, Ilfeld, Hohlstedt, Quedlinburg, Trautenstein, Regenstein, Wickerode, Gross Werther, Artern, Rottleberode, Nixei, Osterhagen, Woffleben, Bleicherode, Tettenborn, Mackenrode, Walkenried, Klaissingen, Sonderhausen, Ilsenburg, Ballenstedt, Sollstedt and Niedersachswerfen.

ing machines, sheet-metal-formers and work benches. Along Tunnels A and B ran standard-gauge German railroad track plus a modern assembly line. And overhead, massive gantry cranes whirred smoothly.

By May 1944, the month that found Nicholas plunged into the thick of the horrendous demolition-and-digging work, and a mere nine months after General Kammler had launched the gigantic project, 300 V-2s — assembled from Peenemunde-manufactured components and parts — rolled down the Mitterwerk mass-production line for experimental testing.[2]

In a year's time, within the space of 45 football fields, Kammler was raising a new Peenemunde from the ashes. He was obsessed with achieving that goal. "Never mind the human victims," he ordered his subordinates within the Kohnstein," the work must proceed and be finished in the shortest possible time!"

His exhortation wiped out any remaining doubts about the fate of the undernourished, overworked and sickly slave laborers. Merely keeping them alive would place an enormous burden on Dr. Kahr's rag-tag team of doctors and their pathetic store of mostly useless palliatives.

Kammler's order would also transform Johnny Nicholas in the months ahead in ways that he could never imagine.

As *helf artz* on the sick-call desk, Nicholas commanded a unique perspective on Camp Dora. His patients arrived from every tunnel, every work detail, every workbench and every assignment across the sprawling camp. They represented almost every facet of the massive Mittelbau complex. To satisfy his voracious curiosity about everything, Nicholas endlessly pumped them through casual conversation, which is how he kept abreast of the amazing transformation taking place beneath the Kohnstein.

How was it possible? The gigantic rock and rubble piles that he had had to climb over were gone! The demolitions had stopped, the dust and debris had settled. Picks and shovels, wheel barrows and *bascules* had

---

2 The completed rockets arrived at the south end of Cross-tunnel No. 41 for final testing. This was a special excavation more than 50 feet in height so that the rockets could be tested in the vertical position. One side of this tunnel consisted of multilevel inspection scaffolds. These permitted technicians to measure fluid levels and gyroscopic functions that could not be checked when the rocket was in the horizontal position.

been set aside, and prisoners now hunched over thousands of work bench-es, making parts and subassemblies — all under the training and supervi-sion of German civilian technicians.

Tunnel B had two primary assembly lines running for almost half a mile, from Cross-tunnel No. 21 to Cross-tunnel No. 42. At the end of these as-sembly lines the sinister-looking, finned, 46-foot-long behemoth V-2s rolled out of the Mittelwerk on their way to winning the war for *Der Fuehrer.*

He could see the difference at sick call: The numbers were decreasing as the murderous tunnel boring began to wind down. Yet the work of transport-ing the huge mechanical equipment to equip the factory was exceedingly dangerous — even if the men had been healthy. Hardly a day passed without five serious accidents.

As one of the *helf artz* summoned into the tunnels to treat the victims, Nicholas could see how dangerous tunnel work still was.

The prisoners had to manhandle into the Mittelwerk all the equipment used in the manufacturing process. They used handcarts, block-and-tackle, huge skids pulled by teams and temporary narrow-gauge railways employing "skips" — small rail cars. The most lethal moves involved mas-sively heavy, 20-foot-tall Weingarten hydraulic presses for stamping out the sheetmetal fuselage sections of the V-2.

Nicholas could extrapolate from the evidence of his own eyes only so far. What happened beyond the end of the twin assembly lines, when the monster rockets emerged from Mittelwerk and were loaded onto freight cars and battened down under heavy tarpaulins, was every prisoner's guess.

The V-2s were being shipped by rail to Holland, to the 15th Army Group. German soldiers had started training in September 1944 to fire the weapon at England.[3] The firing batteries were encamped in the heavy woods of The Hague's biggest city park, the Haegsche Bosch, which was sited within the mandatory 200-mile range of London.

---

3 The basic instruction manual, the *A-4 Fibel* (primer), turned out to be an unorthodox document for the *Wehrmacht*. A creative writer had juiced up the arid technical jargon with embroidery-sampler homilies, inspirational verses, illus-trations of buxom *frauleins* in negligees and swimsuits and bucolic sketches of German villages. For a military field manual, the slim volume acquired an unprec-edented popularity with the soldiers.

And there were other sites in Northern Europe. Designed to be fully mobile, the V-2 moved on a long flatbed rail car. It could be quickly erected at any location with a hard surface, ideally an aircraft runway or a highway intersection. Immediately after launch the crew march-ordered in minutes and sped to another location.

Rapid mobility made the launchers almost invulnerable to retaliation from enemy aircraft.

On Sept. 6, 1944, the Haegsche Bosch crews lobbed their first two V-2s. The target was Paris, which had been liberated a month earlier by the Allies. Both rockets exploded in mid-air. Two days later the crews adjusted their firing orders and arced the first one into London.[4]

The monster V-2 terrorized the English much more than the infinitely less vicious V-1 flying bomb. Britons' fears soared in the knowledge that V-2s traveled faster than the speed of sound; that they gave no advance warning. Therefore there was no defense against them short of bombing the launch sites — if they could be detected.

Hitler vowed to escalate the terror to avenge the Allies' devastating round-the-clock fire-bombings of major German cities. He ordered 5,000 V-2s for a mass assault on London scheduled for February or March 1945. In response to this directive, by October 1944, when von Braun was fully satisfied with the V-2 design, Managing Director Richkey tooled-up for a production quota of 900 rockets a month.

---

4 The intended target was about a mile from Waterloo Station. Instead it landed in Chiswick, leaving a 30-foot-diameter hole, demolishing six houses, killing two people and injuring 10 more. Accuracy of the weapon was limited to a range of about five miles. If it were aimed at a military target, chances were very good that it would hit a civilian target. The V-1 and V-2 campaigns against England lasted approximately seven months. In all, 5,823 V-1s and 1, 054 V-2s landed. In addition, 271 flying bombs and four V-2s fell into the English Channel. Total casualties numbered 33,442, with roughly half of all bombs and rockets falling on London.

Although the primary target for Hitler's Vengeance weapon was the English, he also intended to retaliate against the Americans for their daylight air raids on Germany. For the United States he was preparing a deluxe V-2 — the A-9/A-10. It, too, was the brainchild of von Braun. His A-9/A-10 blueprint proposed a quantum jump in the ballistic-missile concept. The weapon — gigantic for that era — was designed to soar to an altitude of 110 miles, sprout wings and glide into New York City at more than 3,000 miles an hour. Fortunately, the design lay fallow on von Braun's drawing board while he lavished top priority on the mass-production of V-2s.

Nicholas' euphoria over his deliverance from the tunnels wouldn't have lasted long; guilt over his "luxury" life would inevitably have begun to nag him. His Christian upbringing, deeply planted by his parents and assiduously watered by the French Brothers of St. Louis de Gonzague, would have sneaked back into his life. How much longer could he revel in his incredible good fortune while the miserable wretches of sick call lined up outside the dispensary-barracks door?

Other worries may have nagged him. A stern conscience would have informed him that, even though the SS doctor, Lt. Kahr, technically was "the enemy," he was indebted to him for his good fortune. He must have admired the Austrian's relentless and heroic efforts to improve prisoner health care. Yet how would he have squared his admiration with the loathing that every prisoner was expected to direct toward anyone wearing the hated SS uniform?

He must also have mulled the fact that patients lying in the wards of the *revier* and, in a sense, enjoying Kahr's protection, were plotting to sabotage the V-2 mass-production line. How could Nicholas keep faith with the patients by keeping his mouth shut about sabotage plots — and still keep faith with the SS medical officer?

It had taken Nicholas only a few weeks to discover that, despite its implacable death rate, the *revier* was one of the safest havens in Dora. SS men were loath to enter it because they dreaded the overpowering stench of gangrene and death, and they were petrified at the thought of picking up any of the myriad of communicative diseases that plagued the patients.

Ironically, this formed a protective cocoon around the *revier*, allowing it to function as a sanctuary wherein prisoners could congregate and communicate with less risk of being seen or heard by the SS or their *kapo* functionaries. Apart from the odors, it was an ideal breeding place for sabotage plots.

Few prisoners ever appreciated the immense power concentrated in the *revier*, which explains why the Communists who controlled it would — and frequently did — kill to hold on to that power, the prime requisite for which was its relative freedom from SS interference. And because every prisoner, whether tunnel rat or prison councilor, sooner or later passed through the *revier*, it developed into a clandestine central-intelligence message center for all information affecting prisoners' lives.

It exercised an even more direct impact on them: Because prisoner-doctors had access to lethal chemicals and hypodermics, they were frequently directed by the prisoner government to prune the prisoner ranks of informers and spies; of prisoners who ratted on their friends to the SS; of the hated Criminals who preyed violently on others; of the *kapos* whose power had gone to their heads.

The target was inveigled to the *revier* on some medical or health pretext and given — either by fraud or force — a lethal injection. And in case the SS might inquire, an autopsy was performed and a death certificate completed.

Prisoner-doctors, including Nicholas in all likelihood, who worked at the pleasure of the Dora's prisoner council, thus were routinely forced to function as gardeners selectively weeding the prisoner population to preserve the balance-of-power *status quo* among the camp's ruthlessly feuding political, ethnic and criminal factions.

As for the saboteurs?

Even as late as the third quarter of 1944, when few prisoners remained in the tunnel dormitories and the vast Mittelwerk plant was up and running, few — if any — inmates knew what kind of weapon the V-2 was or how it was to be used. They had never seen a rocket before. The elaborate security system devised by *Kommandant* Fourschner prevented any single prisoner from seeing the big picture. Sitting at — sometimes chained to — his workbench in the cross-tunnels, an individual could identify the only component that he was working on, such as an electric motor, wiring harness, fuel tank, large sheetmetal cylinder, sheetmetal fin, radio and gyrocompass, for example. But that was a far as he could project. Anything he knew about his part/component was told to him on a need-to-know basis. And to keep the entire work force individually insulated, isolated and in ignorance of the true nature of The Weapon, prisoners on and off the job were prohibited — under pain of execution — from talking to one another.

As Managing Director Richkey stepped up the pace of production, the *revier* blossomed as a hotbed for sabotage plots.[5] Out of these came such tac-

5 Benjamin Jacobs, a Polish dentist, recalled when he and his brother were conducted by SS guards to the tunnels for the first time. On the way they saw a huge bullet-shaped object [a V-2 rocket] covered with canvas roll slowly past them on the adjacent railroad track. "We were led into a tunnel built into the mountainside," Jacobs said. "It was nearly dark and freezing inside ... a strong smell of sulfur was everywhere. Above a water tank was a warning in German: *'Nicht trinken!'* (Do not drink!) The end of the tunnel was not in sight.

"As the foreman led us in deeper, we saw prisoners at work benches surrounded with bins that held strange-looking parts. Many gave us the thumbs-up sign. We

tics as urinating on complex electrical wiring, causing circuits to short out when energized; welders purposely botching seams, causing rocket fuselages to split open and/or tail fins to fall off in flight.

Sabotage carried a hanging penalty, making conspirators extremely careful not to be overheard. Occasionally, however, patient-conspirators, too confident of the protected environs of the *revier*, talked too loudly. Inevitably some of them would be overheard by some starving and demoralized eavesdroppers ready to betray them in exchange for the promise of half a loaf of bread or a less hazardous work detail.

Nicholas would have hovered on the periphery of these sabotage conspiracies, waffling over the question of whether he was "in" or "out," agonizing over the conflict of his loyalties to his fellow-prisoners and the Allies, on the one hand, and his ties to Dr. Kahr on the other hand. No matter how he would have sliced his dilemma, however, the Austrian physician still came out a "German," an SS man, one of the "enemy."

"Denunciations," as betrayals of saboteurs were called, meant automatic death sentences on them.

Mass hangings were one of the few routine events that temporarily transformed all prisoners in heroic efforts to unite in self-defense. The society's ethnically fractured and politically segregated nature made it extremely difficult for it to react cohesively and punctually to emergencies threatening the common good.

---

continued further into the tunnel, and a foreman ordered my brother and me to work with three prisoners already at work there.

"They looked frail. One of them was barely skin and bones. We asked them what we should do. As soon as the foreman passed, they stopped working and said to us: 'Don't do a thing. Just act busy when a German comes by.' ... They spoke German to us with a heavy French accent. Besides the sulfur smell, this place reeked of ammonia, each breath we took hurt.

"When a foreman approached us, the three Frenchmen reached into a bin, picked up a few parts that were already clean, wiped them again and tossed them into a second bin. We mimicked them for the rest of the day. I wondered how long they had been faking and how we could get away with this charade."

The Germans regarded this comparatively innocent goldbricking in the same category as urinating on electrical components and slipshod welding practices; they were all considered acts of sabotage punishable by death. To guard against being caught in the act, the tunnel slaves had worked out a secret code for monitoring the whereabouts of SS guards and *kapos*. "Fifteen!" for example, meant that danger was on its way; "eighteen!" sounded the all-clear.

Confronted with mass executions, the mission to save the lives of very important prisoners temporarily suspended all other considerations. Greens helped Reds, Politicals of the Right reached out to those of the Left; Norwegians to Slavs, Danes to Russians, Frenchmen to Poles. At Dora, prisoners from some 26 nations rallied under the supra-nationality of human survival to attempt to defeat *Kommandant* Fourschner's mass-execution lists.

The *lagereldtester*, conceding the impossibility of saving *everyone* on the list, concentrated on the most politically and/or morally important among the condemned. He chose whom to try to save, whom to let die. Time was always critical — mere hours between discovering the names of those to be executed and the time of execution. The *lagereldtester's* choices flashed along the prisoner grapevine to all *kapos* and other prisoner functionaries to alert those to be saved.

Sometimes immediate transfers to distant subcamps were conjured. Or they were hidden in the space above the rafters of a barracks and rotated from one barracks to another.

Or the body switch was used: The *revier kapo* found a corpse whose physical features resembled those of the condemned man. When the SS arrived to claim the victim, the *kapo* produced the look-alike "corpse." If a suitable corpse wasn't available, a dying prisoner of the same general appearance was selected, a *helf artz* gave him a lethal injection, and he was sacrificed as a substitute, although there is no evidence Nicholas did this.

The body switch was always worth a try. Despite its complexity, it often succeeded. When it didn't, the SS added the conspirators' names to the execution list....

Public hangings in the tunnel didn't take place every day. The gallows on the *appellplatz* was a more convenient venue. However, when acts of sabotage — real or imagined — kept increasing in number, *Kommandant* Fourschner felt that turning executions into public ceremonies would drive home his message more succinctly. The first public mass hanging in the tunnels, with every living soul in the camp present, had taken place as early as March 1944. Now, as the blizzards of November 1944 blew into December, Fourschner felt the urge for another demonstration.

Suddenly the public-address system blared: *Achtung! Achtung! All work will cease immediately! All detail leaders will assemble their formations and march them into the tunnels immediately! All NCOs will report to the gatehouse! On the double!*

Within the Kohnstein labyrinth thousands of prisoners converged from all over the camp. SS guards herded them into the southern end of Tunnel B, where whirring machines fell silent. Conveyor tracks clattered to a stop. All manufacturing ceased. In the massive caverns the shuffling of thousands of wooden clogs on concrete shattered eardrums.

Thousands or more bodies crammed around the intersection of Tunnel B and Cross Tunnel No. 41, the apex of the event.

Nicholas' height would have enabled him to see over most heads and have a clear view of the hangings.

In the center stood a platoon of SS. Above whirred a gantry crane. From it dangling as many nooses as there were victims. In the hushed silence the nooses twirled in the tunnel's air currents....

The SS squad moved apart to make way for an NCO followed by a line of shuffling prisoners. They were halted beneath the massive crane as it whirred into position.

An SS officer read aloud from a sheet of paper: *The following haeftlinge have been tried and found guilty of criminal acts resulting in the reduction of production quotas of the Mittelwerk. These crimes come under three specifications: the deliberate introduction of foreign objects into components and assemblies so as to cause malfunction; unlawful acquisition and possession of property and materials belonging to the German government; and chronic malingering.*

The SS officer called out the names of the condemned, then concluded his proclamation: *The accused have admitted their guilt and have been sentenced to death under the general charge of sabotage. By the order of Heinrich Himmler, Reichfuehrer of the Schutzstaffel.... Proceed with the executions!*

The executions used "a block-and-tackle from which a long and heavy iron bar was hanging," remembered a former German prisoner, Karl Feuerer. "The [men to be executed] were lined up one next to the other with wire nooses around their necks. The nooses were tied to the 15-meter-long iron bar. The moment the bar was hoisted — by means of this pulley system, all the people met their deaths simultaneously."

As a warning, the SS left the dead untouched. And for days prisoners hustled back and forth past the corpses, dangling five feet from the tunnel floor, on the way to and from their workbenches.

CHAPTER THIRTEEN
DR. KAHR

Dr. Kahr had become a familiar figure on the Dora landscape, hobbling awkwardly across the grassy terrain of the Kohnstein from the SS camp to the four-barracks cluster of the prisoner hospital. Typically he rushed along with head bent, a little out of breath, eyes angled down as if the worries that hunched his shoulders were concealed in the toes of his muddy jackboots.

In the fall, however, he was moving more slowly, more deliberately, taking time to ponder the rows and rows of barracks rapidly rising out of the chaos of the vast construction site; watching the heavily laden trucks groan under massive loads of logs as they plowed cruel furrows in the earth; staring at strings of stick-thin prisoners rushing back and forth from the railroad spur to Nordhausen, struggling under loads fetched from freight cars choked with cement, construction equipment and mining supplies.

The Austrian doctor's waking hours were monopolized by medical concerns, so he might have failed to note the veritable circus of corporate logos of famous German companies strewn across the camp. The bonanza of building material that increasingly engaged his attention, from cement bags and corrugated-iron sheets to cranes and steamrollers, all bore the stamps, decals or trademarks of major industrial concerns.

At least a score of the major names from the equivalent of Germany's Fortune 500 List were either contractors or subcontractors engaged in constructing Camp Dora, Mittelwerk and the rockets shuttling smoothly down its twin assembly lines in Tunnel B. For what Dr. Kahr was thinking, however, he wouldn't have had corporate logos on his mind; he would have been more focused on the predatory SS men, machine pistols suspended from shoulder straps, lounging at their posts or sauntering along, shopping for targets of opportunity....

When a junior officer directly disobeys his commanding officer, it's always bad for the officer — particularly when both sport the skull-and-crossbones SS insignia on their lapels. The impending clash was fraught with more serious consequences for the doctor, despite his recent promotion to captain.

The Hippocratic Oath had trapped him in the classic conundrum of immovable force meeting the irresistible body: He needed more barracks to house the increasing tide of desperate patients that was routing to him from sick-call, and Kommandant Fourschner, who could have authorized their construction with no more effort than signing a work order, just didn't give a damn: He couldn't see how Kahr could get so worked up over *haeftlinge*; there was an inexhaustible supply. The kommandant's credo was that they were fodder for the V-2 assembly.

When Kahr came to Dora in February 1944, he testified at the Nordhausen trials, "four [hospital] barracks, which contained approximately 350 beds, were standing ... but they were only sufficient for a small number of prisoners, perhaps for 25 percent of the strength. I realized immediately that a large extension was necessary ... and ... I tried, first of all, to make the kommandant ... realize that the continuous state in the tunnels was detrimental to the health of the prisoners. The kommandant ... didn't want to listen...."

Because he was making no headway using the direct approach, he began firing memos directly at SS medical headquarters in Berlin, pleading for relief. *Kapo* Ackermann, a German communist and the *revier* clerk, typed all of Kahr's correspondence. He duly whispered around word of the gutsy Austrian's memos. And they did require guts: Fourschner could court-martial him for insubordination, and Berlin could demote him for the mortal military sin of failure to go through channels.

The doctor might as well have saved his courage: Berlin proved to be deafer than the kommandant to his entreaties. Meanwhile, the *revier's* patient-to-bed ratios were rising frighteningly, so he concluded essentially: *To hell with Fourschner. I'll build the barracks myself.*

Behind his mild manner and pleasant, non-threatening countenance, Captain Kahr concealed a stubbornness and resourcefulness born of having spent many months in front-line combat, continually having to make life-saving decisions in the absence of higher authority. He had done it so successfully and so often that it had bred in him a very high opinion of his ability to do so. As he saw it, in circumventing *Kommandant* Fourschner, he would merely be applying the lessons learned in combat.

Another factor was the congenital contempt that Waffen SS had for their brothers in the Concentration Camp Branch SS. Not only did combat SS have an immense reputation within the Fatherland as skillful, determined and resourceful fighters; they were the very last opponents that Allied soldiers, given a choice, wanted to come up against. By contrast, Concentration Camp "soldiers" were an anathema to him.

As a combat veteran he might have set the mystique aside, but apparently he hadn't — or at least not completely. His leg was crippled, but his *Waffen* persona remained alive and well and persistently irritated by the slovenly military bearing of the Dora SS. He had no hesitation in calling them up short when he judged them delinquent. He had already developed a reputation for reprimanding enlisted SS for failing to salute him when their paths crossed, or when their salutes were not rendered in the traditional manner.

He held socializing with Kommandant Fourschner and his brother officers to an absolute minimum; and when he acquired the use of an automobile, it dropped to zero. He preferred to spend his off-duty time in his barracks apartment, which he had begun sprucing up a little with some wood paneling contraband that he had laid his hands on, or on the diversions that nearby Nordhausen offered.

If the insubordination with which Kahr was toying were discovered, it promised a court martial for him. And it begged a bullet for the prisoners about to be talked into joining his dangerous scheme. They would have to steal the building supplies and "borrow" the heavy construction equipment. They would all enter the conspiracy quaking in the knowledge that Fourschner cried "sabotage!" every time a prisoner grabbed a length of waste electrical-wire off the Mittelwerk floor with which to tie his wooden clogs on more securely.

By the time that Kahr began firming up his plan, Nicholas had been working in the prisoner-hospital dispensary barracks for about six weeks. The doctor would therefore have had ample time in which to observe his new *helf artz* in action, fashioning bandages out of paper, making splints from cardboard and adapting crude carpentry tools to reduce simple skull fractures.

The "American" had a good brain and was fast on his feet. An improviser *par excellence* with a can-do mindset, he was precisely what Kahr had to have on his team if his perilous plot to bamboozle his boss were not to backfire.

The doctor's proposal was as simple as it was audacious: Steal building materials stashed in super-abundance all around the base of the Kohnstein. Persuade qualified prisoners to volunteer their off-duty hours for construction. His reasoning was that, on a noisy construction site, bustling with men, machines and equipment constructing roads and pathways, details of prisoners hustling here and there with timbers and logs, the sounds of buzzing saws and clinking hammers filling the air, and scores of new "legal" barracks sprouting across the grassy field, no one was likely to zero in on three or four "illegal" ones.

Prisoners on their off-duty hours? Which prisoners? What off-duty hours?

Prisoners holding convalescence slips. Some months more than a thousand slips were dispensed. Slip holders were permitted to go back to their barracks or to the prisoner canteen[1] and rest. (The kommandant's rules, however, forbade them from lying down; they had to sit erect while "convalescing.") Obviously most convalescents would be too exhausted to volunteer, but surely a handful would be willing — and physically able — to do so during their rest time in the noble cause of building desperately needed new hospital facilities to benefit *all* prisoners.

And who was to recruit these volunteers?

Johnny Nicholas.

By virtue of his personality and position, no one was better qualified. In just a few months his grin and gift of gab had garnered him such acclaim that patients had started calling him "St. Nicholas." He was hugely popular with the sick-call regulars, and he kept track of those to whom he awarded slips.

---

1 This was a large warehouse that included several smaller storerooms, a kitchen, a food-preparation room, a day room and an office. Officially, prisoners who had money could buy items such as oysters, mustard, lemonade, toothbrushes, soap, soap powder, buttons and smoking materials. Practically speaking, supplies were never dependable.

Kahr surely perceived canonization of his black *helf artz* as a heaven-sent credential for enlisting barracks-building volunteers. But how was he to approach the *haeftlinge?*

The occasion called for extreme tact, mutual confidence and trust. All he knew about him was that he was a doctor — or claimed to be — from America. There was a lot of mystery about him. A lot of uncertainty about who he really was, and where he really came from. Yes, they had their medical calling in common, which was a beginning. But slave-labor-camp social etiquette ruled off-the-job contacts with prisoners. It wasn't a simple matter of buttonholing the *schwartze* after sick call some morning and laying it on him. The strictest rules governed the most casual contact between masters and slaves.

How was Kahr to approach him? With every caution. *Kommandant* Fourschner had promulgated a one-page typewritten sheet covering all the dos and don'ts for officers: No talking to any *haeftlinge* unless the subject involves work; no accepting gifts from him; no fraternizing; no expression whatsoever of sentiment toward him; no inquiry into the state of his health....[2]

Nicholas relied on no typewritten sheet to explain his social standing vis-à-vis any SS officer — commissioned or noncom. A graduate of Buchenwald, it had been drilled into him that *haeftlinge* had no rights whatsoever; they existed solely at the sufferance of the SS.

A prisoner never spoke to any superior — prisoner-government lackey or SS — without being spoken to first. Having been addressed, he removed his cap, stood at attention, identified himself by name and number, then asked for permission to respond.

Nicholas followed the ordained servility in his dealings with Kahr. When others were present, the doctor addressed the black man by his serial number. But the give-and-take of working side-by-side daily with sick and injured allowed him a little slack for social maneuver.

Despite the rules, their relationship would have ripened over time, and within the context of their deeper rapport the doctor would have risked making his pitch.

---

2 Every SS officer had to sign an agreement that he would never reveal anything he had seen or heard during his service at Camp Dora. Violation of the agreement was punishable by execution.

To any wretched soul languishing in sick call, the *helf artz* at the head of the line exercised the power of God Almighty. Nicholas' convalescence slips came as major miracles. If he couldn't wangle them a slip, a scarce pill or a salve ranked as a supernatural phenomenon of a lesser rank. And when he had exhausted his supply of these, he excavated for petty gratuities — maybe a few spoonfuls of soup or a couple of cigarette butts; but always his ever-ready infusions of the will to hang on and the certainty of Allied victory.

And if it came to recruiting volunteers for a worthwhile cause, he would have had few qualms about cashing in on the goodwill banked in the hearts of thousands.

Yet Nicholas may have been motivated by more than "cause"; bizarre as it may seem in the slave-master society of Dora, he may have identified with the young SS captain, who was only a few years his senior, for what he was attempting to do.

In his mind Kahr's hated SS uniform may have been canceled by the revered profession that he followed. All his life Nicholas had demonstrated the pedestal on which he placed those pledged to Hippocrates. As a child he had wanted to become a physician. In Paris his insatiable curiosity about the workings of the human body had driven Pape and Coicou crazy. On official documents left in his wake, the "profession" blank is always filled "medical student."

Identification is kin to admiration. That he could easily have experienced, too.

Trading life-saving rest time to build hospital barracks would have bulked as a no-brainer to any slave laborer. But Nicholas, convinced either of "the cause," or of Kahr's backing, or conceivably riding an adrenaline rush over the chance to one-up Fourschner, was too cocky a con man to let a little "hard sell" stand in his way.

On the other hand, he'd certainly have voted against Kahr's bringing *an SS man* into the act — Master Sergeant Rudolf Jacobi.

Jacobi, a carpenter by trade in civilian life, had served with an SS combat engineering battalion on the Russian front. As strong as a bear and hard as granite, he headed Dora's construction department and was in charge of all barracks building. More important for Kahr's purposes, he controlled — and knew the locations of — the immense dumps of lumber, corrugated iron, cement and other building materials scattered around the base of the Kohnstein. The doctor reasoned that to steal the material in broad daylight, Jacobi had to be either bought, pulled into the plot or blackmailed into looking the other way; that the SS master sergeant's well-recognized face was their passport to impunity.

Combat on the Russian front had left the SS master sergeant a moody man lashed by hidden demons inciting him to sudden and brutal assaults on any prisoner within striking distance. Overnight the storm blew itself out, and tomorrow always found him leaning contritely toward the opposite horizon, prostrating himself in mawkish sentimentality toward his victims of yesterday's tirades.

One didn't need an M.D. to tag Jacobi as an emotional basket case, a grenade with the pin pulled. Kahr — unless, as a relative newcomer, wasn't privy to the master sergeant's history — must have recognized a schizophrenic when he saw one. So why was the doctor so hot on the bastard?

There weren't too many SS that caused Nicholas to quiver in his boots; with his excellent German, he always figured he could talk his way out of anything, just as he had that day at roll call, when the B-17s were flying over and Brauny had drawn a bead on him. But Jacobi would have given him the shakes: All it would take would be for Jacobi to go nuts on the construction site one morning. He'd blow their cover, and they'd all wind up swinging from the crane.

Jacobi's lethal instability would have already been well documented for Nicholas: He'd have heard it first hand from survivors of the SS man's attacks whom Nicholas treated after they were carried, limp and bloody, into the hospital. No way would he have opted to do business with Jacobi. His gut told him the man was crazy, a disaster awaiting its cue.

But, as Nicholas would have reminded himself, Jacobi wasn't his call. He was the *schwartze haeftlinge*; Kahr was team captain.

Nicholas wouldn't have known, however, that the two SS men had already done some shady business together. In the normal course of their SS duties, a medical officer and a construction chief NCO followed very different paths around the camp and seldom rubbed shoulders. But they had already met — secretly. Kahr had tapped Jacobi for some sheets of wood paneling. He wanted to spruce up the drab apartment that he occupied in one of the SS barracks, and Jacobi had delivered.

That transaction, however, relatively innocuous on its face, had made both of them complicit in an illegal act: In the kommandant's catalog, appropriation of government materials for personal use was the equivalent of sabotage. They had co-opted each other, but they were in no immediate danger as long as neither one talked.

Beyond its decorative utility, the paneling's value to Kahr lay in the demonstration that Jacobi wasn't troubled about breaking camp rules. In the hospital-barracks scheme, however, the doctor had a more elaborate transaction in mind, and if Jacobi had been co-opted once, he could be a second time.

Kahr, of course, couldn't have disclosed to Nicholas the reasons why he was confident that Jacobi was the man to ramrod the project. Nicholas would simply have had to accept the doctor's judgment.

Still, Nicholas' stubborn feeling wouldn't have let him give up without trying. Navigating cautiously within the straight-jacket constraints of SS-prisoner decorum, he may have attempted to warn Kahr, employing the stilted third-person address dictated by the circumstances.

Prisoner No. 44451 requests permission to speak, Herr Doktor.

Permission granted.

Herr Doktor, accounts of Hauptscharfuehrer Jacobi circulate in the revier. With the Herr Doktor's permission, the prisoner feels it would be in the Herr Doktor's interests if he were made aware of these accounts.

Accounts? What accounts? Explain yourself, 44451.

With the Herr Doktor's permission: Prisoner Jay, the carpenter, has built barracks under the supervision of the Herr Hauptscharfuehrer for nine months. Prisoner Jay has personally observed the Herr Hauptscharfuehrer's relations with the haeftlinge who work for him. Prisoner Jay would be a first-hand source of information, Herr Doktor....

But whatever course their exchange may have followed, they would have been ultimately forced to concede that, given the rapidly narrowing window of opportunity, they had no other choice: It had to be Jacobi or nobody. Now or never.

Whose judgment should be followed?

Let Lady Luck make the call — a characteristic Nicholas' solution in tight spots. He'd probably have slipped his lucky *pfennig* from his pocket — and more than likely called the toss.

Sometime between late July and early August of 1944, a window of opportunity chosen to coincide with *Kommandant* Fourschner's absence from the camp, an uneasy alliance of sick prisoners began constructing additional hospital barracks under the direct authority of Dr. Kahr. "I started to build ... on my own responsibility," he testified at the Nordhausen trials. "I, for instance, stole, together with the prisoners, parts of barracks from some unused dump.... We stole the metal parts mostly from the Mittelwerk, and we took the wood mostly from the various construction sites that were in the vicinity of Dora....

"I had ... the support of the prisoners. I needed the carpenters, the locksmiths and other workers in the camp and all those people, at least the carpenters, were under Jacobi, who was a very strict disciplinarian."

From his window in the dispensary Nicholas looked out across the heavily obstructed construction site. A few meters away the first of the "illegal" structures, indistinguishable from the vast crop of "legals" going up all around, was already taking on its familiar shape.

Informants for the Nordhausen Notebook[3] agreed that the black man was at his best leading the pack; at his worst following, looking on, powerless to intervene. If he watched Brauny or Simon, the arch haters and despisers of convalescence slips plus their signers, dispensers and recipients, poke around suspiciously on the illicit site, asking questions, he'd have been hard pressed to let happen whatever was going to happen. That wasn't his style. He always had to be in control — or not *in* at all. It was his other religion. *When you're in control, you make things happen to the other guys. When you stand pat, the others make things happen to you.*

He wasn't in control in this caper; he was sweating it out and he was miserable, they said. And when he couldn't bear the strain of his impotence any longer, he turned from the window and went back to his sick-call patients.

Germany mass-produced two main types of barracks: one for air force enlisted men; the other for Labor Service workers. Both types arrived at

---

3 Matthews and others involved in the 1947 Dachau Trials.

Dora's railhead as crates of prefabricated parts packed into open freight cars.

Kahr had authorized four new barracks. He had calculated that 20 convalescent *haeftlinge*, working under one Jacobi, could construct *one* new barracks per week. The one piece of power equipment on the site was a "borrowed" steamroller for leveling the building sites. The rest of the work — sinking deep holes, pounding thick tree-trunk sections into them, bolting heavy planks across the butt ends to support the floor — would be done manually.

The task demanded that each frail convalescent coax 2,000 calories out of the 1,200 or less he was fed daily. Any calories left over were burned up in fighting the extreme fear of discovery.

Don't worry, it'll all be done before Fourschner ever gets back, Nicholas had promised his "volunteers."

But everybody knew that Fourschner was totally unpredictable. He had returned ahead of schedule before. What if it happened this time? Then what?

From tall guard towers armed SS sentinels gazed down on the sprawling construction site. Ambulatory SS roamed the vast dumps of material, tugging on the straps of their machine pistols, seeking relief from boredom. Periodically officers in high crowned caps, clipboards thrust in their armpits, strutted confidently through the chaos. They would stop to study progress on individual projects, make notes, move on to evaluate other projects, pausing to study Jacobi and his trembling crew but never interfering.

The bear-like Jacobi bestrode the hospital-barracks site like a Colossus, swearing at his crew, screaming them on to more effort, more speed, lashing them with profanity. Gradually it percolated the awareness of the stress-ridden convalescents that their crew boss's domineering-badgering-blaspheming presence functioned as camouflage against opportunistic SS busybodies. His performance deflected the curiosity of even the most predatory SS, such as Brauny and Simon, on their frequent appearances.

But Jacobi's crew suffered a near-fatal relapse, Matthews was told, when Fourschner's deputy, carefully navigating a safe approach for his gleaming jackboots through the constructional squalor, stumped on site one day. Like many a deputy, Captain Stoetzler was bucking for his superior's job, so it behooved him to out-Fourschner Fourschner when standing in for his *alter ego*.

Throughout the course of the barracks project, said Matthews's informants, Nicholas spent almost as much time at the dispensary window, checking the progress of his convalescents, as at his desk. Had he spotted Stoetzler that day, he must have wondered how much longer before the beast in Jacobi might slip his leash?

Saws snored. Hammers clinked. Log upon log ... plank by plank ... day after day....

The first barracks was completed.

As success materialized before the eyes of the incredulous convalescents, the volume of their apprehension of Fourschner catching them in the act toned down to a mere descant to their doubts. Yet they could never dislodge their fear completely — because it was completely justified.

The *Herr Kommandant* was a horse rider with equestrian pretensions. The same eyes that couldn't watch a magnificent stallion suffer, however, were blind to the dangling saboteurs obstructing his view as he arrived for work in the tunnels each morning.

His office was in the Zero cross-tunnel which, since its days as one of the four dreadful dormitories for prisoners, had been salvaged from total esthetic desolation. It wasn't the I.G. Farben executive chambers, but a modicum of paving and plastering plus heating and air conditioning had elevated it to a state in which desks, chairs, long drafting tables, typewriters, copying machines and standard office repertoire did not feel completely awkward.

From this headquarters Major Fourschner ran his command — part of the SS Construction Branch — while dreaming of riding high on the coattails of his patron, General Kammler.

Many of his discussions with the general of late had been about sabotage in the Mittelwerk. Indeed, quite recently Kammler had recognized his protégé by saddling him with an additional responsibility; one with crucial significance for Kahr and his conspirators: The general had invested him with the title of Deputy Chief of Counter-intelligence for Mittelwerk. Thus hunting down saboteurs had become both professional duty and avocation. Not surprisingly, he would have been hunting the wherewithal to demonstrate to Kammler that he had tapped the right man for the job.

Meanwhile, from the dispensary barracks window Nicholas charted the daily progress of his convalescents. But he lacked the stomach for watch-and-wait, friends said. The only fuel he ran on was action and adrenaline. Passivity occluded the vessels feeding his spirit. He may have considered himself above hammering and sawing, but at least those activities couldn't completely demoralize him the way that juggling pencil and paper did, compiling long lists of possible volunteers culled from each morning's sick call.

Still, his was absolutely essential work; work that only he could do.

The Labor Allocation Office kept scrupulous track of convalescence-slip holders to prevent anyone oversubscribing his quota. If a name showed up too often or too long, its owner was automatically under suspicion, red-flagged and likely flogged by either Brauny or Simon. Programming a single team for the duration of the project would have drawn Labor Allocation's suspicion too intensively on team members and imperiled the project. Prudence would have told Nicholas to lower the suspicion-intensity index by recruiting several separate crews and rotating them regularly.

While testimony in the Nordhausen trials touches on Dr. Kahr's conspiracy to illegally construct prisoner-hospital barracks, it is silent on details as to how it was actually implemented. Certainly the plot relied on some kind of flim-flam in connection with the convalescence slips. And almost certainly Nicholas was best endowed as the flim-flam artist. But he could not have pulled off such intensely nerve-wracking conniving without leaning heavily on help from prisoners all over the camp.

Few of them were not, even in some minor way, indebted to him for some medical service that he had performed for them, some joked that he had told them about how stupid the SS were, or a crust or cigarette butt that he had palmed off on them. So he could count on a network of friends in key places around the camp who, through the prisoner grapevine, flagged him when he was in danger.

He had friends working in the Labor Allocation Office as clerks, floor sweepers and general gophers. He would have relied on these friends to warn him of any sign that Simon or Brauny was likely to uncover anomalies in the distribution of convalescence slips.

If he received such a warning, however, the question would always have been what was he going to do about it? His only fall-back position would have been Dr. Kahr. But if Kahr had also become *persona non grata....*

It was best not to think of that. Besides, had he been anxiously observing his first crew at work, through the dispensary window, he could not have avoided the persistent reminder that he still had several more crews to recruit.

If Brauny and Simon were not to tumble to the scheme, additional crews were a No. 1 priority. Only when he had taken care of it could he have returned to the next most important priority in his new life — coming to terms with the nonmedical machinations of life in the *revier*.

The *revier* was the seat of prisoner political power in Dora; a Red island in a sea of Green criminals. He had discovered that there was a lot more to preserving his privileged new existence than glib talk and a glad hand at sick call. Above all he desperately needed a crash course in The System — the ceaseless power struggle among Dora's competing political and criminal factions. Otherwise, his ignorance could kill him — literally.

He had already discovered some of the cost of his ignorance, his and Dr. Kahr's.

Both men had been painfully naïve about prisoner-hospital protocol: Jobs in the *revier* — all of them highly coveted — were automatically handed out by the hospital's government to prisoners of its own stripe. The government was a council of Communist prisoners obligated to ensure that only fellow Comrades filled those jobs. Kahr, in unilaterally nominating Nicholas, a POW, as *helf artz*, had innocently infiltrated an equally innocent non-Communist into the *revier's* Communist turf. The prisoner hospital's councilors now found themselves politically bound to oust Nicholas in favor of a comrade.

And they'd kill him if they couldn't find a "political" way to remove him. It was the inevitable fate of any prisoner either dumb or daring enough to try bucking the Comrades' iron-willed hegemony.

These political assassinations were carefully engineered to appear as death from natural causes. The target was lured into the *revier* on some pretext and "diagnosed" with a highly contagious disease. A prisoner-doctor, under direct orders of the Comrade councilors, "treated" him with a syringe. A Comrade-clerk made out a phony death certificate to satisfy the paperwork requirement of the SS, then the corpse was carted up the hill to the crematorium.

Against this System, Nicholas wouldn't have stood a chance. All the street savvy he'd picked up in the back alleys of Port-au-Prince and refined in the shadier sections of Paris totaled zero in Dora's treacherous underworld. He could easily have been the Comrades' next set-up if Dr.

Kahr, who was equally system-ignorant, hadn't packed the immense power of his SS commission.

In Dora, as in every German concentration and slave-labor camp, even the lowest SS trumped the highest-ranking prisoner. On the power-distribution curve Kahr, as a recently promoted captain, scored in the upper-percentile range. For Nicholas this translated into protection that the Top Comrades could never have challenged without risking a date with the crematorium for themselves. Consequently they had no choice but to adopt a hands-off policy on the "American prisoner-of-war" while figuring out their next move.

While ruminated, however, something happened that caught them totally by surprise: Nicholas rapidly shaped up as the most effective sick-call *helf artz* that the *revier* had ever seen. His popularity with the sick-call prisoners quickly burgeoned, and Dr. Kahr, indifferent to the strictures on relations between SS personnel and *haeftlinge*, was soon circulating fulsome reports on his medical performance.

This unexpected development acted to chip away at the Comrades' solidarity for ousting Nicholas. Their initial resolve bogged down in grudging acknowledgment of his surprising medical prowess, and gradually the motion to terminate him slipped between the cracks of their implacable ideology and seemed to have been forgotten.

Maneuvering himself into the *revier* job slot had forced Nicholas to dredge up every scrap of medical knowledge ever to pass his way; everything he had picked up in the hospital in Martinique; all that he had learned from his intense, wee-hours-of-the-morning marathon inquisitions of his medical-student friends, Pape and Coicou, and the medical office he established in Paris. But none of it would have been enough had he not put it into practice with gargantuan self-confidence and the consummate skills of a professional actor.

He succeeded in amazing the *revier's* ruling councilors with his medical performance, yet he never completely disarmed them. He had earned their respect, but they could not let themselves forget that politically he was still an alien in their midst. Apparently they were still against involving themselves in any scheme — such as the barracks-building project — in which he was engaged. Their position seemed to be that political action encompassing any prisoner on the *revier* staff was the prerogative of its ruling Comrades, not some Johnny-come-lately POW.

Kommandant Fourschner was none the wiser when, sometime during September, Kahr began moving patients into the unauthorized hospital barracks.

For all the prisoners in on the plot, the creation of the four squat, one-story structures, undistinguished from the scores of others dotting the landscape at the base of the Kohnstein, ranked as an accomplishment on a par with one of the Seven Wonders of the World. For a brief spell in their sentence in Hell they had found remission; they had defied everything that the SS stood for. They had stood up and reassured themselves that within each of them there still resided a glimmer of self that was unalienable, unaffiliated and untouched by the incessant assault on their humanity.

Other than fleeting glances exchanged or whispers *en passant*, there could have been little overt recognition of reassurance confirmed. All celebration would have had to be private and personal, secret and internal.

But sweet as their celebration was, it was diluted by the reality that it could only be short-lived: Dora was plagued by the peril of prisoners who ratted on their fellow prisoners to ingratiate themselves with the SS. In the long run it was impossible to cover up "sabotage" on such a calculated and blatant scale.

Nicholas would have been as aware of this as anyone, but nothing is known about how he may have processed that awareness. Based on his temperament and personality, one may speculate that the irrepressible gambler in him blocked out the possibility of his ever being caught. Abetting that grand illusion must have been the narcotic "high" that success would have pumped through his veins and distorted his sense of reality.

But long before reality crashed down on him, rumors of what Dr. Kahr and his co-conspirators had accomplished would have leaked from slave to slave until it energized, renewed and empowered most of the prisoner body.

That astounding transformation of lowly, contemptible *haeftlinge* — much more than the stolen building materials — would have been reason for Kommandant Fourschner to make the harshest example of the "saboteurs."

Each of Kahr's four new hospitals had room for 200 narrow beds stacked two tiers high. By autumn's ebb the sun of evening slanted through their windowpanes on sick prisoners who, in their previous overcrowded quarters, had been dying naked on the floor.

By October 1944 all building construction at Dora ceased. In the comparative quiet of the fields at the base of the Kohnstein, the Austrian SS doctor could contemplate with justifiable pride the overflowing population of sick and injured whom he could now treat adequately.

The hospital-barracks coup constituted an immense and — until now — unrecorded triumph of the human spirit on the part of Kahr, Nicholas, Jay and numberless other prisoners whose names — but not their deeds — are lost to history.

Regrettably, though, the triumph would turn out to be temporary.

CHAPTER FOURTEEN
BEAT OR BE BEATEN

It was SS Corporal Paul Mainschein's morning to harass Nicholas at sick call.

The corporal's hair-trigger anger and his brutality toward prisoners were so legendary at Dora that they dubbed him *Main Schwein* (Chief Pig). He jerked open the dispensary door to admit a fresh batch of patients. A chorus of sustained hacking and coughing wafted through the predawn darkness. Mainschein snarled his standard greeting: *Six more! Six more! Shoes off! Get your damned shoes off!*

The corporal's official assignment was as a medical orderly in the SS hospital. This aseptically clean, well-staffed-and-appointed facility, strictly in accord with the high medical standards that the SS lavished on its own troops, was more than 200 yards away from the *revier*. This was as close as most SS voluntarily got to the dreaded contagion infecting the *haeftlinge*. True, there were exceptional times when the SS stormed into the *revier* unannounced on raids. They would tip over the beds and toss the ailing prisoners onto the floor in their hectic searches to root out threats real or imagined. But left to themselves, the SS men generally gave the prisoner hospital and its cesspool of gangrenous, tubercular, typhoidal and dysenteric occupants a wide berth.

Mainschein, however, was one of the exceptions. For reasons that initially baffled Nicholas and the other prisoner doctors, then gradually became clear, Mainschein was drawn to the stench as a bee toward the smell of honey — especially during sick call. He invariably showed up at night, and his excuse to Nicholas was that he "just wanted to help out."

The corporal had been a baker's helper in civilian life. In his early 30s and small in stature, he was a flaming transvestite who surfaced in the SS barracks in wig, painted face, falsies and bar girl's dress, "pretending" he was "available." He was also a chronic drunk who, on the slimiest whim, had inflicted the most bestial assaults on innocent prisoners.

Mainschein's behavior was so bizarre that even the SS complained about his exploits. He would arrive at the NCO mess early, eat his own meal then eat the meals of others who arrived late. He habitually held prisoners up at pistol point and robbed them in broad daylight. *Haeftlinge* seldom had much of value beyond a fountain pen, in one case, and, in another, a can of sardines that a starving prisoner had gotten from home that, by some miracle, had managed to get past the package pilferers in the Dora post office. In Mainschein's mind that made them fair game.

As the chief physician on the post, Dr. Kahr was the pudgy little corporal's boss and therefore held responsible for his behavior. He repeatedly had to straighten out Mainschein's messes and hoped to transfer him to some place where his warped personality would wreak less havoc.

Mainschein habitually left the SS hospital late at night and staggered over to the *revier*, where his presence terrified prisoners. In "checking" them, the medic-corporal's only examination consisted of inserting a tongue depressor and saying: *Open wide!* Far from probing for infection, he was actually panning for gold — gold teeth. When he found it, he demanded that the prisoner or prisoners identify themselves. They could not refuse the order of an SS man and duly disclosed their names and serial numbers. But unwittingly they had already signed their own death warrants. It was only a matter of time before their bodies were added to the mound of corpses accumulating outside the *revier*.

Before they were hauled off to the crematorium, however, Mainschein was sure to return on another late-night visit, when, with the surgical pliers that he always carried, he would yank the target teeth.

Nicholas and the other prisoner doctors appealed for help to Dr. Kahr, who immediately proclaimed a ban on SS entering the prisoner hospital without his permission. But by this time Kahr's stock with Kommandant Fourschner had plummeted in value because he issued too many convalescence slips, which minimized the labor force in the tunnels at a time when V-2 production demanded it be maximized. So Kahr's ban wasn't worth the breath expended in announcing it.

When the drunken SS corporal started showing up at morning sick call to "help out," Nicholas had to run interference.

In the predawn darkness Nicholas watched through an open door of the barracks dispensary as Mainschein walked slowly along the ragged, sinuous line of sick prisoners, playing his flashlight beam on furtive faces.... He halted by one bent figure and punched him. *Damn Jew!* he shrieked. *You're not sick, you bastard! Get the hell out of here!* He punched another crumpled old man. *You're a Jewish pig, too. Get out!*

It was the autumn 1944, and Managing Director Richkey had extended the tunnel workers' 12-hour shift in order to speed up the pace of rocket manufacture. But his tactic backfired: Extra hours piled on the boney shoulders of the malnourished workers pushed too many of them too far. The monthly death rate had climbed toward 1,000; the sick-call line had lengthened alarmingly.

To shorten it Kommandant Fourschner banned all Jewish prisoners from reporting to sick call.[1]

Mainschein delighted in enforcing the ban.

The sick men trembled at the sight of his shadow. Many fled in sheer terror back to their barracks, leaving ragged gaps in the line. It reformed after Mainschein cursed his way back to the barracks entrance, where he yelled: *Only six of you swine at a time! Six at a time! Single file! Single file! No shoes! Get your filthy shoes off! Move! Move!Move! ... Line up and strip. Clothes will be properly folded and placed on the floor in front of you so I can see your triangle and read your number! Mach schnell! Mach schnell!*

The sick men complied in dumb haste. In half a minute they shivered stark naked before the big Green *kapo* in bodies that caricatured scarecrows. Goiter-sized carbuncles bulged under mottled skin. From winter's frost, chilblains still rent like split sausages festered on hands and feet.

Their owners coughed rhythmically and deeply, barren rib cages ballooning hideously as if about to burst. Terrified to spit, they gulped down stringy sputum only to cough it up again. The flesh on their fac-

---

1 Statistics supplied to the Nordhausen War Crimes Tribunal by Wincenty Hein, a Polish prisoner-clerk in Dora's revier, show that Jews constituted 4.5% of a daily average of 4,197 prisoners recorded at a Dora subcamp at Harzungen from 12/20/1945 to 3/20/1945. Also, 10% of a daily average of 17,147 prisoners recorded at Dora during January 1945 were identified as Jews. A report covering January-March 1945 shows Dora's Jewish prisoner constituent at 9%. Death rates for the three-month period, however, reveal Jews dying at a much higher rate than their percentage of the prisoner population. Of 1,090 deaths during the quarter, 22% were of Jews.

es had wasted away, hollowing their eye sockets and lending them the wide-eyed look of shocked children.

Injured to the left! Ill to the right! shouted Mainschein. *Move, you foreign swine! Move!*

The hapless men shifted turgidly as if invisible mud clung to their feet and minds. They scraped up their clothes and shuffled mutely toward Nicholas table.

Line up! Mainschein bellowed.

On Nicholas' table stood a dozen glasses filled with a white opaque liquid. Each glass contained a cylindrical wooden plug drilled down the center and fitted with a thermometer. Several feet of string connected the ends of the plugs to a row of nails in the wall. He dipped each of the thermometers into a can of oil.

Bend down! He went along the line, inserting the thermometers. ...

Waiting for the mercury to register, he sat down behind his desk again and began filling out blank forms.

Name? ...

Number? ...

Age? ...

Nationality? ...

Block Number? ...

When were you last on sick call? ...

What was your complaint? ...

What medicines were you given? ...

When he had finished recording particulars, he questioned them about symptoms.

In any other setting they would have presented a hilarious picture — nude near-skeletons, strings dangling from their rear ends.

He removed the thermometers, replaced them in the glasses and recorded the temperatures.

Prisoner-doctors apprenticed in a hurry under a qualified physician and a crude commandment: Above the belly — aspirin! Below the belly — castor oil! From such primitive beginnings they quickly graduated to specialties in surgery, internal medicine, otolaryngology — and whatever else the duty called for.

Mainschein snatched the sheets of paper off Nicholas' table and stared intently at them. Suddenly he screamed: *This temperature is only one hundred!* He glared at the six naked prisoners, who shrank to their smallest, their Adam's apples bobbing.

Mainschein focused accusingly on one prisoner, then rammed his fist into the man's belly, collapsing him on the floor. *Let that be a lesson to you!* He stared at Nicholas. *You, too, schwartze! This revier is no place for slackers!* He exploded in a tirade against Nicholas for babying prisoners with convalescence slips.

Walter Pomaranski, a young Polish prisoner, was toiling in the tunnels when an SS guard smashed his head in with a rifle butt. The assault was so savage that at midnight, when his shift ended, comrades left him for dead where he had been struck down, at the intersection of Tunnel "A" and Cross-tunnel No. 42....

When he opened his eyes, he was in the prisoner-hospital, and a large, black-skinned man was looking down at him.

Pomaranski, a strapping 19-year-old, was new in Dora and didn't know anyone outside his own Polish group. He asked the black man who he was, and Nicholas identified himself. He told Pomaranski that his Polish friends had taken a huge risk in sneaking into the tunnels at night to bring him to the *revier*. Nicholas explained that prisoner doctors were not allowed to treat prisoners outside sick-call hours; that if the SS caught them, they both would suffer.

Pomaranski wasn't feeling much pain: Nicholas had given him a shot of an almost unheard of commodity at Camp Dora — morphine. Then, using carpenter's tools, he relieved the Pole's depressed skull fracture and splinted his broken leg using a cement bag.

While he worked, Nicholas kept up a steady flow of conversation, Pomaranski recalled. "He told me that he was an American Air Force major and a doctor. He said that my injuries were serious, but I was young and strong and I would recover."

Pomaranski remembered that Nicholas brought him up to date on the progress of the war and concluded by giving him a pep talk: "He told me: 'Just remember you're a Pole. There are thousands of Poles fighting all over the world. Keep your spirits up. Don't give up hope. We're all going to back home one day.'

"He gave me some food and cigarettes and told me to say nothing to nobody. Then he picked me up and put me in a bunk."

After the war, when Pomaranski had resettled in Terrace, British Columbia, Canada, he filed a claim with the (West) German government for reparations for his sufferings in Camp Dora. Hoping to document his injuries, he wrote the U.S. government for help in locating a former U.S. Army Air Force doctor, a Major John Nicholas, who had treated him in Camp Dora in 1944. He never got a reply.

"If it wasn't for him," said Pomaranski, "I might not have gotten out of Dora alive. He was either a very sincere man or a good actor."

Or, it might be added, a bit of both.

Because of Mainschein, Nicholas' gesture to Pomaranski backfired.

Fear of the SS corporal became so intense that many non-Jewish prisoners in serious need of treatment refused to show up at sick call. Comrades of these desperate men appealed to Nicholas to come into the tunnels and treat them. He consistently declined their appeals, citing the dire penalties that threatened him and them.

But you broke the rules for Pomaranski, they countered. *C'mon, Johnny! You're a good man, Johnny! You can do it, Johnny, can't you?... Okay, Johnny? Please, Johnny! Just for my comrade, Johnny! He's in very bad shape. He's going to die, Johnny, if you don't.*

Camp rules narrowly restricted a prisoner-doctor's movements. He wore a special badge that got him access to the tunnels to treat casualties of rock falls, machinery accidents and SS beatings — as long as they occurred during the 6 a.m. to 6 p.m. shift. Otherwise *helf artz* were banned from the tunnels.

For Nicholas to ignore the ban was to court suicide, so he refused the pleas. Probably he felt bad about turning them down. However, something was about to happen that would change his mind.

A week or more passed during which Mainschein had failed to barge into the dispensary to monitor sick call. Nicholas would have guessed that maybe Dr. Kahr's complaints about SS harassment in the *revier* had finally registered with Kommandant Fourschner. Several more uneventful mornings passed, and Nicholas would have found himself further encouraged. Morale in the terrorized sick-call line was recovering, and Nicholas may have flirted with the dream-wish that the problem had been taken care of; that ideally the chubby little SS transvestite had died a most painful death and gone straight to hell.

But his wish list collapsed when Mainschein stumbled into the dispensary a few mornings later, reeking alcohol, jabbing an accusing finger at six prisoners bent over Nicholas' desk, thermometers sticking out of their rear ends.

Schwartze schwein, did you ask if any of them is a Jew? Mainschein shrieked.

Nicholas tried blinding him in a blizzard of doubletalk. The hapless prisoners cowered in terror. But Mainschein just wouldn't be snowed. He whipped around to the prisoners and screamed at each in sequence: *Are you a Jew? ... Are you a Jew? ... Are you a Jew? ...*

One trembling, emaciated prisoner finally blurted out that he was a Jew.

Mainschein glared at Nicholas murderously. *"You were told no Jews, schwartze! NO JEWS! ... Beat the Jew, schwartze!*

Nicholas didn't move.

BEAT THE JEW!

Nicholas still didn't move.

Mainschein fumbled his pistol out of its holster, cocked it and pointed it at the black man*! ... BEAT THE JEW!*

Nicholas would have known that he was seconds away from a bullet through the head. He began punching the unfortunate Jew. Then Mainschein joined in.

Valtenin Kovalj, a 35-year-old Ukrainian and a patient in the dispensary's temporary ward, watched through an adjoining window. "Mainschein and a great big Negro were beating a man until he remained lying [on the floor] like a log," he told the Nordhausen tribunal. "First they beat him in front of the door. Then they beat him in the dispensary. He was dragged away by the legs. We knew already when anybody is dragged away by the legs he finally comes to the gas chamber."

Beat or be beaten! Hang or be hanged! Shoot or be shot! Kill or be killed! It was the law of survival in Dora.

By late summer of 1944, V-2 production had taken most suitable tunnel space in the Mittelwerk. But tunnel boring still went on — albeit on a relatively minor scale — because Mittelbau GmbH had several military projects that could benefit from the protection from aerial bombing that the Kohnstein provided. So lesser tunnel systems were continually sprouting off the Mittelwerk complex like roots growing from a tree.

At times when the barracks outside were overcrowded, these latter-day tunnel-borers, as their predecessors in the early days, were forced to live in their own excavations. Mainschein phobia had terrorized some of these prisoners from reporting to sick call. Was it their desperate need for treatment, or Nicholas' desperate need prove to himself that *he* was still in control, that changed his mind about breaking the rules?

Sometime after midnight he stole out of the dispensary barracks and walked warily across the grass. An old canvas bag hung from his shoulder. Machinery sounds from the tunnels hummed softly through the night as he stole toward the electrically charged barbed-wire fence. The heavy odor of cheap cigarette smoke, then glowing butts in the inky darkness, confirmed the presence of the familiar Ukrainian SS men patrolling the fence.

Talking his way through the fence was the least of his problems; the big one was gaining entrance to the tunnels.

You can never be sure about these Ukrainians. They'll shake your hand as quick as they'll slit your throat. They wear SS uniforms but they're not Germans. Wearing German uniforms is the way they hate the goddamned Russians.

The Russians had forcibly annexed the Ukraine. When the Germans invaded the Soviet Union in 1941 and rolled into the Ukraine, the people had welcomed them as liberators, not as conquerors. Tens of thousands of Ukrainians had rushed to join the Germans in defeating their common foe, the Russians.

So the German High Command formed a special ethnic division of Ukrainian SS volunteers. But instead of assigning these hardy Slav peasants to front-line combat against their despised Russian conquerors, the SS generals had insulted them by assigning them to guard concentration camps.

The fence was guarded by demoralized Slavs. They performed their duty half-heartedly. For something to break the boredom, they shot at anything that moved. The only other relief from their drudgery were prostitutes. Dora's existence was Top Secret, yet the ladies had managed to rendezvous conveniently at nearby Nordhausen to tap the SS trade.

For his madcap scheme to work, he had to talk his way through the continuous line of sullen, trigger-happy Slavs encircling the prisoners' camp. And he did.

How? One theory is that he turned the incidence of venereal disease among the Ukrainian SS to his advantage.

VD was as common as athlete's foot among them, and *Kommandant* Fourschner was known to strip the hide off any SS man under his command found infected. For this reason, symptomatic Ukrainians dreaded reporting for treatment at the SS hospital: In a matter of hours their names, serial numbers and diagnoses duly surfaced on Fourschner's Morning Report. So the wily Slavs secretly sought out Nicholas for treatment.

Typically they showed up at the dispensary late at night, where he treated them — or put on an excellent pantomime of doing so. Sometimes they brought their own medicines with them. Most of them, however, showed up empty handed, and he "treated" them with whatever he could improvise or looked convincing.

Nicholas may have conducted a thriving, confidential, strictly-after-hours private practice in treating Ukrainian SS suffering from VD. He may have scheduled his nocturnal excursion into the tunnels for a particular night when Ukrainian patients were on fence patrol. He could have negotiated his safe exit and return through the gate on the basis of a simple *quid pro quo*: He kept their secret; they kept his.

Once through the gate, he walked free along the base of the Kohnstein until he arrived at the gaping, 38-foot-diameter mouth of Main Tunnel "A" concealed behind a vast camouflaged awning of canvas. Behind the awning stood a shack manned by four German SS backed up by a heavy machine gun on a tripod.

Something had to have clicked in Nicholas' mind following his forced beating of the Jew. *I'll show that bastard Mainschein who's boss. I'll show Brauny. I'll show Fourschner. I'll show all the SS sons-of-bitches.*

But *they* would never *know* that he had showed them. Only *he* would know. Yet maybe *his* knowing was enough. Maybe that was all that *he* really needed.

A man of Nicholas' bizarre temperament periodically had to reprove to himself that he was still Number One; that he was master of any situation no matter the odds stacked against him. Sometime in the fall of 1944 he put his life on the line when he visited sick prisoners in a small secondary tunnel system inside the Kohnstein.

The bulk of the prisoner population had, by the late summer of 1944, been moved out of the tunnel dormitories and into regular barracks on the outside. But a small prisoner group still bored tunnels within the Kohnstein and lived in them: New, but much smaller, tunnel complexes were being continually bored for a variety of ancillary manufacturing purposes.

Nicholas ventured into the midnight blackness of these tunnels, co-author Matthews was told in the Nordhausen Notebook. Prisoners stirred in their tortured slumber to whispers they could not believe: *Johnny's here! Dr. Johnny's here! ... Wake up, for chrissake! The crazy American's here!*

Along the rocky, stench-ridden aisle between the four-tiered bunks the black man groped his way, they told Matthews. Hands clutched at him in the inky dark. Voices cracked with emotion as he shot the breeze with them, seeking out the sick and injured, dipping into his battered bag, slipping them nostrums for the body and potions for the mind: *Don't let the bastards get you down, guys! They're almost finished. The Americans are halfway to Berlin! We have 'em on the run! Hold on! We're all gonna get back home, guys! Real soon!*

According to the Nordhausen Notebook, the subterranean drama played out near the intersection of Tunnel "A" and Cross-tunnel No. 42, where the SS had almost beaten Pomaranski into the next world. Here stood a vast metal reservoir of water visible from the mouth of the cross-tunnel where Nicholas hunkered down, staring at it. ...

A sign, illuminated by an electric light dangling from the tunnel ceiling, proclaimed in large letters: *NICHT TRINKEN!* (DO NOT DRINK!) Smaller print declared the reservoir water strictly reserved for mixing cement and promised summary execution for *haeftlinge* caught drinking it.

Nicholas and the prisoners hunkered around him as he intently watched an SS guard, a machine pistol slung from his shoulder, slowly patrolling back and forth along the reservoir....

Hey, Johnny! Where are you going?

I feel like a swim. Nicholas began peeling off his sweat-soaked uniform.

Don't be crazy, Johnny!

He edged toward the tunnel mouth, where he shucked the rest of his clothes.

What's that crazy fucking American up to now?

He began edging toward the reservoir.

Holy Jesus! He really means it!

That idiot's going to get himself killed!

The prisoners watched in horror, powerless, barely breathing....

Nicholas reached the reservoir unobserved. He hunkered down in shadow as the guard walked past him and continued on his beat. He waited until the guard reached the far end of the reservoir, then he climbed nimbly over the side of the reservoir and quietly lowered himself into the water. The prisoners froze as they watched the nude black man thumb his nose in the guard's direction, then leisurely cavort in the water, pantomiming a back scrub and a shampoo.

After this colossal caper, which, had there been the slightest miscalculation, could have gotten them all killed, Nicholas casually eased himself out of the reservoir as if emerging from a swimming pool, sneaked back to the speechless prisoners, where he put his clothes back on. They stood around him, stunned, shaking their heads in disbelief.

"He was crazy," Boruch Siedel, a 17-year-old Jewish prisoner, told the Nordhausen Tribunal, "he was completely crazy."

CHAPTER FIFTEEN
THE DISTANT RUMBLE

It had happened so swiftly. His mind must still have been spinning as he huddled in the back of the truck taking him away from Dora, SS guards riding tailgate.

It had been so abrupt. No warning. No explanation. No time.

You are going.

What? ... Now?

Ja, now! Immediately!

But Herr Doktor, I ...

No more questions! This instant! It is all arranged. You will be in charge.

But Herr Doktor, the prisoner wishes to ...

You will find some former acquaintances ... Mach schnell! Mach schnell!

He would have thought that he knew Kahr; that he would at least have dropped a hint beforehand. He would have assumed that by this time they had reached a genuine understanding. But then he maybe wasn't as smart as his ego said he was.

If the prisoners riding with him had heard his thoughts, they'd have laughed cynically: A *haeftlinge* and an SS officer having "an understanding!"

They froze in their frayed uniforms. The guards squatted in their bulky greatcoats.

The thick layer of snow on the road concealed a mirror of ice. The driver eased his truck cautiously through twists and turns, then entered a peaceful farming village of 400 population and 20 steep-roofed houses mantled with snow. About 600 feet on the far side of the village, the truck slowed down as it approached a large, shabby-looking, brick building with a tall chimney.

It was an abandoned factory. Coils and strands of barbed wire embroidered the top edges of high walls enclosing the building. Hundreds of its tiny, square broken windows were patched over with scraps of wood and cardboard.

Then came the inevitable pudding-bowl helmets, zebra-striped sentry boxes and the pungent smell of carbolic....

St. Nicholas is here!!! St. Nicholas is here!!!

The shouts ricocheted off the walls of the old abandoned factory building that was Subcamp Rottleberode, one of 31 subcamps of Dora. The news flashed around that Dr. Kahr had assigned the black American to take charge of the subcamp's *revier*. A small number of ex-Dora prisoners had been transferred to Rottleberode. The exclamation drew them out of their wretched bunks to greet him and shake his hand.

He discovered that Rottleberode already had *two* prisoner-doctors. And one was a *real* physician, the other a *real* medical student. Both were eminently more qualified than he or any of the pretenders back at the Dora *revier*. So why had Kahr drafted him so precipitously?

He met the two prisoner-doctors, Dr. Fernand Maistrioux, a Belgian, and Robert Gandar, a University of Strasbourg medical student. They wasted no time in getting to the basics.

Who runs this place?

The Greens.

Sonofabitch! No need to ask what kind of operation they run.

You don't, Monsieur Nicholas.

So where do they work?

The tunnels. They march them there every morning, back every night.

I make it twenty kilometers each way.

Twenty-two.

What time are they through with roll call at night?

You don't really want to know,

How many guards?

About 120.

Nicholas and the two prisoner-doctors made rounds on each of the three floors of the dilapidated old brick structure and found 1,200 men crammed in bunks like bananas in a crate.

The prisoners bombarded him: *What brings you here, Johnny? How's the war going? When will it be over? When are your soldiers going to come for us?*

The *revier*, located on the second floor, had 20 beds occupied by double that number of sick. But turnover was quick — 25 to 30 corpses a day.

A small hut outside the main building functioned as a morgue. The SS hanged prisoners in a nearby underground cave with bad lighting. And they had a pack of mad dogs that had ripped to death prisoners dumb enough to try escape.

With 1,200 prisoners, the two prisoner-doctors explained to Nicholas, Rottleberode had reached capacity. They could manage the current sick-call load and the long-term patients provided the total population didn't grow any more. But they knew it would.

In the dormitories stood wooden, two-tier bunks jammed so closely that a prisoner struggled to walk between them. Many bunks touched, with three patients occupying the space intended for two.

No indoor latrines. Any prisoner caught relieving himself outside after lights-out risked a bullet. So they urinated in rusty cans and jam pots that brimmed over by morning. The dormitories reeked. Conditions begged for an epidemic

The prisoners worked a 6 1/2-day week, with Sunday evenings off. They marched off *einhocken* (locked elbows) each morning toward the tunnels at Dora, returned long after dark, numb with fatigue, to an hour-long roll call, a slice of sausage and mug of weak soup less nutritious than the swill served back at Dora.

No tables. No plates. No knives, forks or spoons. They ate sitting in their bunks gulping soup from rusty old tin cans. The ate solid food out of their bare hands.

The *revier* occupied a section of the third floor. It was partitioned off from the rest of the dormitory by walls of scrap cardboard. The beds were choked with prisoners suffering from malnutrition, typhus, dysentery and tuberculosis.

Medical supplies remained pathetic, grimly laughable. The hospital's inventory listed one sunlamp, one sweatbox and one closet of ancient medical equipment.

Maistrioux and Gandar answered Nicholas' questions forthrightly but volunteered little: Newcomers always had to break through a solid wall of suspicion to be accepted. "Prisoners didn't fully trust other prisoners in the camp, only those whom they had known on the outside," Gandar explained nearly 30 years later.

Dr. Maistrioux, the Belgian, hailed from the town of Beauriang. He had been in charge of the *revier* until pleurisy had knocked him flat on his back. Maistroux conjectured that as the explanation for why Dr. Kahr had dispatched Nicholas: To fill the temporary vacancy.

It sounded plausible but was way off the mark. Nicholas would be stunned when he discovered the real reason.

Gandar, a skinny Frenchman, was as tall as Nicholas. A member of the French Resistance, he had been captured at Clermont-Ferrand.

Nicholas eyeballed both prisoner-doctors. They looked okay, sounded okay. But 11 months in the system had taught him to assume everyone you encountered was lying until they proved they weren't.

Gandar spoke fluent German. The Rottleberode SS trusted him enough to send him *alone* on trips back to Dora for medical supplies. That would have instantly struck Nicholas as suspicious: Wasn't that a long leash for a German to put on a member of the hated French Resistance?

The caution and doubt were mutual, explained Gandar, who became a professor of gynecology at the University of Strasbourg after the war. "Some of my friends told me that [Nicholas] was a Martiniquean who had been arrested for dealing in the black market in Paris."

After Nicholas had settled in, the French medical student confronted him with the rumors. "He told me on his honor as an officer that he was indeed an American citizen," said Gandar, "that he was on a secret mission for the Allies, and that for security reasons he could not tell me about it."

Nicholas was sticking to the story he had repeated so often at Buchenwald and Dora, and his legend grew with each retelling.

Andre Sabliere, a French prisoner from Lyon, remembered Nicholas from Rottleberode. "He was in charge of medical care and first aid under the command of an SS man," he recalled after the war. "Drugs were quite rare. The sickest ones lay in the infirmary. The less sick ones got one or two days of rest.

"It was very difficult to be found sick. However, he never said no when I asked him for a rest day. That meant life, especially at the beginning, when I had to work and walk every day to and from Stampeida, where [another] underground factory was being built."

At Rottleberode, Sabliere remembered, tin cans and glass jars used by the prisoners to collect their soup ration were in extremely short supply. "After having broken my glass container," he said, Nicholas "gave me his own mess tin, which was vital for me to get a liter of soup."

Bak, the Polish electrician, first met Nicholas when he went to the *revier* at Rottleberode seeking treatment for a severe cold. "He told me ... that he was a major and a pilot in a U.S. airplane shot down over France," he said. "He gave me no medicine but he gave me three days off work.

"In camp he was known as a doctor. He wore a special sign on his uniform that meant doctor's helper. He was completely educated like a doctor."

Gandar returned one night from a routine trip to Dora with more than additional medical supplies; he brought back stunning news: On the same day that Dr. Kahr had abruptly dispatched Nicholas to Rottleberode, Fourschner had discovered *Doktor* Kahr's illegally built barracks and summarily banished him back to his old combat unit fighting the Russians.

The Comrades at Dora's *revier*, who always seemed to know everything, Gandar explained, didn't know where Nicholas had gone, and he — Gandar — hadn't bothered to tell them. Why not? Because he didn't like Comrades. All they knew was they had heard on the grapevine: Kahr screwed up the paperwork on the transfer and the "American" *helf artz* was unaccounted for.

Nicholas could only hope it stayed that way.

Had he been any other prisoner in the maze of the Dora complex's 40,000-some prisoners, running him to ground would have been a needle-in-the-haystack situation. But a black prisoner? Dora's only one? He'd have realized it was only a matter of time before they grabbed him. He'd have felt his belly tighten every morning as his chances for remaining "lost" decreased with every roll call.

If Fourschner didn't get to him first and put a bullet through his head, his old nemesis going all the way back to Buchenwald — Brauny — would.

Which was the other piece of bad news that Gandar had brought back with him: Brauny had been appointed the new kommandant at Rottleberode; the same little *feldwebel* who kept ripping up the convalescent slips that Nicholas handed out; who had threatened to shoot him if American planes ever bombed Buchenwald.

If?... Hell, the Americans had *already* bombed it, Nicholas would have told himself. And not just once, either. Several times. On that basis, Brauny should have shot him a long time ago.That is if he'd really intended to shoot him in the first place.

Whatever the diminutive *feldwebel* had up his sleeve, Nicholas could be sure of at least one thing in his new billet: Kahr had been shipped back to the Russian front. He, Nicholas, had no one running interference for him any more. He was strictly on his own now.

Lying was a way of life in the netherworld of concentration camps. It was a fictional nimbus within which each prisoner clouded himself for his own survival, his primal directive. That meant you never disclosed your last name to any other prisoner unless you had to. Last names made a prisoner vulnerable, pointed an arrow at his family back home. From prisoners and *kapos* on up to *lagereldtesters*: First names only, last names on a need-to-know basis only. Or a phony one.

Lying yesterday to survive today. Lying for that amorphous tomorrow when you'd never have to lie again.

Nicholas wouldn't have argued with that — except that everyone seemed to know *his* last name. Institutional lying seemed to explain his wariness in dealing with people like Gandar, who wandered on too a long a leash for Nicholas' comfort. It tainted everything the French doctor said or did.

So was Gandar really on the level: The stuff about Kahr? Or was he trying to set him up for something?

A few other select prisoners "enjoyed" similar freedom of movement between Rottleberode and Dora. It may have been one of them who came back a few days later with a scuttlebutt update: Jay had disappeared.

Jesus Christ! First Kahr. Now Jay. What the hell's happening?

The Jay news had to have hit where it hurt: Sure, he'd started out a loner and promised himself he'd stay one. But somewhere along the way he'd started looking forward to sneaking their inconsequential little exchanges during roll call. Somehow he'd developed a soft spot for the little Englishman. The thought of him going up the chimney....

Despite his daily dose of self-admonition he'd allowed him *and* Kahr get into his blood stream.

Kahr he'd have admired — SS uniform or not — for bucking Fourschner. Kahr rated tragic and heroic. Besides, he'd always had a thing for doctors, for doctoring, for healing.

That was his mother in him. She and her voodoo herbs and potions. Don't laugh, kid; they worked, didn't they? That's all that counts. *Momma, if you could only see me now....*

Kahr. A guy with real balls.... *Nice try, Herr Kapitan — even if you did keep calling me by my goddamned serial number.*

And now Jay. He'd miss him — even if he didn't understand what the hell he was saying half the time. He always called people "blighters." Standard Cockney. "Poor blighter" this, "poor blighter" that.

Not much to get between. No time. Wrong place. Keep it light. Safe topics. Lousy weather. Lousy food. But he'd have always been curious about what goes on inside the head of an Englishman with a wife at home in a Third Reich getting bombed to Hell by Americans planes and two sons fighting in the goddamned *Wehrmacht.*

He knew where Kahr was — or was said to be. And Jay? A hundred-to-one said he'd gone up in smoke. *See you on the other side some day, Herr Blighter.*

A notice appeared on the camp bulletin board: Kommandant Brauny wanted volunteers for a camp symphony orchestra! Christmas was coming, it proclaimed, and he wished to encourage prisoners to perform a program for the holy season. Volunteers would be excused regular duties for rehearsals!

Had the little sadist undergone a Yuletide conversion? He who'd lashed men on the *bock* until exhaustion? Who'd beaten prisoners to death with a piece of cable? Or was he simply a music lover plagued by bad dreams about former sins and, with the war winding down, freshly repentant and seeking forgiveness?

It seemed like one shock after another: Time was when execution was the price a prisoner paid for getting caught with a radio. Now Brauny was piping official German radio newscasts over the public-address system!

This told Nicholas that the war's end wasn't far off. He tried to tease the truth from claims of massive Allied defeats and masterful strategic withdrawals by heroic German armies.

Surely even diehards like Brauny couldn't deny that the Third Reich was *kaput*. And could he *really* think that after a few Christmas carols everybody was going to kiss and make up?

Nicholas and his prisoner-doctor colleagues kept busy. Their stock-in-trade was carbuncles — the occupational ornament of all slave-laborers. The size of small melons, they spurted pus three feet across the ward when lanced, leaving large cavities that laid bare the bone.

Few instruments were sterilized; hot water was almost unobtainable. The *revier* was forced to get by on a single pair of dull scissors. No cotton batten. They reserved their meager supply of clorethyl for major surgeries, which meant that carbuncles were lanced and scraped clean without anesthetics. Screaming patients were held down by comrades during the crude repairs.

At night men wasting away from dysentery, tuberculosis and pneumonia risked a bullet when they staggered outside the factory into extreme cold to use the latrine. Nicholas scrounged empty oil drums and located them at the far end of the ward.

Weak prisoners sometimes fell into the drums. They had to be fished out and cleaned off — in freezing water. It was impossible to do the job properly; there wasn't enough soap to go around. If they recovered, they stank so badly that they became lepers shunned by the other prisoners.

As the dull December days dragged by, the *revier* became packed beyond capacity. The seriously ill overflowed out into the dormitories. Nicholas, Maistrioux and Gandar worked around the clock.

The outlook was grim, yet the sight of Nicholas, stiff-backed and formidable, always boosted morale. He seldom held court without a clean uniform and his red *helf artz* brassard. And on the long, chilling Sunday evenings that winter, when prisoners stood down from their labors in the tunnels, he ambled through the packed factory building shaking hands, bantering in several languages, glad-handing like a politician up for re-election, always flashing a smile, exhorting the prisoners to hang on a little longer, assuring them that the American Army was on its way, that they would all soon be free men again, home with their families again.

Good theater, and very plausible too: U.S. bombers could be seen and heard regularly high overhead on missions stabbing deep into the German heartland. For many a woebegone prisoner, the contrails streaming in the stratosphere from those B-17s and B-24s streamed into his heart, funding him with hope to last him through another day.

As the only American — or so they believed — that they had ever seen, they reached out to touch the symbol of the deliverance they prayed for.

Christmas came, and they slid their bunks back into the corners of the dormitory to make room for the Rottleberode Symphony Orchestra.[1] Someone had dragged in a fir tree. Margarine threaded with string mimicked candles. For presents they wrapped cigarettes and pieces of bread in chalk-covered paper. In breaking voices they dared to sing of love and hope and goodfellowship; and from across the barbed wire separating them from the SS drifted voices joining theirs in "Silent Night," the Everest of man's most sublime aspiration:

> *Stille Nacht! Heilige Nacht!*
> *Alles schlaft. Niemand wacht.*
> *Nur das traute hochselige Paar-*
> *Holder Knabe in lockigem Haar*
> *Schlaft in Himmlicher Ruh,*
> *Schlaft in Himmlicher Ruh ...*

By January 1945 Rottleberode's prisoner population had swelled to 1,700. That wasn't Nicholas' rudest shock: SS Corporal Mainschein, the gold-tooth-prospector, transvestite and all-around *schwein*, showed up to fill the position of "camp physician." His arrival seemed to coincide with a sudden upward jump in the numbers of healthy, gold-toothed prisoners reported by Mainschein as defying sanitary regulations. He ordered the offenders into the *revier* for shots "to prevent them from catching disease," although it has never been established who administered these injections. Minutes after they died, he inscribed spurious causes of death on their records. Later that night he was reported rummaging with his pliers in the makeshift mortuary outside the building, practicing his dentistry skills.

---

1 It was organized and conducted by Marian Krzyzanowski, a Pole related to Chopin's mother.

Back at the Kohnstein, Fourschner's volcanic fury at having been bamboozled had finally run its course. He had decided to let the illegal hospital barracks stand.

Ever since Kahr's precipitous departure the previous November, they had been the responsibility of the new medical officer, 42-year-old Alfred Kurzke, an SS master sergeant with an M.D. degree. Now, sadly, Kurzke stood glumly in the heavy snow of late January, contemplating the imminent the collapse of the 11-building hospital empire that the Kahr-Nicholas conspiracy had plotted so resourcefully to create.

The direct cause of the disaster was the rapid approach of avenging Russian armies along Germany's eastern borders. The indirect cause: Tens of thousands of evacuees fleeing German concentration camps in the path of the Soviet advance. Massive populations from the death factories of Auschwitz and Gross Rosen were now refugees flooding into all the western camps, bringing their sick and injured with them, and Dora's prisoner hospital was being swamped.

December 1944 had closed on a daily patient head averaging 700 and conditions gradually improving overall. Now, because of the massive influx from the East, the January counts were registering peaks of up to 1,400, this at a time when there were 700 to 800 beds in the entire hospital, forcing two and sometimes three patients to share the same bed. February's projections warned of catastrophe.

If Captain Kahr, wherever his unit was fighting, had not already been crushed under the unstoppable Russian steamroller, this would have crushed him.

As the snows of March blew through the broken window panes of Rottleberode's crumbling and drafty old factory building, the *revier's* tiny wood stove glowed ever more feebly in the center of the floor. Nicholas had burned up all available fuel. How long would the 60 dying men he had squeezed into his little cardboard-walled cubicle last? Within a week most would be in the mortuary, their damp beds already loaded with replacements.

Four months had passed. Surely by now Fourschner had managed to trace him! What was the *kommandant* waiting for? What was Brauny waiting for? They both had declared open season on his hide. They'd had four months to do it. Why hadn't they?

Soviet armored columns in northern Germany were now probing dangerously close to the Peenemunde V-2 research center. General Kammler ordered complete evacuation to the south of von Braun, his research-and-development personnel and families — more than 5,000 people. By mid-March, with the Russians just 25 miles away, the final contingent of Germans evacuees slipped away to relocate in the Harz Mountains area, in a cluster of villages around Nordhausen. Von Braun took accommodations in the hamlet of Bleicherode, eight miles southwest of Camp Dora, close to the V-2 production line.[2]

---

2 Of the 52,000 workers Managing Director Richkey had at his disposal, about 12,000 were German civilians, most of them in supervisory and technical positions over the prisoners. In his stampede to buy more time, he teased the civilians with production bonuses running as high as 50 percent of base pay. To 40,000 *haeftlinge* working 15-hour days and longer, he gave nothing.

Prisoners fell behind on their assigned work quotas at grave risk. On Richkey's watch sub-par production was tagged sabotage.

At the Nordhausen War Crimes trials in 1947 he would be indicted for production speed-ups causing the deaths of thousands of slave laborers. He would also be charged with "making accusations of sabotage for the most trifling incidents which resulted in the hanging inside and outside of the tunnels of hundreds of workers." The indictment would read that "... by failing to use the power inherent in his position (he took) a consenting part in the death by exhaustion and other means of many hundreds of prisoners."

During the entire existence of Dora (August 1943 to April 1945), the SS officially recorded about 15,000 deaths, but witnesses told the war-crimes tribunal that actual deaths numbered between 18,000 and 20,000. The monthly death toll varied, depending on prisoner population, working conditions and medical treatment. It was highest during Stage One, the construction phase of the project (August 1943 to March 1944), when the men toiled in demolition blasting and rock handling and slept in the tunnels. It dropped substantially in Stage Two (April to August 1944), when they were moved out of the tunnels into barracks and V-2 production began to phase in, but it never fell below 500 to 800 deaths per month, despite Kahr's best efforts.

The SS headcount for the prisoner population of Dora and its 31 subcamps on April 1, 1945, a little more than a week before liberation by the U.S. Army, was 40,202. But it has been estimated that a total of some 60,000 prisoners of 26 nationalities sampled its horrors at one time or another during the 19 months of its perverted existence.

The remains of the camp have been preserved by the German government as the Dora-Mittelbau Museum and is open to tourists. In April 1995 some 600

Asleep in the crowded *revier*, Nicholas jerked awake at the sound of a bunk rattling violently. He looked over and saw Alois Josiek, a Pole, writhing wildly in his bunk; he had a 104-degree temperature and oozing eruptions on his face. As the night wore on, the rattling worsened, rousing the sick patients from fitful slumber. Abruptly Josiek leaped out of bed and savagely attacked his neighbors.

Nicholas grabbed him and tried to subdue him, but Josiek had gone berserk and was dribbling syrup from his monstrously pocked face all over the other patients. Nicholas slammed him on the jaw, and the Josiek folded. Nicholas slung him over his shoulder, then talked his way past the SS guarding the old factory building by telling them that the Pole had died from typhus.

Once outside, Nicholas headed for the mortuary hut and laid his inert charge on a mound of corpses. His intention was to keep the deranged Pole in cold storage until his fever passed.

The next morning, however, a report that Nicholas had carried a *dead* Josiek out of the building during the night reached Mainschein's ears. The SS corporal exploded and had the black man dragged before him. He didn't care that Josiek was dead; he was apoplectic because Nicholas and Josiek had left the building *without his permission*. He told Nicholas that he was going to shoot him. First, however, the *schwartze schwein* was to return Josiek to the *revier*. Then he'd shoot him.

Josiek's fever had subsided overnight, and the Pole was back to normal when Nicholas entered the makeshift morgue to get him. Astonished prisoners observed him carry Josiek back from the morgue and deposit him in his sickbed in the *revier*. Immediately the word flashed around the camp: *St. Nicholas brought Josiek back from the dead.*

As April dawned, the inmates of Rottleberode heard the distant rumble of artillery as they stood outside at roll call. Upstairs, as he prepared for the sick call avalanche, Nicholas could hear it too.

The line of scarecrow figures waiting at his cardboard-cubicle dispensary at one end of the *revier* snaked all the way downstairs and outside to the roll-call area.

As they coughed and hacked, wheezed and groaned, they could find no solace in the *revier*. Patients were jammed two and three to a bunk.

former slaves rallied at the museum to observe the 50th anniversary of their liberation by the U.S. Army.

The flimsy cardboard walls bulged. Sick men stumbled off to their dormitory bunks to die in their own filth. The less seriously ill huddled on the floor, poking predatory fingers into stinking vegetables, indifferent to the cloying odors of decaying human and vegetable life all around.

It was still dark on the morning of Wednesday, April 4, 1945, when SS guards stamped thunderously into the prisoners' dormitory. *Alles aus! Alles aus! Alles aus!* They rushed from bunk to bunk, hammering the occupants with rifle butts, prying them out onto the floor. *Mach schnell! Mach schnell!*

Nicholas, Gandar and several prisoners helped carry the sick down the stairs and out onto the parade ground, where they found Rottleberode's 1,700 prisoners and a hundred or so SS staff already assembled.

On the far side of the roll-call area Nicholas would have seen *Kommandant* Brauny at a podium with several officers and NCOs toting machine pistols. One of them was Mainschein.

Brauny *and* Mainschein! Both had threatened to shoot him.

This is it! ... They're going to do it? ... Sonofabitch! This time they're really going to do it!

CHAPTER SIXTEEN
OPERATION COMMANDO 99

"Rottleberode was evacuated at dawn," remembered Sabliere, the Frenchman. "I walked out with a thousand other deportees, and Johnny stood there with the sickest ones from the infirmary. ... I do remember him with gratitude."

Rain drizzled on the shivering prisoners, all the more miserable because their bellies were empty. A detail hurried up and down the ranks, handing out half a loaf of bread and a 1.5-pound can of meat per man. They hadn't seen rations like that in years. They were instantly suspicious. Rumors rustled. ...

The guards barked orders, dividing the prisoners into four separate formations.

Achtung! Achtung! Achtung!

The formations snapped to attention. Brauny emerged from a huddle of black uniforms and announced that the camp was being closed.

The hearts of 1,700 prisoners fluttered. Evacuation? Why? To where? To what? We hear Americans are nearby, but where?

Nicholas, at the head of the sick prisoners, marched off in with one formation, Gandar and Maistrioux in another.

On situation maps at Berlin SS Headquarters, junior officers worriedly slid colored arrows representing the U.S. Army's 1st Division closer and closer to the Harz Mountains.

For *Sturmbannfuehrer* Ludwig Wiegel, who was entrusted with security for slave-labor camps in that area, the time had come to implement Deputy *SS Reichsfuehrer* Himmler's order that no live prisoner be permitted to fall into the hands of the Allied armies.

The order was based on two considerations: One, extreme embarrassment that the walking scarecrows would demonstrate to the world how incredibly inhuman the civilized Germans really were; and two, thousands of Dora slaves carried in their heads pieces of the secret of the Kohnstein and could not be allowed to betray it, even though Hitler's vivid V-2 dream was rapidly fading.

Wiegel telephoned phoned Dora and ordered "Operation Commando 99" into action.

This was a secret, handpicked detail of hardened Greens promised freedom in exchange for herding the inmates of Dora and its subcamps into the tunnels. Bulldozers were to seal off the main tunnel entrances and exits, and poison gas was to be pumped in via ventilation shafts. The bodies were to be entombed within the Kohnstein forever.

In line with this plan, the SS began a massive round-up on the evening of Wednesday, April 4, 1945. On foot, by horse-drawn wagon, truck and train a mass migration of slaves swarmed from the rim of the far-flung Mittelbau complex toward its Kohnstein hub.

The closer the innocent hordes converged on their rendezvous, the denser grew the congestion in the network of country roads leading to the mountain. A colossal jam quickly developed.

From high in the clear blue sky, predatory American fighter-bombers, lured like sharks to blood, relentlessly dive-bombed and machine-gunned the ripening embolism of men and machines glutting all roads and rails into Dora.

The Nazis' grand plan for mass murder in an orderly manner was disintegrating into chaos.

The telephone line hummed between Dora and Berlin. *Sturmbannfuehrer* Wiegel was informed that enemy air attacks were escalating; that a lack of bulldozers and explosives made it extremely doubtful if the tunnels could be sealed off and their occupants entombed as planned. Simply mowing them down with machine guns where they stood was not feasible, Wiegel was reliably informed; it would take too much time and too many SS. Besides, it would litter the idyllic Harz countryside with incriminating evidence for Allied war-crimes courts.

Wiegel switched plans: Forget the Kohnstein! Evacuate *haeftlinge* by all possible routes to central Germany for extermination at Bergen-Belsen, Neungamme, Ravensbrueck and Sachsenhausen, where the mammoth extent of Nazi atrocities could be conveniently concealed in the ashes of crematoriums.

The column in which Nicholas marched numbered about 350 men. All day and into the night they slogged toward the Kohnstein, each prisoner hoarding his private fears. Nicholas, Gandar and Maistrioux walked with the sick, who rode in wagons pulled by fellow prisoners. The sounds of creaking wagons and droning Allied bombers filled the night. The horizon sparkled intermittently with the flashes of artillery fire and exploding bombs.

In the van of the column limped a World War I retread, 60-year-old SS Sergeant Friedrich Teply. His guards rode herd on the flanks.

Teply had ordered silence, but the prisoners murmured excitedly among themselves, relaying to their comrades Nicholas' unrelenting promises that the end was near, that "his countrymen" were not far away, that freedom was just around the corner. These and many more of the "black American's" morale-building assurances were related to co-author Matthews in the Nordhausen Notebook.

After years of captivity, thoughts of freedom bubbled in the anxious prisoners' brains like champagne on empty stomachs. But their excitement sobered in the realization that they were still under SS control; that they knew too much about the V-2 for the SS to let them fall into enemy hands alive.

Teply's old injury slowed him down. Every few miles he halted the column for a rest. Whenever he did, panting prisoners collapsed into the thick grass and heavy bushes by the roadside, where whispered escape plans flared like sparks in dry hay.

And Nicholas? Plans for his personal escape certainly hatched aplenty in his fertile imagination, but they would have collided with the sick. If he made a break for it, he'd have to leave them, and they'd surely die. So what? *Moun fet pou mouri.* Right? Man is born to die.

Every time Teply stopped the column for a breather, impulsive prisoners wriggled off into the uncertain night. Some made good their escape. Some didn't. The guards' hoarse shouts. The typewriter clatter of machine pistols. The crack of rifles. The tormented screams of ragged men leaking lifeblood into darkness.

The pace quickened as Teply detoured his column off the road and through fields and woods. If the enfeebled old SS sergeant was wearing down, it was devastating for the emaciated men heaving the sick wagons.

Gandar's column arrived at Niedersachswerfen, a hamlet two miles northeast of Dora, and marched into the railroad station. Standing on the siding were several trains of open freight cars loaded with prisoners from other subcamps. Men in the various trains began calling out to the prisoners in Gandar's formation. Soon they were shouting greetings and information back and forth at one another. "Many of these prisoners were from Dora," Gandar recalled. "And when they heard we were coming from Rottleberode, they asked: 'Where is Johnny?' He was well known in Dora."

The spirited interchange among the prisoners ended when Gandar's train pulled out of Niedersachswerfen, but there was no sign of Teply's column.

Not until dawn the following day, Thursday, April 5, did Teply's group finally troop wearily into the village. It was one of many railroad junctions designated by the SS as marshaling points for the exodus. The march should have taken Teply's prisoners a few hours, but massive gridlock and relentless American fighter-bombers had bogged them down in a long, time-consuming detour. To the American pilots the railroads were worthy targets, but it's not known whether they were aware that the prisoners were becoming "collateral damage."

The April sun had barely cleared the horizon at Niedersachswerfen when Teply's exhausted formation straggled onto the railroad station platform. Suddenly the public-address system screamed: *Achtung! Achtung! Air raid! Air raid!*

Angry sirens shrieked as silvery airplanes streaked down on the village, scattering bombs and spitting bullets. As they pulled up from their screaming power dives, the planes were close enough for prisoners to see their U.S. markings, read their fuselage numbers and note their distinctive twin tail booms.[1]

The American pilots caught the station platform choked with several thousand prisoners from Rottleberode and other Dora subcamps. The terrified men scattered through showers of zinging lead and ear-shattering explosions. Hundreds cowered helplessly under the station's corrugated-steel cover. Others dashed frantically along village streets to dive headlong into store doorways for cover.

Ammo expended, the American's circled and zoomed homeward, leaving the railroad tracks choked with debris.

---

1 Lockheed Lightning P-38s.

When they left, SS guards rounded up the widely dispersed prisoners and bullied them back into their original formations on the station platform. A senior SS officer stepped forward and barked an order. The prisoners sluggishly climbed down from the platform and began clearing the tracks.

It was mid-morning, and the tracks were clear. Teply hobbled around, out of breath, culling his prisoners from the tangled mob milling around the station. He was standing with Brauny at his elbow when another train puffed into the station. A 15-car freight loaded with more Dora prisoners, it ground to a stop next to Teply's reassembled column, where Nicholas was standing. A few of the new arrivals immediately caught sight of him. According to the Nordhausen Notebook, they waved and called out: *Hello, Johnny! Hey, what's going on, St. Nick? Where are they taking us?* Matthews' informants said that Nicholas didn't respond, which was ominously uncharacteristic of him.

Brauny hovered in the background, leaving Teply and his guards to herd his column aboard empty freight cars hurriedly hooked to the newly arrived train. Fearing the return of the American planes, the guards worked frantically, packing the prisoners aboard. They jammed them in, 120 to a car that could sit 40 in comfort. So everyone had to stand.

Teply ordered a separate detail to load the sick into two canvas-covered freight cars at the rear of the train, and Nicholas climbed aboard one of them.

Gandar and Maistrioux, the other two prisoner-doctors, had disappeared. If Nicholas called out for them, he would have received no answer. They had escaped during the chaos of the air attack, leaving Nicholas on his own with an estimated 200 to 300 sick prisoners.

Brauny climbed up into the locomotive cab with the engineer and fireman and ordered them to move out.

The train chugged out of Niedersachswerfen and headed due north for four days across the rolling Harz landscape under continuous American fighter-bomber attack. Time and again the train halted to avoid jumping the tracks because of bomb craters pocking the tracks. Each time a crater was spotted, the engineer braked hard and backed up — sometimes for 15 or 20 miles — until he reached a railroad junction, where he would take off on a new track, hoping that *it* hadn't been bombed, too.

In the open cars the prisoners, packed in the standing position, froze in the chill night air of early spring. Lacking water, many fainted. When they did, they collapsed onto a metal floor flowing in human waste. During air attacks the sick cowered on their mat of shit-soaked straw still frozen from the plummeting temperatures of the previous night. By day the weak April sun bathed the sick cars' bullet-ridden canvas covering, incubating the stench. The malodorous wretches breathed their last miserably. All Nicholas could do, Matthews was told, was stack the dead in the rear of the car to make more room for those about to die.

Whenever the target-hungry American fighter-bombers screamed down with machine guns belching, Brauny, riding forward in the cab, screamed for the engineer to halt the train and leaped for the thickly overgrown embankment. Scores of frozen, fear-crazed prisoners followed his lead, scrambling stiff-legged for the cover of the surrounding woods with guards pumping volley after volley after them.

It was hard to miss at such close range — for either the SS or the American pilots. When the all-clear sounded, corpses littered the embankment. But with every attack a few more prisoners made the mad dash to freedom.

The SS didn't bother to bury the dead. They probed questionable casualties with the toe of their boot. If an eye blinked or limb twitched, they stitched the owner with lead to make sure. All the while the surviving mass of prisoners burrowed madly into the brushed-tangled embankment like maggots in a chunk of cheese, terrified that their time had come.

When screams and smoke abated, survivors staggered back aboard the freight cars as docile as sheep herded by a barking dog.

The terrible tableau of air attacks repeated several times daily throughout the four-day train trip, which would end at Mieste, a small farming village and railroad junction about 100 miles north of Nordhausen. In normal times the Nordhausen-to-Mieste train trip takes a morning or an afternoon. Because of the ceaseless air attacks, the Teply-Brauny prisoner train took four times longer; the 15-car freight didn't rattle into Mieste station until 10 o'clock on Sunday morning, April 8.

The village was still billowing smoke plumes following an earlier air attack. Stricken villagers stole from the wreckage and appeared on the station platform to stare at the wasted, filthy hulks in the freight cars. Farm wives, *hausfraus* and doddering oldsters pinched their noses against the rancid stench of the evacuees.

They weren't hostile; just frightened, curious. Some waved at the hapless prisoners. One civilian came up to the side of the freight cars and whispered that the Americans were expected in Mieste at any moment — that they were only eight miles away.

In seconds the incredible news was whispered from freight car to freight car. The mood of the cold, hungry, exhausted, anxiety-ridden prisoners switched from despair to quiet delirium.

Back in the sick cars, Nicholas spread the word. But his charges were beyond despair or delirium. They were bleeding, broken, starving, spent, wasted, useless, hopeless. And they knew it. They were calmly indifferent to the news that wreathed the black face in its famous grin. But no matter what he said, he couldn't stir them from their passivity. The Nordhausen Notebook cites his appeal: "Look, we've gone through so much. The Americans are just around the corner. It's only a question of holding on a few days more."

It was the opposite when Brauny got the word. Realizing that, if captured, he faced a war-crimes court, he exploded into action. He ordered the train's engineer to fuel up on coal and water and pull out immediately. But a stalled ammunition train ahead blocked the track.

Brauny fumed while railway workers toiled desperately to shunt the ammo train off the track.

The prisoners, without food and water for 96 hours, barely moved. In the standing position, packed solidly shoulder to shoulder, they had almost solidified in brisk April nighttime temperatures into single cords of human logs.

Nicholas hunkered in the resignation of the hospital cars. He would have checked out how conveniently close to him the village's homes and stores were. *The right guy could swing himself over the side and lie low somewhere among those building ... A healthy guy. Fast on his feet.*

Sunday night came and went, and if he pondered escape, he still hadn't made up his mind when Monday dawned.

The stalled ammo train still hadn't budged. Brauny, perhaps intimidated by disapproving stares from a continuous stream of inquisitive Mieste civilians, ordered the bone-weary prisoners out of the freight cars — a car at a time — to stretch their limbs. He dispatched guards to forage in the village. They returned loaded with cans of meat, bread, potatoes and vegetables.

The personal side of Brauny ordered the provisions distributed among the prisoners. The professional side set up machine guns and spaced guards on the station platform along the length of the train.

From long experience in controlling *haeftlinge* Brauny knew the wisdom of mixing up the nationalities. United they stand, divided they fall. He had made sure to mix them up during the initial loading at Niedersachswerfen.

During the two-day Mieste stopover, a powerfully bonded Polish group, widely dispersed throughout the freight cars since leaving Niedersachswerfen, plotted to regroup, kill the SS and take over the train. Following each air attack the Poles, who constituted the largest ethnic majority in Teply's contingent, had managed to cleverly concentrate their numbers in several adjacent freight cars. About 80 of them were hatching a mass-escape plot.

Nicholas, either forgetting — or ignoring Mainschein's threat to shoot him — approached the SS corporal/medical officer and persuaded him to form a detail to go through the entire train and transfer all sick and dead to the two hospital cars in the rear.

As Nicholas accompanied the detail on its business, he would have kept his ears cocked.

The Polish conspirators, rallying around a naval officer,[2] had organized themselves into three-man escape teams. They had also hidden potato peelings in their clothes and shaped tin cans, which had contained their meat rations, into crude knives.

The Polish would have pressed Nicholas to join the plot, and he would have declined. Gregarious and outgoing on the surface, the quintessential Johnny was a loner, Matthews' informants insisted. He never fully trusted anyone but himself. The Poles, assuming that the "American" felt it his duty to stay with the sick and injured, would have understood.

Around noon a fresh flight of American planes zoomed down from Monday's sky and started blasting Mieste station apart again. Guards and guarded stampeded into streets, alleys and doorways. A fireball engulfed part of the platform. An ammunition car in an adjacent train exploded, detonating thousands of secondary explosions and spewed fiery debris in all directions.

---

2 Wladyslaw Opiala

Nicholas hugged the hospital car's sodden straw. Raising his head cautiously he saw screaming civilians, panic-stricken prisoners, wild-faced SS milling in the smoke. Utter pandemonium. What was he thinking about at that moment?

His brother Vildebart, interviewed many years later, shook his head. "We led separate lives," he explained. "He never said many things openly to me.

"I know that he had a great admiration for [German philosopher Wilhelm Friedrich] Nietzsche, and he had read [*Thus Spoke*] *Zarathustra*. He would say to me: 'Nietzsche was right: Humankind is divided into two parts — slaves and the master, and I am on the side of the master, not the slave. I don't want to be a slave.'

"I know that he never wanted to stay in one place very long. He was always moving."

Yet slave *is* what he was. And he *had* been in one place — German captivity — for almost 17 months. That would have been a lifetime for a man of his incorrigibly gypsy temperament.

In *Zarathustra*, Nietzsche attacks Christianity for the "error" of preserving the weak to the detriment of the strong. He writes of the "hour of contempt," when man realizes the depths of passivity and omnipotence to which Christianity has reduced him. This realization, according to Nietzsche, produces feelings of disgust and self-contempt so strong as to trigger him to violent action to re-assert his power.

Maybe, amid the crash and thunder of the American air attack, Nicholas, hunkered in the oozy straw, crowded by useless bodies, capitulated to the flood of Nietzschean self-contempt. Arms and legs poling out at odd angles. Pumpkin heads on leek-thin necks. Eyes aglaze. Mouths ajar. Transitory groans, coughs, wheezes, feeble farts separating the living from the dead....

Maybe he needed the violent action that seized and overcame him that day and impelled him to lunge for freedom.

Bak, the Polish prisoner, his friend at Rottleberode, watched him vault over the side of the freight car.

To pilots of the U.S. Ninth Tactical Air Force, German trains offered legitimate targets — especially trains operating in a "redoubt." Redoubts were zones selected by Hitler as strategically suitable for a last-ditch stand by Germany's rapidly deteriorating armies. In the top-secret conclaves of Allied Intelligence the Harz Mountains had earned "redoubt" status. It had been tagged as one of several areas where the German leader's exhausted legions could retreat, re-form and hold out indefinitely.

Nordhausen, approximately four miles southeast of Camp Dora, was the bull's eye of the Harz Mountains redoubt target. The mental picture went airborne when the Ninth Tac's fighter-bomber pilots took off on "armed-reconnaissance missions," which meant bombing and shooting up anything that moved, from trucks and *kubelwagens* to tanks and trains. With the once-powerful German *Luftwaffe* almost completely swept from the skies, wreaking havoc unopposed among Dora's chaotic, gridlocked mass migration was like the proverbial "shooting fish in a barrel."

According to testimony given before the Nordhausen War Crimes Tribunal, over a four-day period, evacuation trains out of Rottleberode were bombed and strafed 48 times by U.S. planes flying at altitudes averaging 90 feet. The American pilots innocently caused death and severe injury to countless equally innocent prisoners.

For Nicholas the tragedy was cruelly compounded: From his earliest days in the tunnels he had repeatedly promised them that "my guys" — meaning the Americans — would be their liberators.

In the month leading up the end of the war in Europe, Mieste lay within the operational radius the 474th Fighter-Bomber Group. Pilots gunned their P-38s[3] down a magnificent concrete runway at a captured German

---

3   Unique twin hulls and sleek aerodynamic lines made the Lockheed Lightning P-38 the most unmistakable combat airplane of World War II. The U.S. Army Air Corps operated 27 P-38 fighter groups around the world during the war, and in Europe the Ninth Air Force operated three of these groups. Of the three, only one P-38 group remained operational through the final days of the war — the 474th. All other groups had transitioned to P-47s or P–51s. The airplanes with U.S. markings observed by prisoners attacking Dora evacuation trains answer the description of P-38s; and according to U.S. Air Force records, the only P-38s in operation at this place and time were those flown by pilots of the three squadrons of the 474th Fighter Group.

Each P-38 packed a 20-millimeter cannon, four .50-caliber machine guns, up to ten 4.5-inch rockets and two 2,000-pound bombs.

airstrip at Strassfeld, climbed and vectored on the Harz Mountain redoubt. From their cruising altitude their targets resembled HO-scale models on a tabletop diorama. But below 100 feet, the recommended altitude for "train-bustin," the young Americans attacking Mieste must have mistaken trains crammed with prisoners in faded zebra stripes for soldiers in the field gray of the *Wehrmacht*.

On the ground at Mieste that April day, when Nicholas made his break, Bak and several other prisoners found themselves torn between shielding themselves from the terrifying flame and fury of the American air attack and tracking the black man's escape route. They watched him pound powerfully along the village street, past coveys of civilians cowering in gutters, past strings of shoppers frantically streaming out of store entrances. They recalled the screams of an SS guard and saw him fire a machine pistol: *Halt! Halt! Stop that man! Stop that prisoner!*

Bullets whizzed around him as his legs pistoned him further and further along Mieste's streets abruptly deserted because of the American air raid.

Months of poor food and lack of proper physical exercise surely curbed his effort. Still, "he was a very tough guy," recalled Vildebart. "Nothing was impossible for him. It was a matter of personal philosophy of Jean to do well in everything; to be master of something or somebody — not a slave."

Bak saw Nicholas brought down by a blast from an ancient blunderbuss fired by an elderly German civilian wearing an armband. He lay where he had fallen until the air raid was over. An SS posse dragged him back to the station and dumped him on the platform, where he sat, hugging a bleeding leg, baring his white teeth with each grimace of pain. ...

Brauny strode up and down the station platform, glaring at dismembered chunks of ammunition train blocking the track while a parliament of railroad officials argued about what to do.

The consensus: Teply's trainload was boxed in for the duration. No backtracking this time; certainly not after a *second* trainload of Dora evacuees had pulled in *behind*, just prior to the air attack.

Brauny took command of both trains and ordered a head count. It told him that he was now responsible for 3,000-plus prisoners — less five *haeftlinge* and seven SS killed in the raid, less an unknown number of *haeftlinge* who had bolted during the raid.

Brauny, Teply and Mainschein huddled in subtone consultation, then broke up. Brauny ordered Teply to line up the prisoners on the debris-strewn platform. The old World War I sergeant staggered off, bawling commands.

Corporal Mainschein, picking a path through the rubble, headed for the rear of the train and stopped by the hospital cars. *Alles aus! Alles aus! Everybody out who can walk! Move! Move!* He plucked the pins securing the hinged sides of the freight cars, and they clanged open.

The sick prisoners barely budged. A few, contorting in slow motion, struggled to their feet and eased themselves painfully down onto the platform. Mainschein, whose capacity for brutality rivaled Brauny's, watched in moody silence.

He didn't rant nor rave. Prisoners read his uncharacteristic restraint as a tip-off to terrible things to come.

The ambulatory sick cleared the hospital cars and stood on the platform. Mainschein ordered them forward to join the main formation already marched-ordered and waiting at the head of the train. ...

Around 2 p.m. on Wednesday afternoon, April 11, Teply marched out of Mieste at the head of a reinforced formation of 3,000-plus Dora prisoners. Nicholas struggled to keep up. About 150 SS guards rode herd on the flanks and rear.

Brauny wasn't with them; he had ridden off on a motorcycle. Destination unknown.

CHAPTER SEVENTEEN
GARDELEGEN

Teply led his column eastward — headed away from the Americans and toward the Russians! To prevent stragglers and escapees, he ordered them to march *einhocken*.

The addled, traumatized prisoners were far beyond awareness of the illogical compass heading; and had they been aware, too spent to do much about it.

The column had barely cleared the outskirts of the village when machine pistols chattered in the rear. Back in Mieste station the SS were finishing off the occupants of the hospital cars. When their smoking *Schmeissers* fell silent, an estimated 200 to 300 striped corpses soaked silently in their own blood.

Teply continued to forge eastward. While daylight lasted, he led his column through woods to avoid the predatory American pilots, but the terrain slowed down the march. At night he speeded up by shunting them back onto open country roads.

Prisoners were so exhausted that when Teply called a rest break, many of them dropped off into a dead sleep. Guards had to batter them awake. With each stop, a few men always managed to sneak off. But just as many miscalculated, were cut down in a hail of bullets and left to die where they had fallen.

The main body of prisoners, however, cowed by exhaustion and fear, did exactly what they were told. During rest breaks they lay sheep-like in the damp woods of nascent spring, hearing their racing heartbeats, ignoring the feeble pleas of the dying, listening to the boom of artillery to the west; wondering where the SS were taking them, what they were going to do with them, what the future had planned for them.

The Americans will find them in time, Nicholas reassured them at every rest break.

Throughout Wednesday night they stumbled on. As the sun came up on Thursday they prayed that this would be their day of deliverance. Alas, posterity had pre-empted them for its own plans. It had assigned them roles in a drama so macabre and so repugnant to the norms of civilized society that the German boys and elderly men who played opposite them conspired to hide it from history.

Master Sergeant Brauny had spun out of Mieste on a motorcycle Wednesday afternoon shortly before the sick had been murdered. He'd been gone for hours, then he'd come roaring back and rejoin Teply's column. He, Teply and Mainschein had huddled in whispers by the roadside, then Brauny had roared off again.

What was going on? That's what the prisoners kept asking Nicholas.

That question would have worried him too — especially now that he was staggering and steadily losing blood from the wound in his right calf.

Some of the guards grew edgier, more unpredictable. In furtive twos and threes they shucked their uniforms and weapons and stole into the darkness. Those left behind were turning trigger-happy, riddling prisoners for the slightest sign of straggling.

By first light Thursday, April 12, the guard force had dwindled to less than 100. The booming of artillery vibrated closer, sounding as if the big guns lay just over the next rise. Lifting fog found Teply's starved, shivering and weary formation trekking over soggy farmland, past large mounds of soil blanketing last year's beet crop.

A clutch of voracious Russian prisoners flung themselves on the mounds, scrabbling for beets like hogs downing truffles. The SS sprayed them until beet juice and Slavic blood commingled indistinguishably.

As darkness fell on Thursday, fog reappeared on Teply's formation as it trudged onward. Gradually other marching columns of striped figures appeared ghost-like out of the mist and, without spoken word, merged silently with Teply's column.

As the night wore on, Teply's charges, now numbering approximately 2,700 prisoners, found themselves repeatedly crowded off the narrow, twisting back-country roads by military traffic rumbling imperiously by in both directions. Sharp eyes among the prisoners detected that convoys observed a half-hour earlier heading in one direction were now speeding back in the opposite direction. Also, they noted Brauny's mysterious motorcycle comings-and-goings increasing in frequency.

What's happening, Johnny?

It meant his Americans were close, he told them. *So hold on! Stick together! Don't do anything stupid! We're almost home. We'll make it.*

His advice was whispered from ear to ear.

Around midnight the ever-winking horizon blazed in vast sheets of illumination. The thundering of artillery rolled ever closer....

Suddenly emerging out of the fog, the lead vehicle in a German truck convoy almost plowed into the front ranks of the column before it screeched to a halt. Teply, striding along breathlessly in the van, and others in the front ranks flung themselves out of harm's way with screams of fear and rage. A long series of chain-reaction tire squeals followed.

A motorcycle with a sidecar made its way up to the head of the convoy, and a German officer passenger shouted: *Who's in command here?*

Teply saluted and identified himself: *Approximately 2,700 protective-custody haeftlinge from Camp Dora en route to Gardelegen, Herr Colonel.*

The unidentified colonel declared that American patrols were reported in the Gardelegan area. He ordered Teply to either turn back or find another route. Then the motorcycle revved and carried the colonel off into the fog, followed by the rumbling convoy.

Teply stood there, undecided.

Rumors rustled throughout the formation.

The roar of Brauny's motorcycle approaching stilled their fearful whispers. The little SS sergeant braked hard and skewed to a stop by Teply. They huddled in low tones, then Brauny revved his engine furiously and tore off again in the opposite direction.

What's going on, Johnny?

Nicholas repeated his mantra: *The Americans are close. Very close. Stick together. Nobody takes off on his own. Whatever we do, we do it together.*
Teply ordered his column off the road and into the fields to spend the night.
Neither guards nor guarded slept a wink for fear of each other.

The prisoners awoke at dawn on Friday, April 13, cold, hungry, shivering in the damp grass. Nicholas' friends noted his injured leg puffed larger. They saw him cough blood and grimace when he tried to stand.
They've gone! ... They've gone! ... They've gone! ... The SS bastards have run off! screamed a prisoner.
Heavy heads slowly tilted on stiff bodies. Was it a wishful cry from a fervid dream? Fearfully they crouched, cautiously scanning the trees, bushes and shadows for the loathsome black uniforms, the machine pistols and pudding-bowl helmets. But there was none to see.
We're free, comrades! We're free! We're free! We're free!
The screamed annunciation turgidly percolated the shaven skulls of men who had been in hell so long that *free* held no meaning for them.
A hoarse command shattered the trance: *Back off the road! Quick! Hide! They could return at any moment! Hurry! Hurry!*
Like clumsy beetles, they wiggled into the thick woods.

Seven and a half miles to the west, the 405th Regimental Combat Team of the U.S. 102nd Infantry Division saddled up for an attack on Gardelegen, an ancient town surrounded by a moat. Everything the division's intelligence section could muster pointed to a bloody battle ahead.
Gardelegen, with its 14,000 population and rustic lifestyle, seemed the model for all the farming towns in the Altmark region. The burghers worked hard from dawn to dusk, esteemed the biblical injunctions of thrift, frugality and charity, and went to church on Sunday.
There the town's Christianity drew a line.
Almost 90 percent of Gardelegen's adults were registered Nazi Party members. Most of the still-not-drafted fathers, husbands and sons belonged to the SS reserve forces — for call-up only in special emergency. Scarcely a teenager existed who didn't belong to the Hitler *Jugend*, an organization of armed youth; and it was rare to find a male over 65 not

proudly wearing the armband of the *Volkssturm* (People's Army or Home Guard) hefting an old shotgun or fowling piece in the crook of his arm.

For a town so devoted to Hitler, 35-year-old Gerhardt Thiele was a textbook mayor Hollywood-cast for the part. With dueling scars on both cheeks, he was a university product of educated arrogance and a messianic belief in the Thousand-Year Reich. Far from being the German backwoods *burgomeister*, he personified the archetype Hitlerite.

And his town bore little resemblance to the sleepy, politically apathetic burgs of the Altmark. Townspeople boasted of their military bastion. They took pride in its renowned officer cadet cavalry-training school and its Luftwaffle field on the outskirts. The town was home to a depot recycling German paratroopers into lowly foot soldiers. Bursting at the moat with uniforms, it personified a TV commercial for the fruits of National Socialism

During almost 5 ½ years of war Gardelegen had fought the cause far from the front lines. Farmers had planted and harvested without interruption. Soldiers and civilians had coexisted with little friction. Even when enemy airplanes started buzzing overhead and, with escalating regularity, the airfield's 88-millimeter antiaircraft batteries had started blasting off for real and not in practice, the soldier-civilian compact had endured magnificently.

All Germans — not only those wearing uniforms — were soldiers, Mayor Theile told his citizens. The prayer offered nightly by all devout Germans civilians, he reminded them, had been answered: Vicariously they, too, had been blessed with the opportunity to defend the Fatherland on the field of battle.

When the sun of the early days of April began warming Gardelegen's rooftops, citizens trembled with news of a horrendous incident reported from the nearby village of Kakerbeck: Ten days earlier, escaped slave laborers had ravaged farmers' beet and potato dumps, murdered them, raped and killed their womenfolk. And now SS Master Sergeant Brauny had arrived with the chilling announcement that several thousand *haeftlinge* were only a few kilometers east of their town.

With the Americans already known to be approaching close from the west, Brauny's report ignited *Burgomiester* Thiele's most inflammable nightmare: His town and its women could be plundered by the *haeftlinge* animals before he had a chance to decide whether to resist the advancing Americans or surrender to them. He lunged for the phone and alerted all local party officials plus the commandant of the cavalry school and the commanding officers of the airfield's infantry and anti-aircraft units.

Gardelegen stood on red alert against the *haeftlinge* threat within an hour.

On Wednesday, April 9, the senior military officer in the Gardelegen sector, German Air Force General von Einem,[1] decided that the threatening *haeftlinge* horde just over the horizon must be brought to Gardelegen — one way or another.

Hours after they had awakened in the woods to find the SS gone, Bak, the Pole, and the prisoners around him still argued vigorously over a plan of action. Many opted for moving on *en masse*. Others argued for staying put and waiting out the end of the war where they were. Impatient with the bickering, a few prisoners started slipping off on their own. But most, paralyzed by sudden responsibility for their own lives, waffled painfully.

Nicholas' swollen leg would have severely limited his options, but it makes sense he would opt to stay put until the Americans arrived.

The rationale for his plan would have been that going it alone was too risky. Angry farmers were likely to shoot furtive individuals in stripes for stealing. Or predatory SS posse would mow them down out of spite. Wandering *haeftlinge* herds would be picked off in ones and twos. Pretty soon there'd be nobody left.

A high-pitched, up-and-down wailing penetrated the noisy arguments. Prisoner lookouts reported a small, olive-drab vehicle approaching at high speed. Watching as it whizzed by, they noted a siren mounted on the fender and a large white star painted on the side. From the front bumper flew a large white flag.

The lookouts counted four passengers in uniforms of the same olive-drab color and wearing round helmets like the ones Russian soldiers wore. But they weren't Russians. They were Americans.[2]

Around 11 a.m. came another shout from the lookouts: *German farmers on the road! They're coming into the woods!*

Kill them!

---

1 First name and precise rank unknown.

2 It was a jeep of the U.S. 405th Regimental Combat Team, its siren going full blast. The passengers included staff officers traveling from a forward combat post to Gardelegen to parley over surrender terms.

No! We should hear what they have to say first!

The farmers, plumpish and elderly, ambled into the fields as if they had all the time in the world on this promising spring day. They "talked in a very friendly way," Bak remembered. "'We know you are from the concentration camps. The war is over. There is no more fighting. Come with us. We will send you to Gardelegen. You will be under civilian control, and the Americans will come for you tonight or tomorrow.'"

The fearful prisoners hesitated.

The German farmers, sensing the disbelief of the *haeftlinge,* asked if they had seen the Americans drive past in their little car? Heard their siren? They offered this as proof that they were telling the truth.

Fear tugged the prisoners one way, hunger and thirst the other. They fingered the knives that they had improvised from the tin cans during the train ride from Niedersachswerfen.

The old farmers urged them not to waste time.

"We decided not to kill [them]," said Bak, who had fought in the Warsaw uprising, "but to keep our knives close at hand."

The farmers said that if the foreign gentlemen accompanied them to the nearby village of Wiepke, they would be provided with horse-drawn wagons to transport the sick and the weak.

The remnants of Teply's column trudged several miles into Wiepke, where apple-cheeked farm girls tossed them words of welcome and early-spring flowers. In the narrow street stood horse-drawn wagons for the sick.

As the prisoner formation emerged on the other side of Wiepke and headed for Gardelegen, the sunny morning lay calm before them. The booming of artillery, a distant descant to their trek ever since leaving Mieste, had been replaced by the shuffling of feet, the creaking of wagons, the clopping of hooves, the chirping of birds.

Nicholas would have been traveling with the sick in the two horse-drawn carts.

"Finally we came to a place where we saw lots of Germans in military pants and civilian jackets," said Bak. "They were on the other side of the road, not bothering us. Everybody was told: 'Surrender! Surrender!'

"We felt everything was okay. There were some women with coffee and sandwiches. But we were not thinking of eating. We were thinking: 'We are here, and we have survived the war.' We started talking about who is still living, who didn't make it. The war is completely over. How are we going to get back home? How are my kids? How is my wife? I'll come and visit you.

"The farmers gave us two big horse-drawn wagons. We are sitting on the wagons — 81 of us on two farm wagons.

"Things seemed upside down. The war is over. People are saying to us: 'Are you hungry?' Women. Young girls. Coffee. But no Americans. Everybody said, 'the Americans will come tomorrow. Gardelegen has surrendered. Sure! Sure!'

"But one thing was really shocking [us]: If the war was over, why was some Polish lady by the side of the road crying? 'Don't go there! They're going to kill you! Don't go there!'

"A few guys jumped out [and took off], but nobody bothered them because there was no military about. And we thought: Well, women will be women. Also, if we go back into the woods, they will shoot us because the woods aren't under civilian control."

Nicholas' wounded leg would have robbed him of the independence that he had treasured all his life. If he walked, he would have had to lean on the shoulders of friends. He would have had no choice but to go where they went, and they had chosen the farmers as their Pied Pipers. He was a cripple, powerless to take the bit in his own teeth — the unfailing primal instinct that had always energized his existence.

Columns-of-fives had been consistently the Dora contingent's marching order. Now that autonomic instinct was crumbling into disorder as wariness waned. Gradually the once-compact formation strung out raggedly along the narrow, country road from Wiepke to Gardelegen.

Around noon on Friday, April 13, they started congregating by a high wire fence surrounding an airfield on the outskirts of Gardelegen. They waited for what would come next; alert and anxious, less suspicious but more exhausted.

Buxom farm daughters and wives clustered at the gate in the fence, smiling and cooing welcome, loading the famished men with food and drink. Black bread and braunschweiger soon bloated shriveled bellies. Hot coffee swilled down their gullets, sweetened tongues and washed down indigestible reservations.

Inside the fence and far away in the distance, German parachute troops in mottled-green smocks and black-garbed SS men lazed and laughed in the sun, studiously ignoring the stinking, bedraggled foreigners.

Outside the fence the Dora evacuees languished in little clutches scattered across a large open field. Some of them stood around awkwardly, like guests who haven't been introduced. Some sat stiffly, unsure of how they should conduct themselves. Many lay basking in the noonday sun.

Conversation hummed. The prisoners' sense of security escalated. They began trading experiences, inquiring about missing comrades, talking of families and homes. Others, unable to cope with the reality of freedom, wept, prayed or stared off incomprehensibly into the distance.

Bak and his comrades stood looking around, taking stock of the situation....

Is that Brauny over there? [3] someone queried.

All eyes focused on a far-distant figure lounging against one of the many buildings surrounding the airfield.

He didn't look like the super-neat, by-the-book little roll call leader; the trim little NCO who stuffed his peaked SS cap to make him look three inches taller; the textbook Nazi whose loathing for Dora's only black man had become part of camp lore. This Brauny lounged capless and unmilitary, his SS tunic wide open at the neck, a cigarette dangling from his lips.

Jesus! There's Ripka!

A well-known Polish prisoner from Rottleberode, Ripka was *also* on the other side of the fence. *What's he doing there? And wearing a German Army jacket too?*

Bak and his comrades started talking about Ripka. He hadn't left with Teply's formation, which had been the first of the four formations to march out of Rottleberode. So how had Ripka gotten to Gardelegen *ahead* of the first formation?

The American air attacks, the chaos and all, someone volunteered. Maybe that had something to do with it. Could be that Ripka's forma-

---

3 During the Nordhausen trials, Brauny was asked by the prosecutor, Lt. Col. William Berman, whether he had ever ordered Johnny Nicholas killed. "No, I did not give the order," the Nazi replied. Berman continued: "You say you last saw him alive at Gardelegen." Brauny replied: "Yes." (File 000-50-37, Volume 34, U.S. vs. Kurt Andre et. al., Federal Records Center, National Archives, College Park, Maryland.)

tion didn't have to make as many detours as the other three formations. Fewer detours meant they got here faster. Right?

Maybe, but that didn't explain why Ripka was wearing a German jacket!

The jacket? Forget about that, said someone. Hadn't they seen all those SS at the end, flinging away their weapons, shucking their uniforms so they wouldn't be captured in them? *Take it easy. Old Ripka probably grabbed one to keep himself warm.*

A rifle doesn't keep you warm. How come Ripka's holding a rifle? Hey, Ripka! Ripka! Over here, Ripka! Over here!

The Pole recognized the caller but seemed reluctant to approach the fence and renew acquaintances with Bak and his buddies.

Hey, Ripka! What're they going to do with us?

Ripka lowered his rifle, as if shooting from the hip, and wiggled his trigger finger ominously.

The banter among Bak and his friends at the fence froze. Someone broke the tension and snickered, reminding them that Ripka had been the resident cut-up at Rottleberode.

Looking through the wire fence, Nicholas would have scanned the perimeter of the airfield: barracks, administrative brick buildings, large warehouses, corrugated steel hangars. Parked military vehicles. Soldiers loitering in suspiciously unmilitary postures.

Another in Bak's group spotted two more familiar figures in German tunics. The very tall one could have passed for the twin brother of another Rottleberode prisoner, Wladyslaw Musielewiez.

Holy Christ! It is Musielewiez. Hey, Musielewiez!

Musielwiez came to the fence. He said that his column had arrived in Gardelegen the day before (Thursday). Because his mother was German, he explained, they'd put him in a special detail and tossed him some surplus German Army clothing to replace his filthy, threadbare stripes.

They gave me an old suitcase to put my stuff in. They fed us and put us up in a barracks with a bunch of young paratroopers. Yes, they've been nice to us. There wasn't enough room for all of us in the barracks, so they put the rest of us in there.

Bak and his friends looked at where Musielewiez was pointing and saw a large, brick warehouse, locally known as a barn, about half a mile away, on the top of a small knoll, all by itself.

And you know something? That bastard Brauny! He gave me his cigarette butt and said he's going to turn us all over to the Americans tomorrow morning.

About two o'clock that afternoon Brauny ambled up to the fence. Still bare-headed and smoking, he acted very relaxed, chatting with prisoners as if roll call had never happened and Dora had been a bad movie. He told them he'd been asked to break up the column up into manageable groups. He asked them to pass the word for all *Reichsdeutsch* (German-born) prisoners to fall out and form up.

The German-born prisoners complied.

Volksdeutsch! said Brauny, addressing prisoners born outside Germany of German parents.

Next he called for *Eindeutsch* — prisoners with one German parent.

Then came *Stammdeutsch* — those claiming some distant German ancestry

Having culled the Dora formation of its "German" content, Brauny marched the four formations away, leaving Bak and approximately a thousand other prisoners unable — or unwilling — to claim German blood in their veins.

And where was Nicholas?

Sources don't agree. His old nemesis, Brauny, testified at the Nordhausen War Crimes Tribunal that he last saw the American black man at Gardelegen, near the barn. However, two other survivors of the Rottleberode evacuation said that Nicholas was in a formation that broke into three smaller columns; that he was in the middle column that bypassed Gardelegen altogether.

Interviewed 25 years later, Bak believed that the only prisoners to escape the fiendish reception organized specially for them inside the barn were himself and 10 others.[4]

What happened to Nicholas?

"He was in the barn," Bak said. "I knew Johnny very well. I saw his picture ... It was a Negro."

---

4 According to the records of the Nordhausen War Crimes Trial, 18 prisoners escaped. For their names, see Appendix.

More than two years later, in August 1947, at the Nordhausen trial, Bak would be shown an 8-by-10 photograph of a corpse found in the Isenschnibbe barn. He would identify it as the remains of Johnny Nicholas.

U.S. Army Third Armored Division Troops entered Camp Dora in April 1945 (above) and were greeted with thousands of dead slave laborers (below) as the Nazis beat a hasty retreat. (National Archives)

Only a small number of Dora slave laborers such as this emaciated survivor remained as the Nazis pulled out, most of them close to death from malnutrition, disease and injuries. (National Archives)

The scorched Isenschnibbe barn at Gardelegen on April 14, 1945, a day after the Nazi massacre that killed more than 1,000 slave laborers. The U.S. Army 102nd Infantry Division's 405th Regimental Combat Team liberated Gardelegen. (National Archives)

American GIs inside the Isenschnibbe barn 24 hours after the Friday April 13, 1945, massacre. (National Archives)

U.S. investigators at first thought this badly charred
body outside the barn might be that of Johnny Nicholas.
(National Archives)

Crosses near Gardelegen of
victims of barn massacre. Some
700 are marked "Unknown"
because they were so badly
burned they could not be
identified. U.S. troops ordered
townspeople to bury the dead.
(Peter Hoffman Photo)

A shrine-sculpture was erected on the
remaining wall of the Isenschnibbe barn as
a memorial to the victims who died there.
(Peter Hoffman Photo, 1969.)

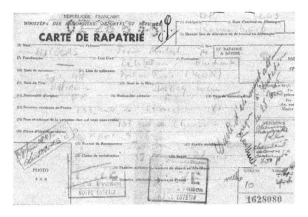

Johnny's French repatriation card after his rescue near
Ravensbrueck as a "DP," or displaced person, in which
he is identified as "Jean Marcel Nicolas." (National
Archives)

COMITÉ INTERNATIONAL DE LA CROIX-ROUGE
SERVICE INTERNATIONAL DE RECHERCHES
3548 Arolsen · République fédérale d'Allemagne

INTERNATIONAL TRACING SERVICE   INTERNATIONALER SUCHDIENST
3548 Arolsen - Federal Republic of Germany   3548 Arolsen - Bundesrepublik Deutschland

Téléphone: Arolsen 434 · Télégrammes: ITS Arolsen

Sz/Go

Arolsen, 16th April 1969

Mr. Hugh Wray McCann   AIR MAIL
1117 Symes Court

ROYAL OAK, Michigan 48067
U.S.A.

Our Ref. : T/D - 603 580
Hist.Nr. 5185
Re : Dr. John NICHOLS

Dear Mr. McCann,

We acknowledge receipt of your letter of 29th March 1969 and
wish to advise you that we have checked our records thoroughly but
could only ascertain the following information :

NICOLAS Jonny, born on 5th October 1908 in Haiti,
Port-au-Prince; Nationality: U.S.A.; Occupation: pilot,
air-force officer; last residence: Paris; was arrested
on 23rd November 1943. He entered Concentration Camp
Buchenwald with Prisoner's No. 44451 on 29th January 1944,
coming from BDS Paris, and was transferred to the Commando
Dora of Concentration Camp Buchenwald on 11th May 1944.
From 13th May 1944 to 5th December 1944 he was in the
"Häftlingskrankenbau Muss. Ambulanz" (sick bay) of CC Buchen-
wald, Commando Dora as camp physician. On 6th December 1944
he was transferred as camp physician to Concentration Camp
Mittelbau, Commando Rottleberode.

Unfortunately we know nothing as to his further fate.

We are not in possession of lists of transports from Concentration Camp Mittelbau, Commando Rottleberode to Gardelegen. For this
reason we are unable to give you any names of prisoners transferred
with these transports, nor the names of about 20 men who, according
to your statement, should have escaped.

We are very sorry that we cannot assist you in a satisfactorily
manner and that we have no further possibility of clarifying the fate
of Dr. John NICHOLS.

Yours sincerely,

A. de Cocatrix
Deputy-Director
of the I.T.S.

Breakthrough letter from the International Red Cross identifying Nicolas as an
American, a pilot and a camp physician. (International Red Cross)

CHAPTER EIGHTEEN

THE SURVIVORS

A stiff spring breeze on a crisp morning carried a malodorous warning to the Americans approaching the Kohnstein. On Wednesday, April 11, vehicles of the U.S. Army's Third Armored Division rumbled cautiously up to the base of the hill. The helmeted liberators stared questioningly at two huge circular holes gaping at them from the side of the mountain slope.

Nicholas, several hundred miles west, continued to hobble along, his spirits no doubt faltering, likely at the lowest ebb of his life. Weak from loss of blood and unable to stand unaided, he would soon find out whether the flowers and food of the ladies of Gardelegen were gifts of compassion or fodder for fools.

Back at the Kohnstein, the puzzled soldiers warily drove their tanks, half-tracks and jeeps toward the prisoner camp. They had to steer through an obstacle course of approximately 600 corpses,[1] most of them

---

1 The liberators of the Kohnstein had been spared the worst; that had been saved for the liberators of Boelcke Kaserne, a Dora subcamp on the outskirts of Nordhausen where SS Commandant Fourschner warehoused prisoners too worn out to be of any value. Of approximately 6,000 prisoners discovered here, nearly 5,000 were dead. "All of them appeared to have been starved to such an extent that there were mere skeletons wrapped in skin," said Sergeant Ragene Farris of the 329th Medical Battalion. "Most of the bodies apparently lay untouched since death had overtaken them, but some were stacked like cordwood under stairways. In almost all bunkers and buildings the living were found lying among the dead.... In one corner was a pile of arms and legs.... [Allied] bombs had ground flesh and bones into the cement floor. Rows upon rows of skin-covered skeletons met our eyes. Men lay as they starved, discolored and lying in indescribable human filth. Their striped coats and prison numbers hung to their frames.... We were battle-tired and combat-wise medics, and we thought there was nothing left in the books we didn't know. Yet in a short period of two

little more than skin and bones, left in heaps exactly where they had been gunned down following the SS decision to kill all who had been missed in earlier evacuations.

The evacuation had begun on April 4. The final transport — of 4,000 — had cleared the gates two days later, and those for whom there was no room on the departing trains or trucks had been murdered.

Major William Castille, an intelligence officer, ventured cautiously into the tunnel and discovered orderly rows of V-2 parts and subassemblies stretching far out ahead of him and in perfect order. All work had come to a complete halt the previous day, but the assembly line had been abandoned with its electric power and ventilation system still running, as if everyone would return after they had eaten lunch. "It was like being in a magician's cave," said Castille.

A quarter of a mile away in the barracks camp, the stunned Americans came upon some survivors. One of them, Michel Depierre, an emaciated French Resistance fighter, lay among 100 prisoners found alive in the *revier*. Between April 3rd and 6th, he told the Americans, the Germans started rounding up prisoners and herding them out of the camp, but that he and the others patients had been too weak to get out of their bunks. The SS abandoned them and cleared the camp on the 7th or 8th. Some 4,500 rocket specialists and German civilian workers had fled the tunnels for their homes in the villages of the Harz Mountains.

---

days I, and many others of the division, saw and lived a story we shall never forget. We found out the full meaning of the words 'concentration camp.'"

"The call went out for medical personnel," remembered Major Edward P. Doyle, the 104th division's Catholic chaplain, "and all units ... were ordered to the camp. Convoys of trucks brought the American troops to assist in the overwhelming task, to save the living if possible and to bury the dead."

Able-bodied German civilians were pressed into service as burial details and ordered to bring with them something with which to transport the bodies. They came with makeshift litters, sheets, pieces of carpet, even doors. They carried the bodies through the town to a prominent hill where a long trench — six feet wide by six feet deep — had been prepared.

"The American GI was superb working under the direction of the equally heroic doctors," continued Fr. Doyle. "Together they saved the savable and put forth their best effort in the cause.... Never have I seen such suffering and anguish. The gun and the pursuit of the enemy were dropped, and all hands turned to the job here and now — helping the helpless.

"It was a busy scene, soldiers as angels of mercy. Their reward, if the patient was able, a smile of gratitude. Deliverance at long last."

Depierre, then 18, arrived in the Mittelwerk in September 1944. He remembered Stage Three as "the most cruel hell. Twelve hours per day or night — 18 hours when we rotate teams — we must carry on our backs extremely heavy equipment in and out of the tunnel. With almost nothing in our stomachs; under the rain, snow, mud; in extremely cold weather, clothed in a poor outfit — wood clogs with fabric on top which gets hooked in everything, and under the beatings of the capos. I touched the bottom of misery and mental distress."

For the next several days the *revier* survivors edged ever closer to death in a maladorous netherworld littered with corpses. On April 11th they thought they were dreaming when they heard the sounds of the approaching Allies. "The first military man that I saw was a Canadian captain who spoke French," Depierre said. "They distributed some food. It was so good, since we were dying of hunger for the past nine months. Only skin was left."

Second Lieutenant M. S. Hochmuth of Ordnance Technical Team No. 1 pulled into the tunnels a few days later, after hundreds of corpses had been removed. He toured the mammoth *Mittelwerk* plant. His report jolted Supreme Allied Headquarters back in Paris: freight cars and trucks loaded with long, slender-finned rockets in "the largest underground plant in the world." [2]

What Hitler's military-industrial establishment had accomplished was nothing short of amazing, revolutionary. The plant's technology was not only light years ahead of the rest of the world; that Richkey had achieved so impressive a mass-production rate under such primitive circumstances in so short a time stunned American Intelligence.

Pentagon brass immediately recognized the massive military advantage that V-2-type weapons conferred on belligerents in any future war.

---

2 U.S. Army war-crimes investigators discovered that of the 58 buildings counted at war's end at the site of the prisoner compound at Camp Dora, eight were prisoner-hospital facilities — the accomplishments of the camp's medical officer, Dr. Karl Kahr, "He was the best of all the SS people, a man with feeling and a human heart," testified former prisoner Julius Bouda of Loyny, Czechoslovakia, before the Nordhausen War Crimes tribunal.

The order was issued to round up what is left of *Mittelwerk*, its product and its scientists[3] and ship them to the United States. On May 22 Special Mission V-2 began evacuating 100 complete rockets from the tunnels and transporting them to White Sands Proving Grounds in New Mexico.[4]

---

3 On April 3 Wernher von Braun, the genius behind the V-2, instructed his personal aide, Dieter Huzel, and the chief designer of the Peenemunde test center, Bernhard Tessman, to gather the blueprints of the rocket and hide them. The two men supervised the loading of three Opel trucks with tons of drawings that had been hidden in an abandoned iron mine at Dornten.

4 Major James Hamill thought that he had adequate time to ship the V-2s back to the U.S. He was wrong. The Allied Powers revised the demarcation lines defining their respective occupation zones, and the Kohnstein was scheduled to come into the Soviet Zone on June 1, drastically narrowing his window of opportunity. In an amazing emergency operation, Hamill drafted GIs with mechanical, engineering and construction skills from all over the American Zone of Occupation to the tunnel factory. His ad hoc army loaded some 300 freight cars with V-2s and subassemblies. Trains cleared the siding at Dora just before the Russian takeover and rumbled across Europe to the port of Bremerhaven. There a hastily assembled convoy of Liberty ships began the transatlantic technology transfer that would one day land American astronauts on the moon.

Hamill neglected to destroy the rockets and parts that he left behind in the tunnels. His failure to do so laid the foundation for the Cold War and the space race between the United States and Russia.

When he left the Kohnstein, Soviet Army Lieutenant Colonel Vladimir Yurasov moved in. He knew nothing about any rockets; he was expecting to find cement-making machinery and equipment because he had been ordered to evacuate a cement plant as part of reparations exacted upon the defeated Germans.

Thus Yurasov stumbled on the second greatest technological secret of the war (after the atomic bomb) by accident. "It's strange," he remarked to his intelligence officer, "this was the most secret German weapon, and the Americans left it for us. Americans are not bad fellows, but somehow too trusting."

Later Yurasov escorted a fellow Soviet colonel through the tunnels. The visiting colonel laughed and said: "The Americans gave us this? But in five or ten years they will cry. Imagine when our rockets fly across the ocean."

The Russians removed all valuable material from within the Kohnstein, rounded up all remaining German scientists and technical personnel and took them back to the Soviet Union. However, even in 2009 some remnants of the V-2 rockets remained inside the Kohnstein.

Shortly afterwards Operation Paperclip whisked von Braun and some 125 of his top scientists to the United States. Bypassing the Immigration and Naturalization Service, they entered the country as guests of the U.S. Army, duly became U.S. citizens and, astride the V-2 and its continually evolving upgrades, formed the scientific spearhead of the U.S. thrust into outer space.

The cost in human suffering and death of that V-2 — and of the triumph for mankind that the rocket made possible — was grimly quantified during the Nordhausen War Crimes trials in 1947.

During the entire existence of Dora (August 1943 to April 1945), the SS officially recorded about 15,000 deaths, but witnesses told the war-crimes tribunal that actual deaths numbered thousands more. The monthly death toll varied, depending on prisoner population, working conditions and medical treatment.

It was highest during Stage One, the construction phase of the project (August 1943 to March 1944), when the men toiled in demolition blasting and rock handling and slept in the tunnels. It dropped substantially in Stage Two (April to August 1944), when they were moved out of the tunnels into barracks and V-2 production began to phase in. Death rates soared again in Stage Three, when production quotas were escalated. The weak and skeletal prisoners could not keep pace with the demand and died.

The SS headcount for the prisoner population of Dora and its 31 subcamps on April 1, 1945, a little more than a week before liberation by the U.S. Army, was 40,202. But it has been estimated that 60,000 prisoners of 26 nationalities sampled the camp's horrors during the 19 months of its perverted existence, and that approximately 20,000 of them perished.

CHAPTER NINETEEN
THE 'BARN' MASSACRE

Romuald Bak had been an electrician in Poland. A natural-born leader, he had been picked as second-in-command by the 80-member Polish group plotting escape on the train trip from Rottleberode.

Intelligent and observant as Bak had been, however, even he had been totally seduced by the maidens, their sandwiches, hot coffee and flowers. "We were in heaven," he said. "We were sure we were completely free."

He had observed Brauny's separating the German formations without hearing any alarm bells. "We figured that maybe they liked to separate the Germans and let them go" he said, "and the foreign people they give to the Americans."

The Germans made no attempt at coercion, he recalled. The prisoners wandered around aimlessly, free to go in any direction they wished. Germans, singly and in groups, kept coming up to them and telling them they would be handed over to the Americans in the morning. "Nobody was thinking about trouble," he said.

The Germans even apologized for not housing them in a regular German army barracks in the town of Gardelegen, which is what they had done for a similar contingent of prisoners the previous night — except for a slight overflow that had slept peacefully in the warehouse, or barn, that Musielewiez had pointed to atop the knoll.

Approximately 15 minutes before twilight, in the company of several other SS men, Brauny appeared again at the gate in the fence around the airport. He swung it open and pointed to the distant barn. You will spend the night up there, he told the prisoners.

They hesitated. Who would be the first to step through the gate?

Brauny said that he wanted to get them all bedded down before dark.

One prisoner stepped through ... then another ... and another.

The SS counted them as they came through the gate.

When approximately a thousand had entered the airfield perimeter, Brauny swung the gate shut, then led them single file slowly along a narrow, worn path up the gentle, quarter-mile incline to the barn.

Once there, he slid two massive doors open and beckoned for them to enter. They hesitated, as they had at the airfield gate, peering nervously into the dark, cavernous interior.

Brauny pointed to the floor, which was thickly covered with straw, and waved them inside.

They huddled hesitantly at the threshold. Why trust him now?

In the deepening dusk an aircraft with American markings droned into the area. When it flew toward the barn, an SS man produced a submachine gun seemingly from nowhere and fired a blast into the sky. Several prisoners screamed and instinctively hit the dirt. The SS man wielding the machine gun laughed and told them to get up. He said not to worry; that he was only firing at the American plane.

The aircraft continued on unharmed and disappeared in the darkness. The prisoners sheepishly rose to their feet and dusted themselves, reassured by the plane's appearance that the Americans were indeed, as they had been told all along, very close.

Brauny stood by the open door, waiting patiently for his Judas Goat....

The Dora men fidgeted on the shoulder of the knoll.

The long line of men, stringing carelessly down the slope into the darkness, slowly wound uphill and fed innocently one by one into the barn's gloom.

Bak entered, fully believing he would be in American hands by morning. "They closed the doors," he said, "and there was enough room for everyone. And maybe after a half-hour everyone was comfortable in the straw. We were happy that maybe it would be a good night's sleep."

It wasn't quite dark when the last man crossed the threshold. The heavy double doors, well greased on their castors, rolled shut, and Brauny silently slipped home the well-oiled bolt.

At the base of the knoll shadowy figures materialized from airport buildings. They were paratroopers. SS. Youths of the Hitler *Jugend*. Old men of the *Volkssturm*. All were armed — including Ripka and 24 other Rottleberode prisoners wearing German Army tunics. When they reached the crest of the knoll, they silently fanned out around the barn, set up *panzerfausts* and heavy machine guns on tripods and aimed them at its four corners.

It was Friday the Thirteenth of April, 1945.

From roof chinks and spaces around the doors the faintest light suffused the musty blackness inside the warehouse, remembered Bak. The farm-sweet smell of straw gradually surrendered to the putridness of 1,016 rancid bodies. In the close atmosphere the temperature rose, incubating the odors, and the ragged men fell drowsy and in twos and threes sank into the soft, two-feet-deep layer of straw.

The kaleidoscopic events of the past nine horrific days since leaving Dora had numbed their minds beyond comprehension. Gray days and chilling nights of standing packed in freight cars. The terrorizing bullets, bombs and rockets of the Americans. Endless nighttime marching. Full-busted maidens. Plump *hausfraus* plying much more food and drink than their shrunken bodies could tolerate.

Over-kill.

They fought sleep, remembered Bak.

Inured to the concentration-camp culture, each man tuned to innate early-warning systems that refused to switch off merely because the war for them was said to be over.

In the gathering warmth Bak and the others began sweating. They started slipping off caps and jackets, uncovering their hollow frames.

The heat, the softness of the straw and the glutting of Gardelegen cuisine conspired in an irresistible narcosis. The drug of long-forgotten comforts seduced their animal wariness. Eyeballs rolled leadenly, and shortly after they had entered the barn, most were asleep.

It was approximately 7 p.m. Twilight time.

Bak remembered a scraping noise — a bolt sliding in its track. A door screeched. He focused on the sound and saw a rectangle of subdued, evening light where one of the twin sliding doors had been pulled aside. A few other prisoners stirred, their watchful eyes fixed on a youthful SS sergeant stepping through the rectangle.

He held something in his hand. He tossed it into the barn, struck a match and jumped back through the opening.

Bak smelled gasoline. A curtain of flame erupted from the straw. Ragged voices shrilled the alarm. A thousand slumbering men exploded to their feet.

"One man was on fire and jumped out through the door," said Bak. "You can see him burning because it was dark. And then another burning man jumped out. Then another, and we hear bang! bang! bang! And so we know we are really in trouble."

A string of desperate prisoners tried to speed through the door but were machine-gunned.

The double doors slid shut, but bullets continued blasting through the wood. The doors opened again. Another gasoline-bomb flew in, exploded into another curtain of fire in the straw.

"But that fire was not stopped," Bak recalled, "and now we are in trouble. The barn is built very solid, so first we organize the Russian guys. They somehow got a door open and started to make a lot of noise. They were very desperate. The door wasn't open, and they were at the door, pushing...."

The Russians rallied as a group. *Urra! Urra! Urra!* they screamed, assaulting the fire with blankets, shirts and jackets, said Bak. When the flames were beaten out, they stood dazed, coughing and gasping from the acrid smoke of burned straw and gasoline fumes.

They're going to kill us!

No, no, the war's over!

I saw the bastard strike the match!

You're crazy! The Americans are coming!

While the arguments raged, one half of the twin sliding doors moved back a second time. Something round, shiny and flaming sailed through and smashed on the ground with the sound of splintering glass, engulfing the front part of the barn in flame.

Urra! Urra! Urra! shrieked the Russians, wading into the flame again, blankets and jackets flailing, feet stamping curling tongues of fire illuminating the terror on their wizened faces.

They're trying to kill us!

The mass of beating, stamping, flailing Russians, now joined by other nationalities, gradually extinguished the flames — and any lingering doubts about what *Burgomeister* Thiele had in mind for them.

The Isenschnibbe barn was a brick-walled building with a tiled roof, measuring 65 feet by 146 feet. Along the inside of the walls stood thick vertical logs supporting log rafters. The only escape route for the terror-stricken prisoners was to break down one or all of the barn's four 14-foot-high, sliding oak doors.

A thousand mouths screamed a thousand suggestions: Climb the vertical logs and break through the roof! Charge one of the doors *en masse* and smash it down! Wait until the Germans open the door again, then stampede through and attack them with mess kit knives and forks, bare hands, anything!

"It was awful," said Bak. "Many people went crazy. They were screaming, praying, swearing, doing everything you can imagine. It was like hell.

"One guy went crazy, and I almost went crazy because of him. He was praying all the time, this Polish guy. I was swearing at him: 'Stop praying! Do something!' I was awful mad at him not because he was praying; he was doing nothing. 'I'm not stopping to pray,' I told him. 'This doesn't help you! Just try to do something!'

"And his praying was most awful for him because I think for almost two hours he was praying. He was not killed, you know. Maybe he was lying between people and accidentally he was not killed."

Seconds previously, freedom and full bellies had anesthetized them. Now the flames roasted them back into the full realization of their deception. They ran around insanely, shouting, screaming, crying, colliding with one another in their terror.

How many times before had each of them stood on the precipice only to snatch himself back — by cheating, by conspiracy, by any means that had insured they would breathe another breath, see another tomorrow?

Outside, *Burgomeister* Thiele stood by his large, black staff car. In his additional capacity as *Kreislieter* of Gardelegen County he had circled the barn with more than one hundred uniformed men and civilians.[1] He and his troop commanders gathered around the car some distance from the barn while SS police dogs yelped and snarled on short leashes.

---

1 The troops surrounding the barn came under the nominal command of a Luftwaffe General von Einem, who was made responsible for the defense of Gardelegen. He had approximately 1,200 troops under his command. In addition he controlled the 101st Airport Maintenance Co., the 73rd Panzer Grenadier Replacement and Training Battalion, *Wehrmacht* military police units at the airport and the Cavalry Remount School. On April 11 an unidentified German general was ordered to Gardelegen. Allegedly he announced to his staff that the prisoners were to be assembled in the Cavalry Remount School and shot, but because the school was in the center of the town and their execution would be too public, it was decided to kill them in the barn. The contingent of troops around the barn seemed to have been token units from von Einem's command, plus those from Master Sgt. Brauny's SS guard force, Thiele's *Volkssturmers* and Hitler *Jugend*, and 25 prisoners who agreed to don German uniforms and participate.

Inside, the crazed prisoners crouched, clutching knives, forks, sticks, stones, anything usable as a weapon.

Gradually the flames were extinguished, and pandemonium abated. Silence engulfed the stygian darkness. The terror-stricken men froze, listening acutely, straining to guess the enemy's intentions. An order shouted. A cough. A footstep. The jingle of equipment.

Far away artillery rumbled.

Where are the Americans?

The desperate men haggled harshly over what to do. They could overcome the teen-age boys in men's uniform and bowl over the old men. But what of the diehard SS men out there?

And if they *did* break out, what then? The barn sat in the starkly flat Altmark meadowland. There'd be nowhere to hide. The nearest woods were hundreds of yards away: They'd be mowed down before they took more than half a dozen long strides.

Unless they waited until complete darkness.

Around 8 p.m. they heard the bolt slide back on the double doors. They saw a hand chuck in another gasoline bomb. The straw again erupted in flames. Fresh pandemonium erupted. They bunched themselves as a human pile driver and rammed one of the side doors, dislodging it from its bottom metal track. They bulldozed themselves through the opening and staggered from the barn in twos and threes with clothes and hair aflame — only to be hosed down by machine-gun and rifle fire.

Blue-and-white-striped bodies fell heavy-headed like wheat before the scythe. But still they came, pushed from behind by screaming prisoners unaware of the pile-up of dead ahead.

Crouching inside the barn, close by the escape hole and screened behind the mound of corpses, the frantic prisoners peered into the darkness outside and sobbed. Freedom was so near but yet so far....

During the lull, some of Thiele's troops crawled up to the dislodged door, flicked meathooks into the pile-up and dragged bodies off into a 50-foot-long slit trench nearby.

For almost three hours the inferno raged. Bullets ripped through the smoke-choked air. Grenades thundered in the confined space, smashing eardrums. *Panzerfaust* (bazooka) rounds tore through the doors. And still the life-hungry wretches lunged through the gap left by the untracked door — only to be shot dead in their tracks.

On the side of the barn opposite the gap, a clutch of prisoners frantically cleared straw from behind another doorway and attacked the earth floor with hands, pieces of wood and tin cans, scraping and burrowing like wild animals to make a fresh escape hole.

"I lay down by a door because there were some holes between the bottom of the door and the ground, and I could get fresh air," said Bak. "I had a knife, and I started to make a bigger hole.... It was easy inside because the floor was dirt, and I was thinking that I could dig a hole and get down below the level of the machine-gun fire."

The doomed men's sunken torsos expanded and contracted wildly as they competed with the hungry flames for oxygen. Dozens capitulated to their terrible exertion and collapsed. Their cries and groans, a vehement chorus of protest and prayer, grew weaker and weaker, until the screams of anguish subsided to a plaintive keening.

Bak continued his furious digging. "I raised myself up momentarily," he said, "and I felt as if somebody had punched me. [A bullet had gone through his jacket and shirt without touching him.] Then a body fell on me. Then another body ... I realize I can get out under this door, but outside the pavement is asphalt. So I cut piece after piece."

Meanwhile, across the barn, near the dislodged door, a mass of men poised as a single muscle about to reflex, clutching crude weapons, ready to rush through. Suddenly one of the front double doors slid open, and a heavy black object flew through the opening.

Grenade!

They dove frantically for the ground.

A deafening thunder sprayed white-hot rain everywhere. Prisoners caught in the sheet of light screamed agonizingly as sticky globs of white phosphorous melted through their flesh.

A thousand miniature straw fires broke out, then coalesced into a single island of flame.

The sounds of snapping blankets, flailing jackets and screams of horror joined the chatter of machine guns and the sharp crack of rifles. Bullets ripped through the doors and tore into their bodies. The prisoners keeled over in droves and fell into the flames.

Courage melted. Discipline collapsed.

The flames feasted on the gasoline-saturated atmosphere. Groups threw themselves uselessly against the massive doors, ripping their nails to blood on German oak. They slapped themselves and wriggled as if ravaged by an itch as the fire licked their bodies and melted their hair.

They milled around in epileptic ferocity in a thousand different directions, wailing and keening. Men with flames dancing on their backs clawed up the vertical logs to get away.

On his side of the barn, Bak continued to chip away at the asphalt. "Finally I broke my knife," he said, "and I thought everything is over for me. So I called out in the Polish language: 'Is anybody still living? Has anybody got a knife?' There were still some people living, and they gave me two knives. The first one broke on the hard asphalt, so I was really careful with the last one while I'm making the hole bigger and bigger. Finally I came to the point where the hole is big enough for my head to go through — but not my ears. And I was thinking: Ears are nothing. You can live without ears.

"At that very moment some grenades exploded close to me, blowing everything in my eyes, and I was thinking: This is the end of the road. But after a few seconds I was still living....

"I'd got this hole under the door large enough for my head to go through. After the grenade was thrown, I couldn't get my head through. [The blast had dislodged the door. Its bottom edge now rested on the ground inside the barn.] I gave up. I was very tired. But a few minutes later a grenade exploded in the same place. Again I was stunned, as if someone had hit me. But I regained consciousness, and I noticed that the door was completely loose on the bottom and still hinged in the metal track on the top. I saw that if I catch the door and pull back, I can crawl under and get out without any trouble. But I waited for some time because it's hard to make a decision to go now or not.

"It was almost dark and I observed that the clouds were very low. There was no moon, no stars and there was a lot of smoke. I was getting a picture of the situation. I could see the Germans immediately outside. About ten of them, maybe 15 feet apart.

"I called out in Polish: 'Is anyone still living? If there is, come here. I have a hole here. Maybe we can get through.' Three guys came. We waited for a while, then we decided to go.

"I pulled back the door, and the first one got out very smoothly. The second one got out very smoothly. I told the third one to hold the door so that I could go. He said no and got very excited. So I told *him* to go next, so I held the door and he got out.

"But it was bad for me: If I had to hold the door for myself, and if it slid back while I was going under it, it would pin me and they'd catch me. I needed someone to hold the door and there was no one. I'd have to do the whole job myself, but I couldn't make a sound because they were very close, maybe 15 and 30 feet away. But somehow I got out.

"When I did, I bumped into the body of the third man out. He was dead. I crawled a little bit further and bumped into another guy. I whispered in his ear: 'You got a knife?' There was still lots of noise — grenades and guns. The massacre was in full swing.

"I started to roll along the ground, meter after meter, and I went through the line. I got dizzy, so I stopped for a rest, and I turned and looked back at the barn. The shooting and all was beginning again, and the barn looked bad. There were many holes in the roof and the doors. There was a lot of light inside. It was just like hell, and I started to run away...."

On Saturday morning, April 14, *Burgomeister* Thiele's car wheeled into the area followed by a truck loaded with elderly *Volkssturmers*. He and several SS jumped out and approached the barn, cans of gasoline in their hands. The previous evening, close to midnight, when all sign of life had vanished from inside, Thiele had inspected the corpses. Several were incompletely incinerated, and he had ordered them doused with gasoline and re-ignited.

Inside, the still-smoking barn lay thick with soot and ash. The inferno had deeply charred the massive vertical logs supporting the roof, some still glowing dull red. Patches of blackened straw still smoked.

More than a thousand ballooned bodies littered the floor in bizarre positions, arms and legs grotesquely intertwined. Phosphorous had eaten through clothes and flesh, laying bare bone. The flames had licked the skin off exposed surfaces, and men who had clutched their faces protectively had pulled their hands away, shedding panes of skin that stuck to their fingers like web in a duck's foot.

Bodies piled in high mounds: Those on the outside layers lay charred and blackened beyond recognition. Those on the inside were less badly burned. Here and there men had succumbed alone, in isolation, the terror on their faces frozen in *rigor mortis*.

Outside the door rammed off its bottom track, machine-gunned corpses lay like human sandbags stacked against a flood. Beneath the bodies, straw had fused with heat-blackened blood and feces extruded during the final agonies.

Thiele nodded to one of the SS, who shouted into the barn: *If any of you are still alive, you will be taken to hospital and given food!*

Several charcoal clods twitched or groaned in response.

The SS man beckoned to an elderly *Volkssturmer* with a machine pistol who riddled those who had naively responded.

When the smoke cleared and the tumult subsided, Thiele ordered the elderly farmer-soldiers to form two groups. One began enlarging the 50-foot-long burial trench prepared the day before; the other started dragging the bodies outside and laying them in neat rows by the barn's western wall.

In the distance, cannon and artillery explosions of the advancing Americans rumbled a descant to the macabre funeral rites. *Mach schnell!* barked Thiele nervously. *Mach schnell!* He watched his men perform their grisly task for a few minutes, then drove off.

The *Volkssturmers* dug and dragged until 5:50 p.m., when the crackle of American M-1 rifles and the thrumming of Sherman tank engines panicked them into flight.

At seven o'clock on Saturday evening April 14, exactly 24 hours after the massacre had begun, the 462nd Regimental Combat Team of the U.S. 102nd Infantry Division moved cautiously through Gardelegen's narrow streets. From alleys and doorways uniformed Germans appeared, their hands in the air, and were shunted off to prisoner-of-war cages.

On Sunday morning, April 15, the combat team's 2nd Battalion was engaged in a reconnaissance of the area surrounding the airfield. Fox Company trudged up the long, gentle knoll overlooking the town, and discovered the blackened brick barn. It stood alone on an expanse of meadowland affording little cover, so the soldiers moved cautiously. The company's point man reached the barn, then waved the rest of his squad forward.

They stumbled upon a trench, three feet deep and 180 feet long, abandoned by the *Volkssturm* diggers. Up through its loose, freshly piled earth poked scrawny arms and legs. Close to the wall of the barn and arranged in neat rows lay bodies blacked, blistered, shriveled, bowed, bullet-riddled — staring skyward through empty eye sockets.

Some of the company's combat-toughened veterans wept openly. The rest were filled with rage.

Divisional commander Major General Frank Keating still had a war to win. Speeding across Altmark at 35 or 40 kilometers a day, his objective was the Elbe River, 30 kilometers east of Gardelegen, and he had little time to spend on the town. Like the dozens of towns he'd already captured, Gardelegen would have to be held by a token force until the rear-echelon troops moved up to secure the area.

But on that Saturday morning, Keating and the assistant division commander, Brigadier General Alonzo P. Fox, had noticed a mysterious cloud of black smoke on the horizon and wondered what was burning. On Sunday morning the report came back that what Fox Company had found demanded the attention of the division's intelligence officer, Lieutenant Colonel Charles Parsons. He, in turn, ordered Captain Horace Sutton, a 25-year-old New Yorker, to investigate.[2]

"When we saw the column of smoke," said Sutton, who commanded the division's Counter Intelligence Corps detachment, "we didn't know what it was. So I took part of my group into town. Nobody was there — no troops of any kind, but plenty of civilians."

Arriving with special agents of his CIC detachment, Sutton got the word that a German force of so-called Werewolves[3] was going to try to retake the town, so investigation of the smoking barn would have to wait.

Before the Werewolves' attack materialized, however, Sutton got a response to his frantic radio call to division for reinforcements. The 462nd Regimental Combat Team detached a force to scout the Gardelegen area and left Sutton with some heavy-duty protection until the full division could move up.

"They were three hairy hours in the afternoon," Sutton said, "when we didn't know what was going to go on. Then these (U.S.) troops came in, and I would judge it to have been ... seven o'clock at night. Then, when the rest of my own CIC detachment came in, we set up command post in a hotel in downtown Gardelegen, sort of like a *gasthaus*, as I re-

---

2 Sutton carried with him a list of more than 150,000 "wanted" Nazis. He worked for the Saturday Review of Literature after the war and became an acclaimed travel writer.

3 Roving groups of armed teen-agers stiffened with SS combat soldiers and used as guerillas behind Allied lines.

member it. A *bierstube* downstairs and a few rooms upstairs. Just a little country hotel.

"We went out to this area and saw a large barn. It was still smoking.

"Inside there were black, charred bodies everywhere, including one that I remember vividly. It kind of reminded me of Rodin's 'Thinker,' with chin on hand and absolutely frozen — if that's the right word. Burned to a crisp. Immolated in that position."

Sutton and his CIC detachment had two immediate objectives: To find the perpetrators and to dispose of the remains of the barn victims. Working through the Gardelegen civilian police chief, he issued an all-points bulletin for *Burgomeister* Thiele and two other county officials believed to have been the ringleaders, then he began questioning other townspeople.

While the interrogations were going on, Sutton's men organized all the local civilians and marched them to the barn. The reason for the object lesson, he explained, was that "... when you went through Germany at that time and you were looking for Nazis, you found no one. No one had ever belonged to the Nazi Party. There was complete disavowal of everything. So when you asked about the [barn-burning] incident, nobody knew anything about it."

For six days following the grisly discovery, troops under the New York captain's command marched apprehensive groups of townspeople — men, women and children — out of Gardelegen along the dusty half-mile to the barn. As they stood there, weeping hysterically and covering their eyes, they heard a grim-faced German-speaking American officer tell them: "You supported and encouraged the regime responsible for this hideous scene."

We didn't know! We didn't know, they protested tearfully.

But the officer pointed to the houses of Gardelegen only 300 yards away. It would have been impossible, he told them, for their occupants not to have heard the screams of the dying.

On April 19, Sutton posted a proclamation in the town square ordering 50 of Gardelegen's wealthiest Nazi Party members to report with shovels to his HQ the following morning at 0800 hours. When the appointed hour arrived, more than 200 stood self-consciously in the street. Flanked by seven tight-lipped GIs from the 327th Engineer Combat Battalion with M-1 rifles, they were escorted to the barn. Twenty minutes later they were exhuming the bodies from the shallow graves and digging new and deeper graves.

At the sight of the grisly remains many wept hysterically.

The tears may have been from sorrow or compassion. But they may also have come from fear that the enraged Americans would do the same to them. To a man, the townspeople turned their heads away, blaming others for the slaughter. A GI guard asked one of the gravediggers, a Nazi Party member since 1934, if he'd known about the mass murder. Yes, he had, the man sobbed, but he'd been powerless to interfere.

The American guards worked the Gardelegen civilians until they were sweating.

Sutton had assigned affluent Party members to unearth the bodies and lower-level Nazis to dig fresh graves. When they saw the grotesque expressions and twisted positions of the dead, practically every man dropped his shovel and protested that he was too ill to go on.

One of the guards, Corporal Steve Bonham, from Wytheville, Va., cursed them roundly and lashed them with the only German word he knew. *"Arbeiten!"* he shouted, pointing toward the trenches with his rifle. "Work!"

The German work party exhumed 574 bodies and carried 442 from inside the barn. Of the total of 1,016, only four could be positively identified by appearance. American grave-registration officers were able to identify 305 by matching still-legible tattooed prisoner numbers with a partly burned prisoner list that was found.

Nicholas' number — 44451 — was not among them.

But 711 of the corpses were ravaged beyond identification. Was he one of *them*, as the photograph that Aalmans, the Dutch investigator, would later indicate to Bak, who would identify it as Nicholas' corpse?

Maybe the black man had been one of the 18, including Bak, who had escaped from the raging inferno. But he is not listed as such in the official Nordhausen archives. Or he could have been among the 711 who could not be identified.

But if Nicholas was not in the barn and had not been found among the dead, where was he?

CHAPTER TWENTY
WHERE'S JOHNNY?

It was too much to absorb too suddenly. They had lolled in the broad, sunswept field within view of their funeral pyre, cruelly tricked by illusion.

Later one wonders how April sun and bloated bellies blunted reflexes honed to razor's edge over years of vile imprisonment. How could slaves sacramentally suspicious of all things German have been blindly led to slaughter?

Especially Nicholas.

Was he also seduced by the lure of comforts long denied? Or did he bypass the barn entirely because his keen instincts warned him? It was too good to be true. Why was Brauny hanging around? Maybe his pain didn't matter anymore. He could try to link up the Americans he knew were only a few miles away. They weren't likely to be U.S. Marines, but they'd do. And they'd see right away from the "A" on his dinghy uniform that he was one of them, and his suffering would be over.

Long after the Gardelegen Massacre two men who knew Nicholas well still couldn't agree on his whereabouts that day.

Bak had known him at Rottleberode. He had always assumed that the "American" had perished in the inferno, yet he had no recollection of seeing him inside the barn. The Pole's assumption had made him certain that the photo he was shown two years later of the blackened corpse in the barn was Johnny.

Roger Arnould, another former Rottleberode prisoner, contended that the formation Nicholas had marched in had broken up into three separate columns as it reached the outskirts of Gardelegen. Arnould, a Frenchman, said that a countryman of his and fellow prisoner observed the Negro in the *center* column; that column had bypassed the barn — never congregated at it or entered it — on its way to the town.

[261]

The only hard evidence of Nicholas' presence at the barn came from his old nemesis, *Feldwebel* Brauny. When Aalmans, the Dutch investigator, was searching for Nicholas, he learned that Gardelegen townspeople had reported seeing a Negro among the prisoners congregated at the fence.

Testing the scenario where Nicholas was last observed outside the barn: We visualize him exhausted by dysentery, ravaged by tuberculosis, hunched on the grass by the fence around the airfield, inspecting his swollen calf, protectively encircled by solicitous friends indebted to him for convalescent slips, many other gratuities and his relentless reassurances that they would survive. Sitting immobile for hours had likely stiffened his blood-encrusted leg. He would have winced and staggered when attempting to stand. It would have been like him to wave aside pridefully the many hands thrust forth to steady him. Some vestige of his famous grin may have hidden the crushing self-knowledge that his impulsive dash for freedom at Mieste, as exhilarating as the rare minutes of freedom had been, had left him a helpless cripple.

He could not have failed to see Brauny on the other side of the fence — nor have forgotten that the little sergeant had threatened to kill him, although why Brauny never carried out the threat also remains a mystery. Surely the mere sight of the hated *feldwebel* had ignited Nicholas' suspicion that something was fishy.

For him, Brauny's transition from swine to Good Samaritan would have been like the eating braunschweiger sausage on a shrunken stomach: too much too soon. What was he up to?

Events would prove how blind the milling prisoner mass was to the most blatant clue of all: Brauny's weeding out the *Volksdeutsche, Reichsdeutsche* and *Stammdeutsch*.

For his unforgivable lapse, however, Nicholas could perhaps be excused. Seventeen months in captivity may have made him sicker than he ever suspected or would admit to himself. He could have contracted a rash of serious ailments from the thousands of sick-call petitioners who had come as supplicants to his dispensary desk. Or just as likely, blood poisoning of his untreated calf wound could have spread. As a victim of general septicemia, his brain would have been functioning far below its peak performance.

If he warned others of his suspicions, no evidence of it has yet come to hand. And if he did, they obviously did not heed his warning. We may have imagined their waving away his admonitions as he had waved away

their offers to help him stand. We may hear them charitably bombarding him with reassurances that after a good night's sleep in the barn they
would all be turned over to the Americans.

As indeed they would. But not in a way those few who survived the
Gardelegen Massacre could ever have imagined – least of all Nicholas.
He would owe his life to a young U.S. Army officer who, in the heat of
battle, would rescue him at Lubz, a town 60 miles north of Gardelegen.

How was this possible, given his wound and physical condition?

Add the numberless other unanswered questions that the young
Haitian scattered behind him on his odyssey from the tropical Caribbean to the bleakness of northern Germany's Luneberger Heath in the
waning weeks of World War II.

The answers may be in his memoirs, which he wrote in English,
French, and German while hospitalized in Paris after the war. But they
disappeared, and until they are found, which is unlikely after more than
60 years, speculation must suffice.

If Nicholas did bend to the blandishments of his comrades and accept the illusory solace of a good night's sleep on the straw, it is not conclusive that he died in the flames: He could have escaped through the
door opening as did Bak and the 17 other known survivors. As for the
handicap of his wounded leg: When life hangs in the balance, adrena-
lin-charged humans have been known to override great physical defi-
cits and perform astonishing feats.

Why did Bak have no memory of seeing Nicholas *inside* the barn?

The terror of burning alive surely monopolized the Pole's every
nerve and sinew. He could not be expected to remember all of the faces
of those around him.

But if Nicholas *was* in the inferno; *if* – like Bak and the other survivors – he got past the mound of corpses piled up by the door opening, and *if* he managed to avoid the withering volleys of the *Jugend* and
Volkssturm, his serious leg wound would have limited his mobility.

If he *walked* to Lubz, away from the advancing Americans, his would
have been a clumsy, beetle-like flight that, in all likelihood, would have
killed him; if not from blood loss, then from the shot and shell of battle:
The path of his flight took him directly into the killing ground between
the U.S. Seventh Armored Division, the German 12th Army and the voracious Russian forces pursuing them.

Perhaps other barn survivors suspended their own fear-crazed flight to lend him their shoulders in gratitude for all that he had given them in his dispensaries at Dora and Rottleberode.

A second scenario assumes that he stayed with his gut feelings, purposely loitered by the airfield fence until dark, then slithered off into the night.

The third scenario places him in the column that bypassed Gardelegen, but Brauny and Bak had seen him there.

No matter which appears more plausible, none explains how, wounded as he was, and seriously weakened from tuberculosis, he traveled from Gardelegen and across the battle zone to Lubz, where a young American lieutenant, in the heat of combat, set aside imminent risk to his own troops to save a stranger.[1]

---

1 Nicholas may actually have traveled much further than 60 miles, which would make his marathon all the more amazing. The Card of Repatriation issued to him on his return to France by the Ministry of Deported Persons and Refugees lists his last place of detention not as Rottleberode but as Ravensbreuck. The hamlet of Ravensbreuck, the site of an infamous concentration camp for women and children, is 35 miles *north* of Lubz. Unless his repatriation card is in error, he traveled not merely from Gardelegen to Lubz but a further 35 miles beyond to Ravensbrueck, then an additional 35 miles back to Lubz — a total of 130 miles.

CHAPTER TWENTY-ONE
ALIVE IN LUBZ

Bumper-to-bumper traffic of the U.S. Seventh Armored Division and hordes of captured German prisoners choked the town of Ludwigslust in northern Germany. Forward movement was barely faster than a man could walk.

The radio in First Lieutenant William A. Knowlton's armored car crackled. It was the voice of his colonel back at division headquarters:

Knowlton, Ludwigslust is as far as we're allowed to go. Our troops are drawn up along a north-south line just outside the town. But I've got a special job for you: I want you to take your troops and contact the Russians. They are somewhere to the east — between 50 and 100 miles. Get someone from their staff and bring him back to me. I want to talk to them.

It's not going to be easy. The German 12th Army lies between you and the Russians. If you get in trouble, I can't send you any help. Don't get too entangled. And let me know your progress. Good luck.

From the turret of his armored car, Knowlton, a slim, 24-year-old West Pointer commanding "B" Troop of the 87th Cavalry Reconnaissance Squadron, looked out on the hopelessly clogged streets.

Fate had arranged for him to meet Nicholas, but their rendezvous would have to wait until he had completed an almost impossible mission.

On Wednesday, May 2, 1945, six days were left before the climactic end to World War II. Several million German soldiers were scattered across northern Germany — all retreating in panic before the Soviets, who had exploded in an orgy of killing, raping, sodomizing, mutilating any enemy soldiers or civilians, children or aged, in the path of advance.

Nicholas didn't know that he was "escaping" into a killing field. Or that his life depended on a young stranger from Massachusetts.

B Troop sallied eastward from Ludwigslust to run the gauntlet between the Sovietss and 200,000 troops of the German 12th Army.

Knowlton's entire force was 95 men, 11 armored cars and 20 jeeps. He had left his assault artillery and half-tracks in Ludwigslust in order to travel light and fast. But speed and mobility wouldn't count against such lopsided odds. His only chance was to stab into the German rear, tag a Russian senior officer and get back to Ludwigslust before the Germans knew he'd even cleared the starting box.

He opened up the siren on his vehicle and ordered his driver to push the pedal to the floor. B Troop tore across the line-of-departure, heading along the main highway running northeast.

It was excellent terrain for a German ambush.

Back in Ludwigslust at division headquarters, radio operators stayed bolted to their headsets as the colonel and his staff paced nervously.

Meanwhile, somewhere in the same stretch of Luneberger Heath, Nicholas would have had to run a similar gauntlet; painfully dragging himself through wooded terrain concealing victory-drunk, trigger-happy Russians and sullen, last-ditch-stand SS.

He'd have moved at night and lain low by day. A stranger in the territory, he'd likely not have had a map. With nothing to guide him but the stars and his intuition, he'd have been a troubled trekker in concentration-camp stripes, fair game for whoever drew a bead on him and brought him down.

He couldn't have known that he was fleeing *toward* his enemies, not away from them: 5,000 Waffen SS infantry and paratroopers of the crack Hermann Goering Parachute Division held Lubz

Others would call his rescue miraculous. Nothing in the Point's textbooks had prepared the young lieutenant for this poker game: Lubz lay *40 miles inside* the German 12th Army's midsection. And 50-to-1 odds favoring the forces blocking B Troop's route to the unknown senior Russian commander with whom he was expected to make contact. To make a bad situation worse, Knowlton had lost radio contact with Seventh Armored HQ in Ludwigslust. He was on his own.

Arriving in Lubz, he found thousands of Germans but no Russians. Should he roll right on through the town and continue his search? No, it would be night soon; he was too vulnerable to ambush in the dark. Better to wait for daylight.

That meant overnighting in Lubz, which had its own dangers.

The town bulged with thousands of surrendered German soldiers who still had their weapons. What if they changed their minds over-night and tried to overpower B Troop? Anticipating this possibility, Knowlton's fallback position was an elaborate masquerade: B Troop would pretend to be the tiny spearhead of a giant Allied armored divi-sion about to thunder into the town at any moment.

If the ruse didn't work, he visualized the corpses of one U.S. first lieutenant and 95 GIs decorating the Lubz town square by morning.

B Troop barely slept. Thoughts of having their throats slit or being riddled was no incentive to slumber. They breathed easier when the sun came up on May 3.

To keep up the charade, Knowlton announced in the town square, which thronged with still-armed Germans, that two B Troop platoons would stay behind to receive the nonexistent armored division. Then, with the little armored-car squadron dangerously depleted, his men rolled out of town. They turned on fake grins for the benefit of stone-faced SS and parachute troops lining the streets. Inside they were pray-ing that they wouldn't have too far to go before they ran into a suitably senior Soviet commander.

On the outskirts of Lubz, B Troop slowed down to make way for hundreds of freed POWs and concentration-camp inmates jamming the highway. Knowlton told his driver to pull over. The bedraggled ex-prisoners clambered around the armored cars and jeeps, hugging and pounding the GIs, jubilantly acclaiming them as liberators.

Wait! called one of a group of escapees[1] huddled by the roadside over a still form. *We have one of your countrymen with us! He won't survive if he doesn't get help! … Can you take him?*

The young West Pointer looked down from his turret at the uncon-scious man. What should he do? He couldn't afford to lose any time on his mission. But the guy was an American; some GI who'd come through hell in a POW camp. *Damn shame if he got this far, then checked out not knowing he'd made it home.*

Decades later, when Knowlton had risen to lieutenant-general's rank and was chief of staff of the U.S. Army's European Command, he recalled "a little southeast of Lubz having a very ill prisoner carted over to our column with a request that we get him back…. We put him on an

---

1 One is believed to have been Jean Haricourt, a Frenchman, now deceased.

armored car until we got him back to Lubz and then may have evacuated him by jeep to a collecting station, where an ambulance was available."

Nicholas' incredible luck had continued to hold.According to the records of France's National Federation of Deportees, Resistance Fighters and Patriots, Nicholas was found by an American "tank" unit on May 3, 1945, near Lubz.

CHAPTER TWENTY-TWO

THEY HARDLY KNEW HIM

To the sad at sick call he was the grinning magician who made bearable the unbearable.

To dispensary confidantes he was an amazing healer.

To others at Dora and Rottleberode he was the mysterious Allied agent captured while on a highly secret mission.

To friends in France and Haiti he was headstrong, brilliant, secretive, untamed and untamable. The youth with the big heart and the grand flair for theatrics whom they "knew like a book" — yet hardly knew at all because deep down he was a loner.

He had the provocative contradictions of that grinning, gregarious type. True, many friends glittered in the orbit of his associations, yet he did not suffer deep relationships. His glad hand, his *bonhomie* and his smile were cosmetics. Behind them he charmingly fended off intrusive associations and preserved his polite, unaffiliated self. They befriended him; he enriched himself on the relationships, amused them but seldom took off his mask.

To family and relatives he was loving son, generous brother, *macho* cousin, troublesome nephew.

To himself, it would seem, he was his restless spirit, forever seeking the reason for everything, impatient with the answers of others, determined to find out why for himself.

And to Uncle Fortune (Bogat), he was a legend.

Interviewed in Port-Au-Prince in1972, the aristocratic old gentleman told the authors that, "Definitely Jean was an Allied agent. He was double agent." Fortune spoke of "high-ranking [German] officers" in "big military cars" that picked Jean up at his apartment near the Eiffel Tower. "He managed to make the Germans believe he was [also] working for *them.*"

What of reports that Jean associated with gangsters and black marketeers in Paris?

"That would have been natural if he wanted to find out [for Allied Intelligence] what the Germans were doing," he replied tartly. "It would not be done by keeping company with the bourgeois and the aristocrats. The fact that he was associated with a certain category of people doesn't mean a hell of a lot because he could get information from them. He could give the appearance of being a black marketeer without necessarily being one himself."

What did Uncle Fortune have to say about persistent reports — despite any supporting documentary evidence — that his nephew had wedged a year of medical training into his crazy-quilt, gypsy-lifestyle.

"Jean was exceptionally intelligent," he contended. "He could have studied a hell of a lot by himself. He could have been further ahead in two years than other students are in four. They told me that he had a [medical] clinic."

Why, when he was arrested, did he give the Germans a Boston, U.S.A., address?

"He *could* have been in the United States. Nobody in the family in Haiti was in contact with him during this time. When he left here, he was in the French navy. But probably he went to the United States, to Boston. He *could* have been there."

When interviewed in 1972, Carmen, his sister, and Madame Nicholas had their own pieces of the puzzle to offer. "He studied medicine in Paris," said Carmen, "and he and Vildebart were in the Resistance...."

"When the Gestapo came to get him," Madame said, "they had surrounded the whole block. He had quite a fight with them. Finally they got him, and he said he was tortured after that. But he always told them that he was working by himself; that he was the only one.

"Vilbebart said that Jean was tortured by the Gestapo to make him talk, but he never did talk. When they found out about his medical ability and the languages he could speak, they sent him to one of the camps and said they could use him."

Madame had gone to her grave believing that Jean had been granted a National Funeral by a grateful government for his war-time services to La Belle France. But no attesting document has ever been found to support her belief.

The last time that she had seen him was in 1937, when he had left for Martinique to enlist in the French Navy. He departed a strapping teen-ager; cocky, strutting, rebelliously impatient with the land that bore him; raging to remake the world in his own, private image. And impulsively, unpredictably affectionate.

Hers was the fretful lot of all mothers who conceive their children in backward islands umbilically tied to poverty and indulge them with liberal educations that abet deep discontent with the limitations of their homelands. And Haiti's slumbering, ancestral inertia dragged as an anchor on Jean Marcel's fretful quest for self-discovery.

A frail woman, Madame Nicolas kept alive the memory of her son until 1974, when, at 84, she died.

Why do birds sing, Moma? Why do doves coo? Why is the sky blue? When will I be big and strong like Uncle Fortune?

Her octogenarian mind echoed with his boyish questions, his restless need to know everything today, his petulance at being told he would have to wait until tomorrow, or until he was a man like his father.

Uncle Fortune could see so much of himself in his teenage nephew that it teared his old eyes. *I'm headed for the USA, Uncle. I'm going to become a Marine. Will you help me?*

Headmaster Tippenhauer, for whom all embarrassment had vanished long ago in his eternal affection for Jean, had been similarly assailed. *Why didn't God ask me if I wanted to be created? ... I would not have done it that way.*

While Madame lived, her son lived on, not only in the family's memories but also within the heavy covers of a thick, glossy-backed album of family portraits as stiff and formal as those of any substantial Victorian family. Within the pictures' scalloped frames he poses at various ages. In one he's about 10 years old, dutifully solemn in a dark suit with knee pants and long socks, an elbow resting on the curved arm of a studio's French Provincial drawing-room chair. In another he's 13, exuding a chubbiness excitable to the maternal instinct; a handsome boy with large, lustrous eyes and a pout accurately portending serious strain on the parental leash.

The memories that she played and replayed as one might replay a treasured old movie were of his pre-teen years, when he was innocent and open. His unfailing smile. His reckless generosity. His extreme vulnerability to the sadness of others. She recalled his compulsive drive to cheer her when she was depressed. A diversionary joke or witty story made up — as often as not — on the spur of the moment.

He worried about suffering and illness in the world. Why had God permitted them? He talked about becoming a doctor and curing the world.

Madame was shown a photograph of him — taken in the late 3os — that she had never seen before. It framed a dapper Johnny in black bow tie and evening dress, cigarette in hand, posing casually outside a Paris emporium, a faint smile on his face. Madame emitted a sustained, high-pitched keening sound reminiscent of an Irish wake. She raised and dropped her head repeatedly as she kissed the 8-by-10 enlargement of the image of the son she hadn't seen in 35 years.

At war's end (May 1945) many Haitians stranded in Paris during the German occupation finally returned home. Several brought reports of him — particularly Drs. Pape and Coicou. The Nicolas family consumed their news ravenously, but, like a meal of empty calories, their stories weren't filling; the picture of Jean that came across lacked coherence and structure. Instead of setting their minds at ease, the accounts of Pape and Coicou raised even more questions about Jean, making his war-time activities more mysterious and him more remote than ever.

Had he been in the French Underground?

"Yes," said Dr. Coicou, who was practicing in Haiti in the 1970s. "He did a lot of work with them." But Coicou would not supply specifics beyond the episode involving the downed American pilot whose escape Nicholas had helped engineer.

Was he a bona fide Allied agent?

If indeed he was, the agencies most likely to have made use of him were the U.S. Office of Strategic Services (OSS), Britain's Special Operations Executive (SOE), the French Section (F) of Britain's Secret Intelligence Service and the *Bureau Centrale de Renseignement et d'Action* (Central Bureau of Intelligence and Action). The *Bureau Centrale*, which was formed by the Free French government in England during the war, worked in limited liaison with OSS and SOE. All four agencies engaged in clandestine operations on the Continent to sabotage the German war effort and gather intelligence.

Until recently the Central Intelligence Agency's Strategic Services Unit was the custodian of the OSS archives. In 1974 the unit's executive secretary, George A. Nole, reported that the OSS had "three individuals with the name John Nicholas" but that "they could not possibly be identical with [Johnny Nicholas] as all were American-born and Caucasian."

That same year, however, a Frenchman, Leslie Atkinson, then representing the Paris office of the U.S. Air Force Escape and Evasion Society, cast doubt on Nole's assurance. During the war Atkinson worked with the famous Comete Line, a highly successful clandestine volunteer force of Belgian women who rescued downed Allied airmen. He claimed extensive first-hand knowledge of French Resistance activities and of the operations of the OSS and the SOE.

He said that the first OSS group of secret agents parachuted into France included a black man.

If true, this would provide a basis for Nicholas' claim to have been a secret agent of the U.S. government, which has never been verified.

A fifth possibility is that he served in one or several French Resistance escape-and-evasion (E&E) networks that, like Comete, rescued Allied aircrews and smuggled them back to England. Therefore it would not be illogical to conclude that his Paris "medical practice" and bogus Heidelberg diploma were part of an elaborate cover for his E&E work. If the Germans were to catch him at it, he likely thought that he would receive far more sympathetic treatment as a POW; by contrast, Resistance operatives usually had all the information they possessed tortured from them, then they were summarily executed.

None of the aforementioned Allied agencies was able to document a record for an operative named Johnny Nicholas, but this is not necessarily conclusive. Thousands of French men and women performed services for Allied secret agencies during World War II. Many of these relationships were formal and contractual, meaning that the individuals were paid and an official record kept of their services. But just as many — if not more — were informal; that is, they were the patriotic gestures of unpaid volunteers whose names were not necessarily recorded.

Nicholas could well have been such a volunteer.[1]

---

1 "No one can even guess the actual size of OSS at its wartime peak. Over thirty thousand names were listed on the agency's roster; but there were countless Partisan workers in the occupied countries whose identities were never known, who were paid OSS money and armed with OSS weapons and performed OSS missions, yet for the most part were unaware that their direction came from Washington. Each field agent employed several local subagents, and they in turn recruited anonymous friends from the surrounding countryside, sometimes numbering in the thousands." — Excerpted from *Donovan of OSS*, by

Europeans would have been more easily taken in by his "American pilot" saga. It would not have been general knowledge among them that the U.S. armed forces were then racially segregated; that the only "Negro" servicemen to receive flight training were fighter pilots; and that those pilots were used exclusively in the Mediterranean theater, never in or over France or Germany.

Only an uncommonly astute prisoner among the many nationalities that Nicholas encountered during his time in Buchenwald, Dora and Rottleberode would have been well enough informed to discover the holes in his story.

Were the German authorities that astute?

Not rank-and-file, concentration-camp-genre SS. However, the officers who interrogated him in Paris after his arrest would have been of a different intellectual caliber. Their stock-in-trade was grilling French Resistance fighters and captured Allied operatives parachuted into Occupied Europe. They, more than anyone else, would have been alert to minute discrepancies in a "cover" story that would have fooled all others.

And yet even *they* were fooled by it, as was Florence, his erstwhile girl friend, who betrayed him. If she wasn't similarly duped, why was he, a hapless Haitian caught innocently adrift in a Paris at war, arrested and banished under the N-N decree?

His apparently was the classic case of the con man: They believed him when he lied and didn't when he told the truth.

Close friends worried that he was working for the Allies *and* the Germans simultaneously. But Dr. Coicou, for one, never bought that idea. "You have to understand that period," he said. "It was a period of great folly. All the French were selling what they called 'wind' to the Germans. They were telling the Germans all kinds of stories.

"And Johnny was a specialist with the story, telling all kinds of things and making believe. He was great with that where the Germans were concerned. But that doesn't mean he was a double agent.

"Maybe he was being friendly with them to get information from them. He lived in a building where they had a radio station — Radio Paris, so he ran into lots of Germans."

What about his relationship with Major Gardemann, *alias* Schmidt?

According to Coicou, there were several hundred Haitians living in Paris during the war, and "they were well protected by a German officer who was on the staff of the German kommandant. This man had married a Haitian ... had lived in Haiti ... We all knew him in Haiti. Johnny knew him well.

"Johnny got all over Paris. He had a car to drive him around. He was using this German. That was part of his personality."

What's the number of the tunnel you work in? What work do you do? What part are you making? What does it do? How does it work? How many do you make an hour? What kind of weapon is it?

These were the kinds of questions that Nicholas sandwiched in with the harmless spiel he transacted with sick-call patients, according to the Nordhausen Notebook. More significantly, they were precisely the questions to which Allied Intelligence desperately sought answers.

Did Nicholas, who consistently identified himself to close associates as an Allied agent, quiz his patients out of casual or calculated motives? This persists as *the* central unresolved question in the Search for Johnny Nicholas.

What was to prevent him from systematically employing his *helf artz* armband to gather V-2 intelligence?

He had the intellect to do it. It would have appeased his quirky temperament as a supreme challenge, a magnificent way of thumbing his nose at the hated SS.

And there *was* a way for him to get his information back to England: A British prisoner, who was – unknown to the Germans – a secret agent in Buchenwald, just 60 miles distant, was in regular radio contract with London. Because the Communists in the *revier* at Dora still maintained communications with their Comrades who controlled Buchenwald, there existed a potentially direct London connection that Nicholas would have needed.[2]

Some years later the tantalizing question whether he supplied the Allies with V-2 information refuses to go away. He had to be aware of the intelligence bonanza begging to be panned at sick call.

However, he may not have been prepared to risk being hanged for it. The quintessential *bon vivant*, he courted the creature comforts.

---

2 Wing Commander Yeo-Thomas, the fabled "White Rabbit" of British Intelligence.

Life was to be lived, not sacrificed. His self-image was narcissistic, not necissarily heroic. He may have been a grateful refugee from the hell of the tunnels, content to ride out his misery in the haven of the *revier*.

From the Nordhausen Notebook repeatedly come the words "crazy" and "mad" in reference to Nicholas' audacity in the most perilous confrontations with the SS. However, those who knew him intimately — as opposed to those who knew him in terms Dora's defensive, guarded, at-arm's-length relationships — invariably reacted to the litany of his "crazy" exploits with a so-what-else-is-new shrug. *If you knew him like we did, you'd know that's just Johnny being Johnny.*

Just-being-Johnny leaped into the Bois de Chene and rescued the drowning victims; stared-down the high-ranking SS officers in the train in Paris; forayed at midnight into the women's camp at Royal Lieu; stood up to Brauny on the roll-call field when the U.S. bombers were overhead; defied the rules when he secretly treated Pomaranski's horrendous injuries after the SS beat him and left him for dead; and skinny-dipped after midnight in the tunnel reservoir....

From Vildebart's letters the family in Haiti learned that Jean had been admitted to the Hopital Lariboisiere in Paris on June 26, 1945 in serious condition with tuberculosis.[3*] "The nurse said that it was the first time they had heard a Negro speak French and German so fluently," recalled Vildebart. "He spoke French, German, English, Spanish, Russian and a little bit of Italian."

Vildebart's wife, Andree, recalled that American officers who visited Jean in the hospital had him recite his story, and that he had done so in several languages and in great detail. [Authors' note: Despite years of searching, these reports have never been found.]

There were few cases of tuberculosis in the U.S. Army in Europe and apparently none in the Hopital Lariboisiere, which had been commandeered by the U.S. Army. Army doctors told Vildebart that they were having special drugs flown in for him from the United States.

---

3 When the war ended and thousands of French prisoners of the Germans were flooding back home, Vildebart began searching for his brother. Eventually the International Red Cross notified him that Johnny was in an American hospital. The French Ministry of Prisoners, Deportees and Refugees issued him Repatriation Card No. 1628080 on June 26, 1945.

When Vildebart and Andree came to the hospital to visit Jean, they were conducted into a spacious ward empty except for a single bed. To isolate the bacillus the doctors had enclosed his bed in a transparent tent. From a nearby metal cylinder thin tubes piped oxygen to his nostrils.

When they first saw him after his repatriation, he looked extremely bloated. They did not specifically recall details about his leg wound, and the hospital could not locate his record while he was there, which may be understandable: It was inundated with ailing and wounded repatriated ex-prisoners during the early months following Germany's May 8 unconditional surrender.

On subsequent visits, however, Vildebart and Andree noticed that he had lost so much bulk that he had become very thin and languished in deep depression.

"That's when the nurse said he started to have hallucinations," Vildebart remembered. "He'd say: 'I gave treatment to this one … and killed this one [with lethal injections.]' He talked as you would in a dream.

"Just a few days before he died he had another hallucination. He saw people burning [alive.] He saw himself killing Germans.

"The nurse came and said: 'Your brother is mad now.'

"He had never told [the nurse] about the [Gardelegen] massacre."

In one respect Nicholas may not have been very different from any other youth: He yearned for a role that would permit him to express his uniqueness and a stage on which to play it out. But there the commonality ends. In one persona he seemingly fused two distinct and often contradictory personalities.

One was the lusty, dynamic, self-aggrandizing, egotistical person well remembered by all who knew him. The second, masked by the *braggadocio*, was a sensitive youth imprinted deeply with a mother's love, a father's sense of duty and the *noblesse oblige* seeded in him by his Catholic schooling as a son in an *elite* family.

Had not the first Johnny, in order to save his life, maneuvered himself into the *revier*, the second Johnny may never have emerged.

Gradually he may have become aware that the sick prisoners, whom he'd initially used as pawns to save his own skin, had come to depend on him for their lives. Perhaps his boyish dream of becoming a doctor and curing the world had not been entirely ridiculed by the stylish cynicism of the smart set in Paris. Whatever was fermenting inside him, it seems to have caused sick-call to become an end for him in itself.

Perhaps his conscience would not let him turn away. Had he become captive to the cunning that had slid him into the *revier*? If so, how ironic, then, that the *helf artz* armband he wore as a prisoner-doctor may have been the most comfortable of all the masks worn in his play-actor's life.

Johnny-just-being-Johnny begs the question: What made *this* Johnny run?

If his friends were ever to comb their memories for a lowest-common-denominator characteristic of him, it would likely be the almost-narcotic-style exhilaration that he got from taking risks.

Psychologists label such personalities thrill-seekers. They are race-car drivers, hang-gliders, sports parachutists, bungee jumpers, downhill skiers and mountain climbers. The class also includes compulsive gamblers and sexual athletes. All in the class crave "life on the edge"; all of them abhor the nine-to-fiveness of everyday life as the grayness of the grave; as the existence of the hermit tethered to a chain forever in a dungeon. They restlessly pursue lives, life styles and hobbies that, unbeknownst to them, infuse their bloodstreams with the hormones that pump them up, self-aggrandize them, inflate them with sensations of omnipotence and omniscience.

But it never lasts, and the exuberance wanes. They descend into the colorless mass of the human herd, where their insatiable addiction drives them, with reckless disregard for danger or consequence, to hunt the "high" all over again.

The syndrome was almost designed to describe Nicholas.

Despite the most modern medical treatment, he grew progressively weaker. In despair, Vildebart revealed to the U.S. Army doctors that his brother was not a U.S. citizen and demanded his transfer to a French hospital. He duly arrived at the Hopital St. Antoine.

As a son of Haiti's upper class, he would have shuddered at the thought of drawing his final breath in a public-welfare institution. The youth who had hungered for excitement and wealth, who had purchased the first at the expense of the second, died on September 4, 1945, at two o'clock in the morning. His body is buried between the graves of two nieces (Vildebart's daughters), who died in infancy, in the Cemetery of Pantin in northeastern Paris.

He had cheated death by four months as a result of his mysterious escape from the barn inferno.

On April 25, 1945, at Gardelegen, 12 days after the massacre, at 2:30 p.m., the U.S. 102nd Infantry Division summoned the citizens of the town and surrounding villages for a full-dress memorial service. It was a Wednesday. The sun flooded from a cloudless sky. The prayer books of a Christian, a Protestant and a Jewish chaplain fluttered in the spring breeze.

Ashes to ashes; dust to dust....

A bugler sounded the funeral dirge. An honor guard in olive-drab woolen shirts stood inside the white picket fence around the graveyard and fired their volleys. Flags snapped as 1,016 bodies — plus two found shot in a nearby woods — were commended to German soil with full military honors.

The division chief of staff, Col. George P. Lynch, addressed the assembled Germans: " ... You have lost the respect of the civilized world...."

As the silent soldiers trooped away and the civilians melted into the landscape, other soldiers erected a sign that reads in English and German:

GARDELEGEN MILITARY CEMETERY

Here lie 1,016 prisoners of war who were murdered by their captors. They were buried by citizens of Gardelegen, who are charged with responsibility that graves are forever kept as green as the memory of these unfortunates will be kept in the hearts of freedom-loving men everywhere. Established under supervision of 102nd Infantry Division, United States Army. Vandalism will be punished by maximum penalties under laws of military government.
Frank A. Keating
Major General
U.S. Army.

Sixty-one years later all that remains of the Isenschnibbe barn is a single wall which the German government preserves as national monument. In front of the wall stands a brownstone sculpting of grim-visaged slaves huddled in agony. Nearby rises a tall metal standard burning a perpetual flame.

Each April 13 Dora survivors from around the world make pilgrimage to the monument. This rapidly-disappearing breed then lingers in the immaculate cemetery abounding in flowers, shrubs and poplars.

Madame Nicolas often pondered the dream she had had before Johnny's birth. The strange man in her vision told her that the child in her womb was a boy and commanded her to call him Jean.

This part of the dream she had related joyfully to all who would listen. But the second part she had kept locked in her heart because the awful images terrified her, sabotaging her peace of mind all during his childhood. And when she had stood at the Port-au-Prince dock with him as he prepared to leave for the French Navy, she had not been able to exorcise the horrific dream from her thoughts.

The stranger, " … was a very sad man," she said in 1972, "and he took me to a cemetery. Not the kind we have here in Haiti, but one with many, many crosses. White crosses. And he told me: 'When Jean goes away from here, you will never see him again.'

"And I said: 'Why do you take me to a place like this?'

"And he said: 'Just remember that you will never see him again when he goes away.'"

The gravesites and layout of Haitian cemeteries are markedly different from those of European cemeteries, and Madame Nicolas had never been outside the Caribbean, yet the scene she had beheld in her dream just before Johnny's birth and described to the authors 27 years later uncannily resembled the Gardelegen Military Cemetery.

How ironic that this talented but impatient youth, who manifested such glowing potential as a free man, would become a legend in the meaningless horror of Camp Dora; would fathom the true depths of his humanity as a *helf arzt* in "the hell of all concentration camps."

And the dream of his mother, *the grand dame* of the herbs, potions and visions, had been frighteningly prophetic: Johnny had remained at the side of the sick during the horrendous journey from Rottleberode to Gardelegen when all instincts shrieked for him to save himself.

Something larger than he had held him there.

And maybe — just maybe — part of what held him was America; or, perhaps more accurately, his heady, invigorating *idea* of the nation he so loved, so ardently wished to be a part of; the impossible dream of an America that became possible to him through the Marines he had known and admired as a youth.

An America that never even knew he existed.

Does Nicholas rate a hero's acclaim?

Hardly does he rank with the Bonhoeffers, the Jagerstatters, the Kolbes, the Niemoellers and those other exemplaries of service above and beyond the call during that period when Civilization faced its greatest threat since Ghengis Kahn and Attilla the Hun. Yet at a juncture in history when cynicism contends with idealism as the New Millenium's coin-of-the-realm, Jean Marcel Nicolas rates at least an Honorable Mention in the voluminous and belated postscripts to World War II now being written.

Although he relished company, loved crowds and courted the spotlight, it was a loner's mask, said Vildebart. He was hunting his niche, craving to be "someone," to be "good" at what he did.

None would have laughed more heartily than he at the idea that he be accorded any acclaim beyond what recitation of his deeds bespeaks of him. In Dora, he would have been the first to acknowledge, he was merely doing what 60,000 other wretches were doing — trying to save his own skin.

His body rests in France, but his spirit may be interred in Gardelegen with his comrades beneath that regiment of Christian crosses and Jewish stars radiating symmetrically across the flat meadowland of northern Germany.

Yet his memory lives far beyond Gardelegen, far beyond Dora. It persists across Europe and North America and around the world in the minds of a waning band of survivors, some of whom still remember him as "St. Nicholas."

"It will have been the emergence of good from evil to establish the exact identity of Johnny Nicholas," said Dr. Gandar, his friend and fellow prisoner-doctor.

"I pay homage to his memory and to the kindness he spread around for lack of appropriate medicine," said Septfonds, his former patient.

Jean Marcel Nicolas left a blizzard of unanswered questions behind him in his restless, questing, intense and often mysterious young life. If the authors could choose one of these questions above all others to be answered, they would pick the question that returns the narrative to the roll-call field at Buchenwald, when Brauny was about to shoot Nicholas because he cheered as U.S. bombers flew overhead.

What did he say to the murderous SS man to cause him to put away his pistol, dismiss him back into the ranks and spare his life?

His exact words, of course, were swallowed up in the majestic, throbbing synchrony of the massive American air fleet overhead, forever lost to history and known only to God. But based on what we believe made Nicholas essentially different from most men of his tender years, we hear him responding: *Herr Feldwebel, if our situations were reversed, and we were in America, and those were German planes flying overhead, I would expect you, as a patriotic defender of the Fatherland, to wave them on enthusiastically to victory just as I did....*

"It would be impossible to meet anyone as extraordinary as Johnny," concluded his countryman, Dr. Coicou. "There was only one man like him in the world."

Johnny Nicholas is buried between the graves of two nieces who died in infancy at the Cemetery of Pantin in northeastern Paris. (Vildebart Nicolas Photo).

Romuald Bak, one of only 18 who survived the Gardelegen barn massacre that killed more than 1,000 slave laborers, emigrated to Canada after the war and operated a motel in Brampton, Ontario. He's shown here with his wife Maria in 1971. (Authors' Photo)

Hugh Wray McCann at the local hospital in Strasbourg,
France, where Dr. Robert Gandar practiced after World War
II. Gandar worked closely with Johnny Nicholas when both
were prisoner doctors at Camp Rottleberode. (Authors'
Photo, 1974).

David C. Smith at the famed Brandenburg
Gate in what then was East Berlin during 1974,
where the bright orange VW he was driving
created a stir. (Authors' Photo)

AFTERWORD
THE SEARCH WITHIN THE SEARCH

For a pair of young journalists The Search for Johnny Nicholas was a challenging, exciting and gratifying international adventure. When we started the Search in 1968 we knew very little about Nicholas. By happenstance McCann first learned meager details about him from South Bend, Indiana, attorney David L. Matthews. A public information officer in 1947 at the Nordhausen War Crimes trials in Germany, Matthews ears perked up when testimony of former slave laborers at Camp Dora, the secret underground complex where the Nazi's V-1 and V-2 rockets were built, repeatedly mentioned Nicholas's name as the only black and only American in the camp. Most of the inmates had never seen a black before, and described Nicholas as "a sensation" who, as a prisoner doctor, was revered for saving hundreds of lives against great odds, assuring them they'd soon be freed.

That was all the information we had about Nicholas. No one knew where he was or what had happened to him. However, Matthews recalled that the chief prosecutor at Nordhausen, Lt. Col. William Berman, had lived either in Portland, Maine, or Portsmouth, New Hampshire.

As we began our search, on a reporter's impulse I phoned Portland information one night. "Yes, we have a William Berman," said the operator. "He's an attorney. Shall I connect you?"

Berman was startled to hear that more than 20 years after the trials he was talking to a *Detroit Free Press* reporter seeking information about Johnny Nicholas. "Yes, I remember his name coming up at the trials, but we couldn't find him. I thought as an American his testimony would be invaluable."

When Berman's 7708th War Crimes Group finished the trials he ordered his Dutch civilian investigator, William Aalmans, to put together a booklet covering the proceedings. "I think I still have a copy in the attic," he told me. "If I can find it I'll send it to you."

[285]

A few days later the booklet arrived, stuffed with information about Camp Dora and its 31 subcamps where 15,000 slave laborers died between 1943 and 1945 from numerous causes including outright murder, beatings, tuberculosis and other diseases and, most of all, malnutrition. Although the crimes were perpetrated near Nordhausen, the trials were held at Camp Dachau outside Munich. Nineteen Nazis were tried and 18 were convicted.

Berman said a photo of a body taken by U.S. Army photographer following a massacre of Dora victims near the city of Gardelegen was thought to be that of Nicholas, but Aalmans reported in the booklet that he was seen elsewhere two weeks later. Where? He didn't say.

Berman and his staff left for the States without solving the mystery of Johnny Nicholas, but McCann and I moved into high gear. We first checked with all of the U.S. military services, likely government agencies, the Selective Service and other sources, but struck out. Because the prisoners had testified Nicholas told them he had parachuted into France on a secret mission, we checked with the Office of Strategic Services (OSS), the Central Intelligence Agency (CIA), and military and civilian intelligence organizations in the U.S., Great Britain and France. None could, or would, claim him as an agent. The French Resistance and Underground organizations we contacted couldn't identify him, either, but as we soon learned the names of most of these freedom fighters were not found on official rosters. The OSS also hired thousands of independent foreign-based agents whose names and missions were never revealed.

We also tracked down other American officers involved in the trials and picked up some valuable information, but nothing that led us to finding Nicholas. We thought Aalmans might provide some leads so we sent a blind note to him in his hometown of Kerkrade, the Netherlands, and heard from his brother, Hans. Yes, William was still alive. He was working at the Dutch Embassy in Madrid. We checked with Madrid and were told he had been assigned to the Dutch embassy in Lima, Peru. We tracked him down there but he never responded. Did he have something to hide?

Armed with the Berman booklet we embarked in spring 1969 for the National Archives in Suitland, Maryland, for four days of intensive research into the Nordhausen case. We were greeted with a massive 13 cubic feet of typed transcripts, some of which were still classified or heavily blacked out. To speed the research we read pertinent passages and testimony into tape recorders, transcribing them when we returned to Detroit.

We didn't "find" Johnny Nicholas, but we collected exhaustive testimony alluding to Nicholas and his exploits. We also unearthed the names and city and country addresses of dozens of prisoners who had known Nicholas at Buchenwald, Camp Dora and Dora's subcamp Rottelberode.

We thought we'd hit the jackpot when we read the testimony of a British prisoner named Cecil Alfred Francis Jay, a carpenter at Dora and the only English speaking prisoner to testify. He knew Nicholas well. His home was said to be Springe, Germany, and that he originally hailed from Plymouth, England. We doubted that he still resided in Springe so McCann placed an advertisement in a Plymouth newspaper seeking his whereabouts. A relative saw the ad and informed us that yes, he lived in Springe and had since the 1920s when he served in England's occupying army following World War I, met and married a German lady, settled down there and was arrested by the Nazis as a foreign national and a potential threat to the Reich.

We next contacted a mutual friend, Peter Hoffman, deputy chief of the McGraw-Hill News Bureau in Bonn. Could he tape an interview with Jay? By all means. When the tape arrived McCann was ecstatic...until he put it in his recorder. "It was 100 miles per hour cockney," he recalled. "I couldn't make out a bloody thing." We bought a rheostat and calmed down Jay but the results were still marginal. When we finally interviewed him during our European investigation in the early '70s, which covered interviews in France, Austria and East and West Germany, we backstopped our taping with notes. Good thing because he still spoke something, but we weren't sure if it was English. Our trip by train from Hannover to Springe also gave us a close-up view of German livestock. We mistakenly took the wrong train and wound up sharing our car with a batch of sheep!

Our next big break came when McCann heard from the International Red Cross in Geneva, which identified "Dr. John Nichols" as Jean Marcel Nicolas, a native of Port-au-Prince, Haiti. The IRC listed his nationality as "U.S.A.," and his "Occupation" as "pilot, air force officer." The letter recounted his arrest and incarceration and his job as a "camp physician" at Dora and Rottelerode. This was the first time he'd been identified as a Haitian, indicating to us that "Johnny Nicholas" was his cover, making our quest all the more tantalizing since the German records identified him as an American and doctor from Boston!

By coincidence, a friend of McCann's, Detroiter Bill McConkey, was planning a vacation in Haiti. Bill contacted a local newspaper columnist for LeNouvelliste in Port-au-Prince who told him that the Nicolas family was prominent locally and supplied McConkey with their names. Yes "Nicolas;" he had added an "h" to his new name.

We contacted the people McConkey had identified, flew to Haiti in spring 1972, and interviewed his mother, Lucie; sister Carmen; Uncle Fortune Bogat, the local General Motors dealer; his nephew Leslie Bogat; and two doctors, Hans Pape and Jacques Coicou, who were friends of Johnny and had studied medicine with him in Paris. We also interviewed his high school teacher, Harry Tippenhauer, and Pierre Gabrielle, who promoted Jean's career at a teenage boxer. Then there was the mysterious "Mr. Williams" who kept popping up from the time we arrived, claiming to be a university student. He was, of course, a member of President Papa Doc Duvalier's dreaded secret police, the ton ton macou, shadowing the Yankee journalists.

Thanks to his Port-au-Prince relatives and friends we gathered stories and anecdotes about young Jean, and photos and other documents that proved invaluable. We were appalled by the poverty we witnessed and were eerily mystified by the voodoo fires we saw nightly above the city. Leslie Bogat escorted us around in his Peugeot. Passing the gleaming white National Palace of Haiti, Papa Doc's home, McCann and I admired the building, which was destroyed in the recent earthquake. "Don't look there too long," Leslie advised. "It's not safe to do so." Welcome to Papa Doc's Port-au-Prince!

And for the first time we learned that a German officer had befriended the Nicolas family when serving at the German Embassy in Haiti in the late 1930s. This was to become a significant angle as the search went on.

Back home the story began shaping up and our reporting steamed ahead, taking us in many directions. The Red Cross reported that Nicholas had joined the French navy in the late 1930s but was injured in an accident aboard his ship and was released. We confirmed that with French officials. From Haiti we developed numerous leads including locating his brother, Vildebart, in Paris, and later interviewing him and his wife Andree on several occasions to help flesh out his activities before, during and after the Nazi occupation. We contacted former prisoners in France, East and West Germany and Canada who had testified against the Nazis including two of only 18 who had survived the Gardelegen massacre where more than 1,000 perished.

We were especially anxious to discern whether Johnny Nicholas had a U.S. medical degree. On a business trip to Chicago I stopped by the American Medical Association national headquarters, but they could find no record of him. While there I asked how I might find a doctor in Austria and was given the address of the Osterreichische Artztekammer — the Austrian

Medical Association – in Vienna. I was hopeful of finding Karl Kahr, the SS doctor responsible for Dora prisoners, who had testified against the defendants at Nordhausen and whose home was Graz, Austria. "Yes, Dr. Kahr still practices in Graz and here's his phone number." I phoned him and, like Lt. Col. Berman, Dr.Kahr was shocked to hear from an American journalist. Since we planned to embark for Europe soon I asked if we could visit him. He agreed and a few weeks later we landed in Paris, interviewed Vildebart and other sources, and then stopped in Strasbourg where we had located Dr. Robert Gandar who, like Johnny, was a prisoner doctor at Rottleberode. When we arrived McCann dropped a few centimes in a pay phone, dialed up Gandar's hospital and asked to speak to the doctor. He spoke no French and the operator spoke no English. She kept asking McCann "Malade? Malade?" Since this was a gynecological hospital, McCann was nonplused. "There's nothing wrong with me" he protested, to no avail. We finally located our translator and were welcomed by Dr. Gandar, who provided a stirring eyewitness account of Nicholas's battle to keep his emaciated and diseased patients alive in the Rottelberode infirmary.

Next we flew to Vienna overnight, planning to catch a train to Graz the next morning. When we arrived at the train station (banhof) the newspapers had blaring headlines, in German of course, indicating that German Chancellor Willie Brandt had gotten caught up in a scandal. "Ah, I see Brandt Was Buggered in Banhof," McCann, a native of Northern Ireland who knew no German, deadpanned.

Arriving in Graz, Dr. Kahr invited us for lunch in his home, serving up delicious locally vinted wine. He described the horrific condition of the slave laborers and how he tried to improve their treatment against strong opposition. He needed help and recruited those with medical experience. Nicholas fit the bill. "He was a very good man…very friendly and always in good humor. In him the prisoners had a friend in the revier (hospital)."

Back to Vienna and then on to Wolfsburg, Germany, home of Volkwagen. A friend at VW offered us the use of a new car to cross the autobahn between West and East Germany and interview a source in East Berlin. It was painted a bright orange. At Checkpoint Charlie separating the two Berlins we were searched, relieved of our tape recorders and watched while the guards jacked up the car and eyeballed the undercarriage with a mirror. Not exactly your friendly neighborhood cops. It was a Sunday morning in East Berlin. McCann had a map and instructed me to turn left at the next corner. Too late we saw we were headed the wrong way on a one-way street. A machine pistol-toting sentry in a black and white striped kiosk screamed at us to halt, but McCann said "Give her hell," and we roared to the next corner and kept on flying. Fortunately there was almost no traffic and we "escaped," pulling up near the Brandenberg Gate directly in front of a Lada car dealership. Lada was a Russian car that looked old when it was brand new. VWs were not available in East Berlin, so ours stood out like an orange in a basket of limes. East Berliners crowded around admiringly for a closer look.

Returning to the U.S. we kept on the phone and continued corresponding with potential sources, rounding up more facts and eyewitness accounts. From Krakow, Poland, we heard from Wincenty (Vincent) Hein, who was closely associated with Nicholas at Buchenwald, from which Dora was spun off, and whose revelations were vital to the story line. It was written in Polish, of corse, but luckily my next door neighbor was a Polish-American and he translated it for us. We also had a friend who translated correspondence from French sources.

McCann delved into Haiti's history and culture to set the scene for the Haiti chapters. We were especially interested in the U.S. Marine Corps occupation of Haiti that began in 1915 and ended in 1934 when President Roosevelt visited there and ordered their withdrawal. We had heard that Nicholas had been seen with Marines in Haiti and the adjacent Dominican Republic and theorized that this may have led to his "Americanization" as "Johnny Nicholas."

Still anxious to fill in all of the holes we visited the National Archives again, rounded up additional sources in Europe and continued to pursue U.S., English and French intelligence organizations attempting to nail down his story that he had a mission to spy for the Allies, as the Red Cross and numerous others had indicated. We also unearthed details of his final days, his rescue near Lubz, Germany, by a U.S. armored column, and his five months in a Paris hospital suffering from wounds incurred when he tried to escape and from TB, by working with his sick patients.

In 1970 we tracked down a Polish prisoner, Romuald Bak, in Brampton, Ontario, Canada, where he owned the Flowertown Motel. Bak had testified at Nordhausen, and emigrated to Canada after the war. He had amazingly survived the Gardelegen massacre. His six-hour account of his escape was brutally emotional. He told us he saw Nicholas in the town just prior to the massacre. Was he among the dead? Seven hundred were so badly burned they were never identified. Like others we interviewed, Bak remembered Nicholas as a free spirit who rallied his patients to not lose faith, the liberating Americans would soon arrive.

We were appalled by the irony that overworked, underfed slave laborers died by the thousands building the underground tunnels to manufacture V-2 rockets, whose technology became the foundation for the U.S. space program when German scientists headed by Wernher von Braun emigrated to America after the war. An engineer as well as journalist, McCann's research formed the basis for the details of the Dora complex.

Information continued to dribble in as we began planning, drafting, rewriting and editing The Search for Johnny Nicholas. Because we were still working full time and had young families, it took about five years to complete the book. We lined up a well known agent, Armitage Watkins, in New York City and had numerous close calls (but no sale) from leading U.S. publishing houses. Watkins sold the story to Sphere Books Ltd. in London. It was published in 1982 and all rights reverted to us in 1985.

What followed was 15 years of on-off interest with scores of Hollywood studios and producers to develop the Johnny Nicholas story for the screen. We sent out hundreds of books and visited Hollywood numerous times to confer with our contacts and agent. All talk but no action. We coined a word for these mostly futile deliberations: "Hollyspeak." Early in the 2000s we returned twice to the National Archives in College Park, Maryland, to gather more information since many of the files had been declassified. We also now had access to the Internet, which wasn't available during our original reporting, and that proved helpful in providing new contacts and background. Then we dusted off our mountain of documents and interviews, leading to the extensive reorganization, revision and reediting of the first book.

We remain excited about the Search we so innocently undertook 40-plus years ago, not knowing where it would lead us. We welcome your comments.

David C. Smith
December 2010

Hugh Wray McCann   David C. Smith
Interlochen, Michigan   Auburn Hills, Michigan

search4johnnynicholas@gmail.com

APPENDIX

PRINCIPAL SOURCES AND REFERENCES

I. FAMILY

Lucie Dalicy Nicolas (deceased), mother; Port-au-Prince, Haiti
Carmen L. Nicolas, sister; Port-au-Prince, Haiti (deceased).
Vildebart Nicolas, brother; Paris, France; Uncle Fortune Bogat and nephew Leslie
Bogat, Port-au-Prince, Haiti.

II. FORMER INMATES OF CAMP DORA AND SUBCAMP ROTTLEBERODE

Romuald Bak, Brampton, Ontario, Canada
Franz Becker, Berlin, East Germany
Jean Berger, Angers, France
Gabriel Boussinesq, Brive, France
Dr. Robert Gandar, Strasbourg, France
Vincent Hein, Krakow, Poland
Cecil A. F. Jay, Springe, West Germany
Pierre Julitte, Paris, France
Fritz de LaCour, Berlin, East Germany
Honore Marcelle, Heinaut, Belgium (deceased)
Roger Maria, Paris, France
Marcel Patte, Paris, France
Thaddeus J. Patzer, Johannesburg, Republic of South Africa
Jean Plus, Landeseuvre-les-Nancy, France
Walter Pomaranski, Terrace, British Columbia, Canada

III. ACCUSED AND WITNESSES AT THE NORDHAUSEN WAR CRIMES TRIAL

Accused:

Arthur Kurt Andrae	Josef Kilian	Willi Zweiner
Erhard Brauny	Georg Wilhelm Koenig	Otto Georg Brinkmann

Paul Maischein	Otto Buehring	Hans Moeser
Heinz Georg Detmers	Georg Johannes Richkey	Josef Fuchloch
Heinrich Schmidt	Kurt Heinrich	Wilhelm Simon
Oscar Georg Helbig	Walter Ulbricht	Rudolf Jacobi
Richard Walenta		

Witnesses:

Dr. Juan Cespiva	Dr. Alfred Kurzke	Walter Ulbricht
Joseph Gastow Coune	Valentin Kovalj	Richard Walenta
Dr. Karl Kahr	Boruch Seidel	Willi Zwiener
Ferdinand Karpik Stanislaw Ziba		

IV. ESCAPEES EN ROUTE FROM SUBCAMP ROTTLEBERODE TO GARDELEGEN

Rene Autard, France
Pierre Ego (deceased), Lille, France
Wilhelm Fentzling, Hamburg, West Germany
Dr. Robert Gandar, Strasbourg, France
Franciszek Krawcsyk, Zory, Poland
Mathiew Lambert, Putten, Netherlands
Ivan Marchenko, Romni, Poland
Jacques Matarasso, Salonika, Greece
David Nahama, Salonika, Greece
Zdzisla Pnjewski, Poland
Rene Thomas, Lyons, France
Waclaw Wochowiak, Lublin, Poland
Ludwok Wrobel, Lecka, Poland

V. ESCAPEES FROM INSIDE THE BARN AT GARDELEGEN

Edward Antoniak, Wielun, Poland
Romuald Bak, formerly of Brunswick, Germany; Brampton, Ontario, Canada
Geza Bondi, formerly of Budapest, Hungary; now living in Australia
Hermann Brandien, Hamburg, Germany
Pietrow Dimitry, Stalino, USSR
Feder Dugin, Bielok Lody, USSR
Armand Dureau, Douai, France
Leonid Kaistrow, Klince, USSR
Enginy Kateba, Szlorucyjuaka, USSR
Mieczyslaw Kilodziejski, Drezewica, Poland
Ivan Matwegeo, address unknown
Momochuk Wasel, Wasel, USSR
Borys Mawjow, Rostov, USSR
Stanislaw Woleszynski, Lublin, Poland

Witold Modzelewski, Warsaw, Poland
Woldzinierz Wozny, Poland
Eugeniusz Sciaiarski, Sosnowiec, Poland
Aurel Zobel, Vienna, Austria

VI. UNITED STATES GOVERNMENT AGENCIES

Central Intelligence Agency
John Bross, Deputy Director
Howard J. Osborn, director of security

Department of the Army
Brig. Gen. William H. Blakefield, commander, U.S. Army Intelligence Command
Col. Robert H. Fechtman, chief, Historical Services Division, Office of the Chief
of Military History
Lt. Gen. William A. Knowlton, chief of staff of the U.S. Army European Command;
former commanding officer of B. Troop, 87th Cavalry Reconnaissance
Squadron
Lt. Col. Harvey M. Ladd, deputy chief, Magazine and Book Division, Directorate
of Defense Information,

Department of Defense
Major Wm. D. Newbern, chief, Foreign Law Branch, International Affairs
Division, Office of the Judge Advocate
Col. Maurice S. Weaver, chief, Field Operations Division, Office of the Assistant
Chief of Staff for Intelligence
Oren Womack, Disposition Branch, Memorial Division, Office of Chief of Support
Services
John J. Slonaker, chief of Research and Reference
Charles J. Simpson, deputy director, Fort Detrick Historical Unit
U.S. Army Military Historical Research Collection

Department of Health, Education and Welfare
William E. Hanna, Jr., director Bureau of Data Processing and Accounts, Social
Security Administration

Department of Justice
Helen W. Gandy, secretary to the late J. Edgar Hoover, Federal Bureau of
Investigation
E A. Loughran, associate commissioner, Immigration and Naturalization Service
Andrew C. Tartaglino, assistant director for Enforcement, Bureau of Narcotics
and Dangerous Drugs

Department of the Navy
W.C. Keene, head, Records Service Section, U.S. Marine Corps
H. F. Ott, head, Disposal Section, Correspondence Services Branch, Bureau of
Naval Personnel

Department of the State
John J. Baker, U.S. Embassy, Prague, Czechoslovakia
Arthur E. Breisky, U.S. Embassy, The Netherlands
Mary T. Chiavarini, American Consul, U.S. Embassy, Brussels, Belgium
Terrence Douglas, American Consul, U.S. Embassy, Warsaw, Poland
Patrick J. Flood, American Consul, U.S. Embassy, Hungary
Alta Fowler, American Consul, U.S. Embassy, Belgium
William D. Heaney, U.S. Embassy, Haiti
Andor Klay, Berlin office of U.S. Embassy, West Germany
Francis G. Knight, director of the Passport Office
Norbert J. Krieg, U.S. Embassy, West Germany
James W. Lamont, vice consul, U.S. Embassy, Greece
Donald Wehmeyer, U.S. Embassy, West Germany
Edward L. Williams, U.S. Embassy, Peru

Department of the Treasury
Foreign Claims Settlement Commission
Dorothy Ladue, Office of Information and Publications, Bureau of Customs
Andrew T. McGuire, general counsel

National Archives and Records Service (Washington National Records Center)
John Taylor
Mark G. Eckhoff
Edwin R. Flatequal, acting chief of Archives Branch
Thomas Hohman
Harry Schwartz
Robert Wolfe

National Personnel Records Center
M.D. Davis, Civilian Reference Branch
M.T. Vranesh, supervisor, Army Organization Records Unit

Office of Strategic Services (defunct)
William J. Casey (deceased), former deputy commander; New York, N.Y.
Thomas C. Cassady (deceased), former head of secret intelligence for France and
Germany; Lake Forest, Ill.
John Howley, secretary, Veterans of the OSS; New York, N.Y.
John M. Wigglesworth, executive secretary, Strategic Services Unit

Selective Service System
Veterans Administration
R. G. Bowman, VA liaison officer, Military Personnel Records Center
Edward P. O'Dell, chief, Contact Division, Veterans Benefits Office

VII. UNITED STATES CIVILIAN SOURCES

Joan Alvarez, Physicians Information Service, American Medical Association, Chicago, Ill.
Warren P. Edris, Kennersville, NC
William Berman (deceased), chief prosecutor in the Nordhausen War Crimes Trials, Portland, Maine
Joseph C. Breckinridge, investigator for U.S. Army's War Crimes Branch; Lexington, Ky..
Ernest L. Chambre, historian, New York, N.Y.
H. Jackson Clark, B. Troop, 87th Cavalry Reconnaissance Squadron; Durango, Colo.
Burton F. Ellis, 7708th War Crimes Group; Merced, Calif.
Alonzo P. Fox, assistant division commander of 102nd Infantry Division; retired lieutenant-general, Wash., D.C.
Earl Harrell, B Troop, 87th Cavalry Reconnaissance Squadron; San Antonio, Texas
M. A. Harris, president, Negro History Associates, New York, N.Y.
Leon Jaworski (Watergate prosecutor), 7708th War Crimes Group; Houston, Tex.
Jerome Kabel, former administrative aide to U.S. Senator Philip A. Hart; Detroit, Mich.
Frank A. Keating, commander of 102nd Infantry Division; retired brigadier general, Clearwater, Fla.
Jacob F. Kinder, 7708th War Crimes Group; Fort Lauderdale, Fla.
George P. Lynch, chief of staff of 102nd Infantry Division; retired brigadier general, La Jolla, Calif.
David L. Matthews (deceased), 7708th War Crimes Group; South Bend, Ind.
Robert G. McCarty, War Crimes Investigation Team No. 6822; Portland, Ore.
Dr. Shelby T. McCloy, Black history authority, Lexington, Ky.
A. E. Schwabacher Jr., F Company, 405th Battalion, 102nd Infantry Division; San Francisco, Calif.
Clio Straight, commander of 7708th War Crimes Group, retired major general, New York, N.Y.
Horace Sutton, Intelligence Detachment of 102nd Infantry Division; associate editor of Saturday Review, New York, N.Y.
Lauren L. Williams, 102nd Infantry Division; retired lieutenant general, La Jolla, Calif.

VIII. REPUBLIC OF FRANCE SOURCES

The American Hospital, Neuilly-sur-Seine
Amicale de Neuengamme et des Commandos, Paris
Amicale des Reseaux Action, Paris
Roger Arnould, FNDIRP, Paris
Edmond Bricout, Amicale des Reseaux Action de La France Combattants, Paris
Dr. R. J. Brocard, (:rdre National des Medecins, Conseil National de l'Ordre, Paris
Jacques Brun, secretary general of Amicale de Dora-Ellrich, Paris La Confederation des Syndical Medicaux, Paris
Jacques Delarue, author of *The Gestapo*; Direction de la Surete Nationale; LePecq
Pierre Dumont, Prefet de la Region du Nord, Lille
Roger Fouillette, Offwiller Federation Nationale des Deportes et Internes Resistants et Patriotes
Nicole Girard-Reydet, vice consul of the French consulate in Detroit, Mich.
Hopital Lariboisiere, Paris Hopital St. Antoine, Paris
Rear Admiral N. M. Eouot, naval attache in the French Embassy, Washington, D.C.
M. R. Mamelet, Ministere de I.a Sante Publique at de I,a Securite Sociale, Paris
Henri Michel, secretary general of the Comite D'Histoire de le Guerre Mondiale
Republique Francaise, Paris
Ministry of the Army, Paris
Ministry of Defense, Paris
Ministry of the Interior, Paris
Capt. Isaiah Olchs, U.S. Navy (ret.), Nice
Prefecture of Police (Archives), Paris
L. Repesse, secretary general of the Union Eationale des Associations de Deportes, Internes et Familles de Disparus
Andre Sabliere, Lyon

IX. REPUBLIC OF HAITI SOURCES

Etienne Bourand School (where Jean Nicolas studied), Port-au-Prince
Dr. Jacques Coicou, Port-au-Prince; Pierre Gabrielle, Port-au-Prince
Msgr. Francois Wolff-Ligonde, archbishop of Port-au-Prince
Dr. Hans C. Pape, Port-au-Prince
Lalier C. Phareau, reporter and columnist for *Le Nouvelliste*, Port-au-Prince
Dr. Raoul Pierre-Louis, dean of the School of Medicine and Pharmacy, University of Haiti.
St Louis de Gonzague School (elementary school attended by Jean Nicolas), Port-au-Prince
Laurore St. Juste, director of the Haitian National Archives
Harry Tippenhauer, principal of the high school attended by Jean Nicolas, Port-au-Prince

X. GERMAN SOURCES
Bundesaerztekammer, Stuttgart-Degerloch
A. de Cocatrix, deputy director of the International Tracing Service, Arolsen
   Deutsche Dienstelle, Berlin
Hans Hueckel, High Court of Essen
Militargeschichtliches Forschungsamt, Freiburg im Breisgau
Zentrale Stelle fuer NS Verbrechen, Ludwigsburg

XI. UNITED KINGDOM SOURCES
J. E. Blishen, Ministry of Defense, London
Thomas Cochrane, deputy director of Public Relations, Ministry of Defense,
   London
Maurice J. Buckmaster, former commander of French Section, Special
   Operations Executive
Library and Records Department, Foreign and Commonwealth Office, London

XII. MISCELLANEOUS SOURCES
Hans Aalmans, Kerkrade, The Netherlands
William J. Aalmans, investigator for the 7708th War Crimes Goup; Embassy of
   Holland, Madrid, Spain
Institute of Documentation, Haifa, Israel
Dr. Karl Kahr, Graz, Austria
Magyar Izraelitak Orszagos Kepviselete Irodaja, Budapest, Hungarv
Jean Nothomb, Brussels, Belgium
Osterreichische Artzlekammer, Vienna, Austria

XIII. HITLER ON PUNISHMENT OF OFFENDERS IN OCCUPIED TERRITORY, DECEMBER 7, 1941
"Night-and-Fog Decree" (Nacht-und-Nebel Erlass). [United States, Office
of United States Chief of Counsel for Prosecution of Axis Criminality, *Nazi
Conspiracy and Aggression*, 8 vols. and 2 suppl. vols. (Government Printing Office,
Washington, 1946-1948), VII, 873-874 (Doc. No. L-90).]

   The Fuehrer and Supreme Commander of the Armed Forces
   [stamp] SECRET

   Directives for the prosecution of offenses committed within the occupied
territories against the German State or the occupying power, of December
7th, 1941.

   Within the occupied territories, communistic elements and other circles
hostile to Germany have increased their efforts against the German State
and the occupying powers since the Russian campaign started. The amount

and the danger of these machinations oblige us to take severe measures as a determent. First of all the following directives are to be applied:

1. Within the occupied territories, the adequate punishment for offenses committed against the German State or the occupying power which endanger their security or a state of readiness is on principle the death penalty.

2. The offenses listed in paragraph I as a rule are to be dealt with in the occupied countries only if it is probable that sentence of death will be passed upon the offender, at least the principal offender, and if the trial and the execution can be completed in a very short time. Otherwise the offenders, at least the principal offenders, are to be taken to Germany.

3. Prisoners taken to Germany are subjected to military procedure only if particular military interests require this. In case German or foreign authorities inquire about such prisoners, they are to be told that they were arrested, but that the proceedings do not allow any further information.

4. The Commanders in the occupied territories and the Court authorities within the framework of their jurisdiction, are personally responsible for the observance of this decree.

5. The Chief of the High Command of the Armed Forces determines in which occupied territories this decree is to be applied. He is authorized to explain and to issue executive orders and supplements. The Reich Minister of Justice will issue executive orders within his own jurisdiction.

XIV. V-2 TECHNICAL DATA

The weapon, called the A-4 by the Germans, was 46 feet long, had a diameter of 65.3 inches and weighed 12 to 14 tons. It was fueled by a mixture of pure oxygen with a 75 percent blend of ethyl-alcohol and water. The fuel was consumed after 66 seconds of flight, when the speed was 3,500 miles an hour and the altitude was 20 miles. Continuing to climb without power, it reached an altitude of 65 miles, at which point it was half way between launch point and target.

The fuel mixture of 8,400 pounds of alcohol and 10,800 pounds of oxygen burned at the rate of 300 pounds a second. The propellant supply was delivered by a turbopump driven by hydrogen peroxide decomposed by a catalyst. Yaw-and-pitch was supplied by graphite carbon vanes in the rocket exhaust.

Ignition of the alcohol-oxygen mixture was by pyrotechnic pinwheel inserted in the motors.

Maximum speed was one mile per second.

Its one-ton warhead, which contained 1,654 pounds of high explosive, penetrated before exploding, consequently it achieved complete destruction of its target, causing a crater 30 feet wide and 30 feet deep. Accuracy was limited to a range of about five miles.

The warhead is contained in a six-foot-long compartment that includes an automatic pilot and radio equipment.

Because the V-2 traveled faster than the speed of sound it gave no warning of its approach, consequently there was no direct defense against it. The only way to counteract it was to bomb the mobile launching pads.

XV. FINAL DEFENSE PLEA: Nordhausen War Crimes Trial
by Major Leon B. Poullada. U.S. Army [U.S. vs Kurt Andrae et al. File number 005-50-37, National Records Center, Suitland, Maryland. Record Group (RG) 338, Vol. 86, (Dec. 23, 1947), pp 7723-7796. Also on microfilm at National Archives, Washington, DC. RG 338, Roll 11, 1079/7723-7769.]

SUMMARY:
Poullada contended that the postwar "war crimes" trials violated basic principles of justice; that the prosecution encouraged witnesses to give false hearsay testimony. He predicted that the decision to try the accused under rules offering them less protection than those extended to U.S. citizens accused of crime set a precedent in international law that the world would regret.

XVI. CAMP MITTELBAU (Dora main camp): Monthly Population/ Death Statistics
(Source: Wincenty Hein, *"Nabitka z Biuletynu Glownej Komisji Badania Zbrodni Hitlerowskich," Tom XVI*; Krakow, Poland)

	Prisoner population	Deaths
August 1943	107	--
September	3300	--
October	4761	18
November	8579	173
December	10,370	672
January 1944	11,352	679
February	11,906	536
March	11,844	766
April	10,723	149
May	11,129	129
June	11,962	136
July	11,575	122
August	12,010	105
September	13,035	122

	Prisoner population	*Deaths*
October	14,514	232
November	24,904	283
December	33,855	571
January 1945	31,815	788
February	37,911	2341
March	39,725	2542
April	40,202	unknown

Total Deaths 10,364

Acknowledgments

We wish to thank our three surrogates for their sterling efforts in accelerating the Search.

James Dunne, a reporter for Popular Science in Detroit, took time out from his responsibilities in Paris to do preliminary interviews with Vildebart Nicolas and his wife.

Wilfred McConkey, manager of employee information services at Michigan Bell Telephone Co., turned his first vacation in Haiti into an investigation of several days. He was ably assisted by William D. Heaney, then a U.S. embassy official in Haiti. Nicolas is an extremely common family name in Port-au-Prince, and it took an exorbitant tolerance for the heat and a lot of pavement-pounding before they found the right family. McConkey's terse communiqué informing us of his success gave a tremendous boost to our morale which, at that juncture, was flagging considerably.

Peter Hoffman, then deputy chief of the McGraw-Hill World News bureau in Bonn, West Germany, spent a weekend in Gardelegen inspecting the Isenschnibbe barn, the adjoining cemetery, hunting for survivors and witnesses of the Gardelegen Massacre and shooting up a storm of pictures. He also made a valiant but unsuccessful attempt to negotiate the snowy Harz Mountain passes in winter to visit what remains of the infamous Kohnstein tunnels: East German guards turned him back at the border. Later he did the preliminary interview with one of the key sources in the project, the Englishman Cecil Jay, whom he found living in Springe, near Hanover. The arrival of his picture and report sent our spirits soaring.

Thanks also to Theodore Szymke (deceased) and Gabriel Werba, our Polish and French translators respectively, for their ready assistance in interpreting documents and tape and letter correspondence.

Also thanks to two men who died before the completion of this book, without whose assistance and advice it might never have reached fruition: Thomas G. Cassady, former head of secret intelligence for the OSS in

France; and Lt. Col. William Berman, prosecutor of the Nordhausen War Crimes trials, who were as anxious as we were to find out who Johnny Nicholas really was.

Also to be thanked are Carmen Nicolas (deceased), who turned over to us many family pictures and official documents relating to her brother Johnny; his uncle, Fortune Bogat (deceased), with vast and valuable perspective about Johnny; to Lesley Bogat, Johnny's cousin, who functioned patiently and uncomplainingly as interpreter, driver and general counsel; and Romuald Bak, of Brampton, Ontario, Canada, whose uninterrupted six-hour monologue of his fight for life inside the burning barn at Gardelegen was astounding in its dispassion and detail.

The penultimate acknowledgment is reserved for our wives, Beverly and Isabelle; our families, who made sacrifices so that we could devote much of our time to the project; our typists of the original manuscript, Laurie and Vickie; and for this revised edition, the journeyman editing of Bruce Smith.

And lastly a special acknowledgment to former Corp. David L. Matthews of the 7708th War Crimes Group. He had hoped for more than twenty years to write this book but could never find the time for what turned into 12 years of international traveling, research, writing and rewriting. When we met him, in 1965, he agreed to share his idea with us.

Without him *The Search For Johnny Nicholas* would never have been finished because it would never have begun.

Hugh Wray McCann
David C. Smith
Interlochen and Auburn Hills, Michigan
December 2010

ABOUT THE AUTHORS

HUGH WRAY MCCANN was a Detroit correspondent for *Newsweek*. He later worked for the *Detroit Free Press* and the *Detroit News*, where his beat was science and space.

DAVID C. SMITH was a reporter for the *Detroit Times*, *Toledo Blade*, *The Wall Street Journal* and the *Detroit Free Press*, where he became business editor. He was editor-in-chief and is now editor-at-large of *Ward's Auto World* magazine.

Both men served in Korea, MCCANN in the U.S. Army and SMITH in the U.S. Marine Corps.

CPSIA information can be obtained
at www.ICGtesting.com
Printed in the USA
BVHW032124131218
535602BV00001B/19/P